Identity Theft in Today's World

Recent Titles in
Global Crime and Justice

IDENTITY THEFT IN TODAY'S WORLD

MEGAN McNALLY

Global Crime and Justice

Graeme R. Newman, Series Editor

 PRAEGER

AN IMPRINT OF ABC-CLIO, LLC
Santa Barbara, California • Denver, Colorado • Oxford, England

Library of Congress Cataloging-in-Publication Data

McNally, Megan M.
  Identity theft in today's world / Megan McNally.
    p. cm. — (Global crime and justice)
  Includes bibliographical references and index.
  ISBN 978-0-313-37588-0 (hbk. : alk. paper) — ISBN 978-0-313-37589-7 (ebook)
1. Identity theft. 2. Identity theft—Prevention. I. Title.
  HV6675.M37 2012
  364.16'33—dc23   2011030646

ISBN: 978-0-313-37588-0
EISBN: 978-0-313-37589-7

16 15 14 13 12   1 2 3 4 5

This book is also available on the World Wide Web as an eBook.
Visit www.abc-clio.com for details.

Praeger
An Imprint of ABC-CLIO, LLC

ABC-CLIO, LLC
130 Cremona Drive, P.O. Box 1911
Santa Barbara, California 93116-1911

This book is printed on acid-free paper ∞

Manufactured in the United States of America

Contents

Part III: Life in Today's World

Series Foreword

WHEN WE THINK of theft we usually think of money, products, possessions. Material things. Megan McNally shows in this illuminating book that identities can be all those things but something more—a lot more. They are ephemeral and at the same time material and tangible. And in this modern age of information, they are very much like money—stored and transmitted at lightning speed in vast electronic networks.

What are identities and how do people—all people—develop and protect them? These are the basic questions with which McNally begins her odyssey to unravel the mystery as old as humans have been able to think, of who we are—each and every one of us—and who we think we are. Societies have helped. They give us names and places and they keep track of us in many ways—through tax collection (perhaps the oldest way), social security, street names and house numbers, bank accounts, credit cards, insurance policies, phone numbers, user names, Facebook pages, and a host of market-related activities. These help us to keep track of ourselves and others. Identity information is everywhere. Everyone has it, everyone trades in it.

It follows that the theft of such a commonly traded commodity should arise simply because it is everywhere. Just like the theft of cars arose once cars were mass produced and became ubiquitous on streets and driveways. Yet in contrast to cars, the essence of human identities is intangible. So what is it that is stolen in identity theft? This is the mystery that lies beneath McNally's dissection of this overrated, overhyped crime that is at the same time devastating to many of its victims.

Homer's *Odyssey* was a search for the identity of Western man. This book may not be quite as historic. But it takes its readers on a journey nonetheless in search of the meaning of identity theft and how it impacts our lives today.

Graeme R. Newman

Preface

AS THE AUTHOR and narrative voice of this volume, its contents reflect my perspective on identity theft overall. I played a small academic role during the American events described herein, but that is not the sum total of my experience with identity theft. While my thinking about the problem remains primarily criminological, and hopefully rational in its entirety, I see nothing practical about this phenomenon at all on any level. We can count rates and pronounce solutions until we are all blue in the face. We can also attempt to control everything that makes identity theft possible, one person and one thing at a time. Since we are already doing both to little obvious avail, it certainly cannot hurt at this point to try looking at the problem differently, and maybe with some better information if possible. That is my universal solution for identity theft in today's world and I believe it has a chance of working for just about everyone.

Although it would have been nice to solve every problem in the world, or even just the one called identity theft, that goal simply exceeds my talents. I am against identity theft, but I am for doing something about the problem. I am just not up for doing anything about everything without some clearer information about the things we have already done, or why. Maybe by the end you will feel the same, or something like it.

I must also admit to some dirty hands in the writing of this volume. A lot of information was lifted from my dissertation, but if you think that is bad, you might instead be grateful for everything I left out. The rest was fashioned using almost any means available. Thus, while I pulled ideas from many different places in order to explain the full wonder of identity theft (to the best of my ability in the space available), I did not fail to cite or misrepresent anything or anyone on purpose. Finally, I happily engaged in many of the practices I decry throughout, even though it was done for everyman's benefit. My intentions were therefore good, but in my own defense, everyone else was doing it and I cannot say that I ever really joined them.

Thanks for everything everybody—you all know who you are, let's keep it that way.

Introduction

IDENTITY THEFT (aka IDT) is an ancient form of social deviance, made new by the trappings of modern existence and a little American ingenuity. The problem on its own, while both intricate and serious, can be grasped fairly easily in rational terms—rational choice being the main criminological perspective underlying the discussion of identity theft in this volume of Global Crime and Justice. The primary obstacle to understanding identity theft in today's world, however, is the largely irrational manner in which this problem has been received.

With regard to the rational side of things, human behavior is consistently motivated to achieve some end that is typically judged to be good in the eyes of the actor. People are also free to choose between good and bad, and deterrence/prevention works by shifting the balance between these options during the decision-making process. Decisions are therefore rational based on how they are reached, not by whether they are independently thought to be logical, moral, or legal. Identity theft, being the result of human choice, consequently acts somewhat rationally on its own within the system of life.

The irrational side of identity theft is embodied by the contemporary reaction to this problem, which in the case of the United States can be classified as a moral panic. Moral panics are probably as old as identity theft, but much more difficult to pin down overall. While the principles of rational choice continue to apply to the actors involved in a moral panic, there is something about this particular collective response to a social problem that is not entirely logical. Although this characteristic irrationality can manifest itself in a variety of ways, many things about identity theft only appear to make sense after all reason has been abandoned. The U.S. example neverthe-less sets the precedent for how the rest of the world might be looking at this problem right now.

America is generally regarded as having been the first nation to discover identity theft, but in terms of the global development of this issue to date, the international community is chiefly in a position parallel to that of the United States during the mid-1990s. Carving out a niche for the real-life victims of identity fraud (IDF) was a lengthy process that gained momentum during the early 1990s and culminated in a succession of state and federal criminaliza-tions that took place between 1996 and 2005. In 2007, the United Nations noted that only 6 member states (out of 192) had relevant legislation, with only 1 (presumably the United States) having criminalized identity theft per se.[1] At that time, the European Union (with a complement of 27 nations[2]) was already in the process of considering whether the criminalization of identity theft was an "appropriate" course of action for its member states.[3] Why might the criminalization of identity theft be inappropriate for other nations?

REASON #1: THE ACTIVITIES THAT COMPRISE IDENTITY THEFT ARE ALREADY ILLEGAL

In the words of the United Nations, identity theft is a "new approach" that criminalizes the abuse of identity "as opposed to the traditional approach of criminalizing other activities committed using false identities."[4] Most if not all countries in the world currently have some legislative means at their disposal for handling cases of identity fraud (part of which became identity theft), and this was also true of the United States prior to the 1990s. Although the U.S. criminalization of identity theft was ultimately deemed necessary in order to legally acknowledge the status of individual victims, there are many associated costs and benefits that must be weighed in this type of decision. Thus, recognizing identity theft as a separate crime may not be a practical or practicable course of action for every country, perhaps even for the United States.

REASON #2: IDENTITY THEFT IS NOT REALLY A PROBLEM

There are several grounds to believe that the American problem of identity theft might be quantitatively and qualitatively different from (i.e., larger and worse than) the one being experienced by other countries. While the issue of identity theft has therefore been sizeable enough to gain international atten-tion and concern, the problem—as it is being experienced at local and na-tional levels across the globe—may simply not be big enough or bad enough to merit independent criminalization, or perhaps any other type of national response such as data collection or victim assistance.

Although identity theft is literally not a crime everywhere on earth, identity theft and identity fraud remain global criminal problems. In the United States, however, identity theft has also been portrayed as something that can happen to or be committed by anyone, which translates into everyone but specifically refers to you—the person with an identity. As implied by the combination of both sentiments, humanity is collectively responsible for the problem of identity theft, but either idea alone represents a logical fallacy. Another type of crime is therefore committed when statements like these are repeated in earnest, which unfortunately happens quite a lot and not just in the United States. In a modern-day environment where most life hinges upon instant communication, these stereotyped bits of misinformation also act like a highly contagious disease, which should not be allowed to spread any further as other nations attempt to discover identity theft for themselves.

Identity theft today is the cumulative effect of many decisions—individual and collective, good and bad. Given that this human process is fueled by information, the goal of the current volume is merely to put what we already know (or think we know) about identity theft into perspective. In today's world, this happens to involve life and the possibility of morality without panic. The promise of prevention is always fulfilled by tomorrow's world, however, so readers will hopefully emerge better equipped to make good decisions about identity theft in their own lives, or for their own nations, in the future.

Part I of this volume begins by establishing the boundaries of identity theft in a rational world. Since mathematics are one form of logic, the meaning of identity theft is examined first with a series of two equations: one that defines the substance of an identity (chapter 1), and another that outlines identity theft as a cyclical process embedded within the larger system of social existence (chapter 2). In chapter 3, the sum of Identity + Theft is then situated within the even larger system—and implied equation—of global existence, which is explained using a different type of logic known as the universal script.

The second part of this volume considers identity theft in an irrational society, informed by a mock trial case study of the U.S. experience. Moral panics have their own brand of fuzzy logic according to scientific lore, but their existence cannot be proven beyond a reasonable doubt to perhaps any but those who already believe in them. Since seeing often leads to believing in rational and irrational terms, chapter 4 reconstructs the basic parameters of a panic in keeping with the framework established in Part I. Morality, however, does not fit neatly into a rational world.

While the systematic logic of a panic is rational to some degree, the human action during a panic appears to be driven by the heart (emotion) rather than the head (intellect), which might explain both the irrationality and the immorality behind this phenomenon. A moral panic can generally be interpreted as a social morality play in which the good guys win a false victory over the bad guys by breaking rules of ethical (and sometimes legal) conduct, thus losing high ground on the slippery slope between good and evil, us and them. This moral transgression might be great or small, intentional or accidental, but it compounds the original badness rather than redressing its harm, usually for the sake of goodness or else under its guise. Therein lies the drama of a moral panic, which simply might have to be experienced in order to be believed. In lieu of a live performance, however, the remainder of Part II narrates the events of the American identity theft panic using a theatrical structure to bridge the gap between the rational and irrational sides of life.

Chapter 5 takes a closer look at IDT (the main character of this moral drama) with regard to its substance, its occurrence, and its embodiment via the label *identity thief*, as well as its separation at birth from the parental problem of fraud. Chapters 6–9 then tell the national story of identity theft from beginning to end, specifically refuting some of the tales that have been told about this phenomenon along the way. Part III concludes by framing the issue of identity theft prevention as a rational (chapter 10) and ethical (chapter 11) choice likely to be faced by everyman in today's world.

PART I

Identity Theft in a Rational World

1 ———————————————————————

The Identity Equation

IDENTITIES ARE COMPLICATED things, part personal and part social. An identity is your person, both inside and out. It is also everything about you, as well as everything you do. At the same time however, an identity is a vital and valuable commodity within societies. While the biological and psychological aspects of someone's identity are bound within his or her physical form, the cohesive identity (or name) by which that body is known functions in the capacity of differentiating individuals from one another within social collectives.[1] An identity is also personal in the sense that it is owned by (or used in reference to) a single individual, but its meaning in the context of identity theft is undeniably sociological in nature. In particular, an identity works as society's link to your physical person, thus fulfilling part of the social contract we all implicitly live under.

The most important tool used for ascertaining the identity of a given person is generally referred to as information, or personal information as it relates to a specific individual. There are also similar qualifiers such as identity or identifying information, which can be used in general or in reference to a particular identity. The various social processes through which other people are identified require an exchange of identity information, but each exchange has different requirements that must be fulfilled. The types of information necessary for identification at the social level, however, are in a broad sense the same as those that soldiers are obliged to provide to their enemies when captured: name, rank, serial number, and date of birth.[2] Taken together, the rough formula for calculating an identity would therefore look something like this: Body + Information = Identity.

BODY

Human existence has a simple story: you are born, you live, and eventually you die. The physical body is therefore the epicenter of existence, and it acts as the anchor for your identity throughout life. If you exist in the physical realm, you have a body, and a particular body at that. Like snowflakes[3] and fingerprints,[4] individuals are thought to be unique, but that does not mean they are unalike—and this is the central problem in the task of identification.

The physical evidence that each body contains or is capable of leaving behind, such as fluids and fingerprints, are integral to the issue of identity theft. This area of physical (or biological) identity also lies right on the border between public and private control; thus, an extremely controversial social agenda exists alongside everything that is identity theft. The physical aspects of existence are only part of a person's identity, however. Since an identity can outlive its body in the social realm, this identity equation needs to be balanced with information about the body and its activities while on earth.

INFORMATION

If you exist in the social realm, then your birth was likely a notable event. Even if the exact details of that event are unknown, some things can be taken for granted if you have a body: You were born on a particular day and time at some relatively fixed location, and you have one set of biological parents somewhere. You were also born with a particular genetic makeup that helps shape what you are. As it pertains to your physical person therefore, identity information concerns your existence (i.e., birth, body, death), not your life (i.e., who you are and what you do while alive). Thus, there is a limited universe of existence information: date, time, and location of birth; date, time, and location of death (as soon as applicable); parents' existence information (or lineage); and a small host of basic descriptives such as gender, height, weight, and coloring (hair/eye/skin). It is important to keep in mind that most physical characteristics can be altered nowadays, even distinctive variations like a birthmark or physical deformity. When it comes to most physical characteristics, however, what you see at any given moment is what you get.

Information about your life (as opposed to your existence) can be sorted according to the remaining aforementioned categories: name, rank, and serial number:

Name

If your birth qualified as a social event, you undoubtedly received a name (first, middle, and last, or something to that effect). Although your given name (or birth name) is vitally important in the world of identification, there are auxiliary names to consider as well, including aliases, nicknames, and married names. Any list of the information that can comprise a person's identity usually begins with their name, because it acts as the primary label for an individual within society. The main problem with using names as the sole means for identification is that they are commonly shared with others, just as two people with no genetic ties may look exactly alike (doppelgängers). Yet since names are attached to bodies, all other types of identity information are typically routed through this single channel of an identity, thereby linking the personal with the social.

A name can also be thought of as a mask for the personality within the body, which hides abundant stores of privileged personal information (i.e., things that only you or someone close to you might know). This image is helpful in the context of identity theft as such supplemental information is often used for the purposes of prevention (e.g., as the substance of passwords and security questions—What is your pet's name? What is your favorite color?), yet may be made publicly available—intentionally or otherwise—through contemporary social network media (e.g., Facebook).

Rank

The term rank outside of a military context can be used to conceptualize an identity in relation to its body's position in the world. All of the variables typically measured by social statistics (e.g., race/ethnicity, religion, education, employment, income, marriage, housing) represent different facets of an individual's identity and diverse examples of the types of personal information that can be used for the purposes of identification. Thus, this category encapsulates a host of socially mundane and often public information that can nevertheless be used to fill out the contours of an individual's identity if his or her particulars are known.

Serial Number

Serial numbers comprise the bulk of personal information normally associated with identity theft, as they can be any type of unique identifier assigned to an individual. Account numbers are one form of serial number, and a single individual in today's world often has several of these linked to their name: bank accounts, credit accounts, loan accounts, insurance accounts, investing accounts, utility accounts, and so forth. Various public and private agencies also routinely allocate serial numbers, with some of the most common examples in the United States being government-issued descriptors such as driver's license and social security numbers. Finally, this category includes addresses, phone numbers, and other systematic sets of information deemed for whatever reason to be exclusive to an individual.

The only real criteria for having an identity in this world is that you exist (i.e., that you have or once had a body), but everyman needs to plug his own personal variables into this equation in order to determine whether his identity is suitable, available, or even desirable for the purposes of identity theft—a topic that will be revisited later on. As a final note, however, all of these identity elements also have associated temporal and spatial dimensions that should be kept in mind. Your identity develops and changes while you are in the process of existing. Some information is fixed in time and space surrounding an event such as death or birth, while other information may legitimately be altered multiple times over the course of an individual's life, especially pieces of information like names, addresses, or telephone numbers. Such considerations factor into the equation at different points when you are trying to solve it, and one day you might be called upon to account for all of it, so it is good to start thinking ahead as well as behind.

THE VALUE OF IDENTITY

Although there are many ways to trade in on your good name in this world, what is your identity actually worth? Universally speaking, the answer might be priceless, but it really depends on the social quality of your identity and everything it is made of. The true value of an identity within a social context must be judged in relation to the object for which it is being exchanged, or through its ability to facilitate a successful trade by the standards of identity theft. Consideration must therefore be given to the specific social needs that demand the exchange of an identity, the forms of identity information required to complete the exchange, and the complexity of the rituals surrounding different types of exchanges. The U.S. social security number may nevertheless stand apart in the world of social identifiers for several reasons.

This nine-digit serial number, after close to a century of being used and misused in a multitude of unintended ways, has become a magical combination that unlocks many doors to the private recesses of the American identity. In particular, the social security number can be used on its own without reference to other linked pieces of information about the identity, like an individual's name. While similar problems might plague the primary identifiers of other countries (for example, surrounding the use of a national identity card), the power and endurance of the social security number is one of the biggest reasons for suspecting that the U.S. problem might be a different beast altogether in the jungle of identity theft.

A given individual is associated with a particular constellation of personal information, but the relative weight of each piece—either alone or in combination—is not the same. To illustrate this point, in the words of one *Washington Post* reader:

> In these days of identity theft, you can never be too careful. I shred everything that has my name and address on it. So now, when I am in a public establishment, I ask to see the phone book. I have learned that my entry is on page 346. I just rip it out and feel so much safer.[5]

While phone books can be used for unscrupulous ends, compare this with the actual behavior of Todd Davis, the former LifeLock CEO who publicly distributed his social security number and challenged others to misuse it in order to promote his company's identity theft prevention services. It remains to be seen how dangerous merely knowing someone's name and address can be, but Mr. Davis's identity was reportedly victimized 13 times during 2007 and 2008, and his company was later found guilty of defrauding consumers and Experian—one of the top three U.S. credit bureaus.[6]

An assumed name might come in handy every once in a while, but hardly anything of value can be exchanged for a name and a handshake alone without any additional information or proof of identity. In summary therefore, an identity is comprised of a body and a name, with name being the general term used to describe the social substance of an identity, which is a network of information categorized in its entirety as being a person's name, rank, serial number, and existence information. With this basic understanding of what an identity is, we can now turn to the issue of how an identity can be stolen.

2

The Identity Theft Equation

THE CONCEPT OF identity theft is not easily defined in a global context, but it can be expressed in simple mathematical terms: Owning Identities + Needing Identities + Acquiring Identities + Misusing Identities + Recovering Identities = Identity Theft. This equation can also be viewed as a social cycle, which seems to have developed in response to the realities of identity ownership in general.

OWNING IDENTITIES

You, as the primary owner-operator of your identity, are responsible for it in almost every way. Your identity is, after all, a social reflection of you (who you are, where you have been, what you have done, who you owe). It also establishes your reputation (i.e., good name) in various social settings, two of the most pertinent to identity theft being criminal and financial. The issue of identity ownership is nevertheless covered under the social contract, and various members of society have proprietary claims over some constituent parts of an individual's identity. In other words, society is a co-owner and co-operator of your identity, whether you like it or not. The issue of who-owns-what exactly when it comes to a person's identity must be settled as a political matter, but its resolution is directly relevant to the topic of identity theft—especially if identities have any value left in this world.

Identification is a central requirement of binding contracts, and social collectives of all kinds engage in very similar activities while routinely performing this function. The social requirements for identification and the related need for authentication (i.e., the process of verifying that an identity genuinely belongs to a body) therefore give societies much control over individual identity. Whatever societies require, however, your identity always leaves you holding the bag. The flip side of this coin, and of identity ownership in general, is that an owner can never be accountable for his or her entire identity because it simultaneously belongs to the society that helped create it. The rights, responsibilities, and privileges of identity ownership may not be split 50/50 between you (the real-life owner) and society (the commercial owner), but they are commonly shared within societies nonetheless.

As for the individual's end of the bargain, identity ownership comes with a number of responsibilities (such as paying taxes and obeying laws) as well as many rights and privileges that vary depending on where you live. An identity typically allows someone to own a car or a home, find and keep employment, travel within and between national borders, and participate in other social benefits, such as the right to vote and receive government subsidies. These are just some of the many benefits of identity ownership and social membership, when and where they are actually afforded.

NEEDING IDENTITIES

Identity theft is the direct result of needing another identity for some social purpose, but perhaps not just any identity other than your own. What a potential offender wants is very different from what he or she needs to obtain results, which in the case of identity theft is dictated by the identity requirements of an exchange. Here is a simple example.

There are many ways to steal a car. You might come across a set of keys by chance or obtain them through dishonest means or outright violence. You might also learn how to start a car without keys (aka hot-wiring). In most imaginable scenarios, what the would-be offender wants is a car (or transportation, or something else that a car or its theft can provide). However, what the would-be offender needs to obtain that goal varies from luck to lies to force to skill—all requiring very different levels of criminal commitment. When it comes to identity theft, however, there are really only two ways to steal a car (or an identity) for any purpose other than a quick joyride: steal the one right under the owner's nose, or procure one from somewhere else under the guise of being that owner.

SCENARIO #1

John Schmidt[1] owns a car, which is legally registered and operated in his name. One day he is stopped for driving a stolen vehicle. How could this be possible? Because someone was able to alter the official information associated with the car. The offender (a male in this hypothetical case) might not have a key to the car, or physical possession of the car, but the car is now legally owned by and registered to him, the fake Mr. Schmidt. Although not representative of identity theft as a whole, this scenario is generally referred to as an identity takeover or hijacking, with the tool of force being information.

SCENARIO #2

The offender—armed with John Schmidt's identity—walks into an auto dealership and purchases a different vehicle on credit, leaving the bill to eventually find its way back to the real John Schmidt (who will then adamantly deny owning more than one car). This represents the worst-case scenario of identity theft: committing new activities under someone else's name, which are disjointed or otherwise disconnected from the realities of the owner's everyday life. The car in this example is not John Schmidt's car, at least not according to the real Mr. Schmidt.

The kinds of personal information required to complete either scenario depends on a number of factors. For example, Mr. Schmidt may own his own car, but may not have the resources available (cash or credit) to buy another one. The effort and proof required to alter the contractual terms of ownership (Scenario #1) might also be more than the average offender is willing or able to provide. In the second scenario, the offender likely knew something about John Schmidt other than his name, or else he would have walked (not driven) away from the car lot that day. But what else exactly does this hypothetical offender know about Mr. Schmidt? This is just one of the many questions about identity theft that may never be sufficiently answered.

The successful commission of identity theft is a mixture of luck, deceit, and skill (if not force at times), yet what an offender needs in both scenarios is information—and not just any information, but the right combination of personal information that will provide access to the many wonders of identity ownership (like driving or owning a car). The desire to ditch your own identity and trade up for a better (or more valuable) model is hardly a modern development: this is a no-no in most societies if not a specific criminal act. Identity theft is driven by a classic cycle of supply and demand however: societies demand identities and individuals are expected to supply them. The process of obtaining another identity for legitimate social purposes is therefore a critical part of how identity theft can be accomplished in today's world.

ACQUIRING IDENTITIES

One of the first things you should know about your identity is that it is vulnerable to many different kinds of attack. An identity is a hot product in contemporary society, and thus someone may try to steal it from you one day. While you will eventually need to take stock of whatever identity information lies within your realm of influence in order to solve the identity equation and help protect yourself, it is best to approach this process by thinking like a criminal.

The matter of whether an identity can actually be stolen (as implied by identity *theft*) is problematic on several grounds, not the least of which is that an identity always remains to whatever degree in the possession of its rightful owner. In criminological terms, however, the minimal requirement for such a theft is the conjunction of a motivated offender and a suitable target. In the case of identity theft, this conjunction of offender and target minimally happens twice: the first time an identity falls into the hands of a motivated offender (acquisition), and the first time it leaves them (misuse).

Motivated Offenders

The people who misuse identities may not be the same ones involved in actually acquiring identities, but these offenders as a group are the people who need a new identity, or else know someone who does. For offenders, identities are typically the means (or tool) to some end; in other words, they are motivated to steal identities by something other than the desire to collect other people's identities. While identity information has been transferred dishonestly for many purposes over the span of human existence, the contemporary phenomenon of identity theft has a distinctively financial flavor that sets it apart somewhat from its past permutations. Nevertheless, motivated offenders may be after more than just the money behind these identities. In particular, there are six categories of targets (money, goods, employment, anonymity, revenge, services) that broadly represent the possible motives (or motivational gears, MGEARS) of identity thieves.

Money

Money may make the world of identity theft go round, but the money of today is not the same as its paper predecessors. It can be plastic or digital, and even virtual in the case of credit when it represents the monies that can be borrowed but not yet earned by the owner of an identity. The security of money in all of its forms and locations is a likely priority for most people in any society, however, despite any additional risks now posed by identity theft.

Goods

Although money is nice to have, there is almost no end to the things it can buy. If an offender has an identity that can be used like cash, he or she can purchase desired targets directly—anything from the basics of life (i.e., food, shelter, and clothing) to all of the pleasures and luxuries it offers (e.g., jewelry, cars, and travel), assuming of course that the identity being misused can afford them as well.

Employment

Some offenders simply want to obtain employment, since for whatever reason (many times related to their immigration status) they are unable to work under their real names.

Anonymity

The desire for anonymity among offenders is arguably universal because it decreases the probability of being apprehended—in theory at least, if not in practice. An offender may also have a particular motive for hiding his or her true identity, thus the need to take cover behind the identity of somebody else. The main acts falling under this category are therefore associated with those who provide false identifying information to any authority upon demand (not in exchange), particularly the police.

Revenge

Another category of offender motivation is revenge, which may be directed toward the owner of a particular identity, or any other party that can be affected by the activities of an offender while under the guise of someone else's identity.

Services

A service is any act that can be performed for money (e.g., health care; car repairs; travel by plane, train, taxi, etc.), or any other social benefit that might be accessible by virtue of being you (e.g., public assistance, the right to vote, community memberships).

It can convincingly be argued that the implicit motivation for stealing identity information is its subsequent misuse, but this is not always true in a strict sense. The motives behind acquiring the identifying information of others may be different from those related to its misuse, particularly if two separate offenders are involved (i.e., one who procures identity information and another who misuses it). The theft of information that occurs may also be literal in some cases, such as when a person's wallet is robbed or a company's database is hacked, but the same result can be achieved in very subtle ways that may not be illicit outright.

To be more precise, the real theft occurs at the moment when an individual with access to identity information decides to misuse it, which may be seconds, hours, days, weeks, or even years after having initially obtained it. In other words, the acquisition of identity information is a necessary but not sufficient condition of identity theft (as herein defined), even though the privacy and protection of personal information in any society are issues of critical importance. Regardless of the specific intentions involved though, there are many people in this world who are motivated to both take and make opportunities for acquiring the different types of identity information necessary for committing identity theft. Their ultimate success in doing so depends on the security of the target in their crosshairs and their own ability to overcome any obstacles that might stand in their way.

Suitable Targets

A given target (or identity information[2]) can be considered suitable in relation to the specific goals and talents of a would-be offender, but its suitability is also determined in part by its form and accessibility. The most valuable targets are usually those containing sensitive pieces of information falling under the category of serial number because they are unique and may provide the most direct access to an identity. However, the physical manifestations of targets (paper, plastic, or digital), and everyone who comes into contact with them (handlers), are also important considerations.

Paper

Paper targets with identity information can be found in all shapes and sizes, from receipts and contracts to bills, credit reports, junk mail, and other types of correspondence. Keeping the identifying information of employees and clients in paper files (i.e., stored records), and issuing paper documents for different reasons (e.g., official certificates and titles), have also been long-standing practices within industries and societies of all kinds. Any individual or entity currently evolved beyond the need for printed records, however, may still have to contend with securing the remnants of old paper-based systems.

Plastic

Some identity information is molded into more durable and deliberately portable forms—typically plastic or laminated cards intended for the purposes of identification or providing access to various services or sectors on a routine basis (e.g., ID cards, licenses, credit cards, security passes). Such cards are usually but not always found together in someone's wallet or its equivalent since they are often intended for an individual's use in a variety of settings, with the general exception of special things not characteristically required of everyday transactions or work responsibilities, such as a passport (which may in some cases be more paper than plastic, but still designed for travel).

Digital

Any identity information that can exist in either paper or plastic form can also exist in digital form, whether on a computer, the Internet, or any compatible storage device (e.g., cell phones, personal digital assistants, portable hard drives, compact disks). There is also a crossover here with the other categories of physical information, because digital technology can be used to enhance the security of paper and plastic documents; one notable example being the Chip and PIN system used in the United Kingdom, in which the authentication process is achieved via the combination of a microchip embedded within a plastic card (also known as a smartcard) and a personal identification number (PIN).[3]

Handlers

Since many types of identity information can be committed to memory and repeated, or otherwise copied from their physical form in material ways, it becomes important to account for all of the people who have access to it in addition to the owner. This means a consideration of anyone that might encounter some piece of identifying information on a regular or even less-than-regular basis, including the owner's family and friends; employers and co-workers; casual acquaintances or strangers; and various agents representing private and public institutions (or collective handlers) of all kinds, such as banks, retail stores, and governments.

Guardians

A given target can also be rendered suitable for attack by either the absence or failure of a guardian responsible for its protection. Handlers are in effect the guardians of identity information, but there may be many others in proximity to the event similarly charged with the safekeeping of identities; thus all handlers are guardians but not all guardians are handlers in a physical sense. Guardians of every type can nevertheless be complicit offenders or victims at this stage of identity theft, depending upon the circumstances in which the information under their watch is compromised. Considering that the same piece of identity information can exist in multiple forms (paper, plastic, digital), a single type of information (like the U.S. social security number) may have dozens of guardians, working alone or in tandem, that can broadly be classified into two main groups: individuals and collectives.

An individual guardian is not only the owner of a given identity, but any person in a position or with a responsibility to guard that identity in absentia. Owners have a personal interest in protecting their own identities to some degree, while others may be under some kind of moral, social, or contractual obligation to do so as governed by the many rules of social interaction. For example, an owner lends her credit card to a friend in order to make a purchase. That friend is a guardian of the credit card (and/or its associated serial numbers) while it is in his possession, but it may be stolen from him (i.e., the friend is victimized) or he may decide to purchase additional items that were not part of the original agreement (i.e., the friend is an offender). Similar breaches of trust resulting in the theft of personal information can also be found at the level of social collectives. When individual representatives receive information legitimately during the course of business, but then secretly use it for their own illicit purposes, they thus breach the contract between the identity's owner and the social collective, as well as the one between employer and employee. In sum, the corruption of individual guardians—whether by human error or design—is a perpetual threat when it comes to guardianship of any kind.

A collective guardian is any public or private entity, jointly comprised of individuals, which serves in some capacity as a custodian for the personal information of others. Many entities have regular security practices in place for everyone's protection, including their own, but there are also different gradations of legal responsibility for the security of identity information, shaped by the nature of different industries and the jurisdictions under which they operate. One of the most important collective guardians is government, because of its often-combined responsibility for the regulation and control of various bodies within society and the protection of individual rights (civil, legal, or human) within its domain.

Identities Lost

The protection of personal information is a contentious issue in America, particularly following the ChoicePoint incident of 2005 in which this data broker legally sold the personal information of close to 145,000 people to an unscrupulous party that later misused it to commit fraudulent acts. According to at least one analysis of this case, an incident like ChoicePoint would be unlikely to occur in Europe given several differences in its collective data protection and privacy laws,[4] but Europe is only one part of the world and the sale of personal information is only one part of the problem where data breaches are concerned.

In the context of identity theft, a breach is a violation of the security of personal information—in any form and under anyone's guard, although this term is generally reserved for a large-scale event like ChoicePoint in which multiple people were affected by a single act of theft. The Privacy Rights Clearinghouse maintains a chronological list of U.S. data breaches that have occurred since the beginning of 2005. Between January 10, 2001, and February 23, 2007, 104,106,513 personal records had been compromised.[5] Its running tally of the number of records breached to date is more than 500 million.[6] To put this figure into some kind of context, however, there are just over 300 million identities living in the United States today.[7]

Although the clearinghouse tally does not account for any collective data breach that occurred prior to 2005, or any of the countless small-scale breaches that have occurred on an individual rather than collective level (such as the loss or theft of a wallet or computer), this example minimally suggests that the problem of breached personal information in the United States might be out of control. However, it tells us nothing about this problem in relation to identity theft, at least insofar as this term can be defined as the acquisition and misuse of identity information.

In short, the risks of losing an identity are different than the risks of losing one to identity theft, as the latter identity is now certain to suffer at least
one more breach in security (i.e., its misuse). Any fair assessment of either the
extent or cost of those risks would therefore require the ability to distinguish
among different classes of breaches in terms of the types and forms of identity information involved (i.e., the social quality of the stolen identity), the
failures of pertinent guardians, and any emergent threats posed by the potential for compromised identity information to be misused at a later date or time
rather than immediately following its disappearance.

Some parties have examined the specific risk for identity theft following a large-scale data breach, but several factors confound a complete assessment of this issue—not the least of which being time, since some valuable
identity information (like the social security number) can have an indefinite
shelf life. To summarize the results of such research to date in the words of
the U.S. Government Accountability Office: "Personal information: Data
breaches are frequent, but evidence of resulting identity theft is limited; however, the full extent is unknown."[8] No similar assessment of this issue has
been attempted at the individual-owner level, yet the same general conclusion
is likely to apply.

While there is no way to comprehensively compare the extent to which
guardians or owners fail to protect all of the identity information under their
respective control, U.S. security breakdowns on both sides (i.e., individual
and collective) appear to contribute in different amounts to the next phase of
identity theft—or the subsequent misuse of an identity. Who loses an identity then? It is still you in the end, but there might be very little you can do
about it.

Consider for a moment the informational residue of your life. If you were
to vanish in a puff of smoke right now, what evidence would there be that you
had ever existed? What if your wallet vanished with you? Your house? Your
car? All of those likely to notice your absence (e.g., family, friends, neighbors,
employers, creditors, governments) have some kind of information about
you right now, but so might many other people and social institutions unbeknownst to you, or long forgotten by you. An identity is yours for life but it
truly has a life of its own, so the person with an identity would do well at this
point to remember the following: Your informational bits and pieces are likely
scattered across the four corners of the earth by now, and all of these seemingly invisible links forge a social chain leading directly back to you (not that
other guy who might one day pretend to be you).

Understanding the personal mechanics of identity management (one implicit responsibility of ownership) cannot truly be compared to an episode of
This Is Your Life,[9] but there is a lot of social ground to cover where identities
are concerned, and accounting for the identifying evidence of your own life
might take a while, if indeed a full accounting can ever be achieved. Wherever
you are, however, take heart—everyman is in the same boat.

MISUSING IDENTITIES

The problem that occurs during this phase is two-sided, one side being how it affects owners (identity theft), and the other being how it affects handlers or co-owners (identity fraud). While many owners may not be aware that a breach of their identity information has occurred, they are usually not aware that their identity is being abused until the act of misuse is a fait accompli. The discovery of victimization marks the beginning of the next phase of identity theft (recovering identities), but the problem of misusing identities is really one of identity fraud, or at least the part of identity fraud in which the genuine identity information of others is exchanged with the intent to deceive. The process of misusing identities is still a stage of identity theft, however, even though the owners of the identities being misused are usually not directly involved in what occurs.

Once obtained, identity information can be transferred by a newly motivated offender to any legitimate third party, thereby defrauding the recipient and making its true owner complicit in all acts that follow. The criminal target at this stage of the process therefore shifts from the identity itself to whatever that identity can be used to obtain (money, goods, services, etc.). In other words, the goal is now to fulfill the primary motivation (MGEARS) for stealing an identity in the first place. Assuming compatibility (or suitability) between the old target and the new target, an identity now becomes a tool for gaining access to some part of an owner's lived existence. It also becomes a cunning weapon in legitimate social interactions. The necessary conjunction between motivated offenders and suitable targets therefore still applies at this stage, albeit in different ways.

Given the variety of exchange options available to offenders within a society, the specific targets at this stage of identity theft can be almost anything or anyone, even though some targets are, in reality, more at risk than others. The complexities of identity theft are nevertheless multiplied at this stage, as reflected by the number and type of victims involved. In particular, the list of victims is now expanded to include the guardians presiding over the security of various social interactions that in some way involve the transfer of identity information.

The Victims of Identity Theft

Identity information—if used in the right combination—can initially unlock one of two main doors on the threshold of your life: the first leading to the personal affairs of existing you (or just plain you; or old you, being the owner of an abused identity), and the second opening to all of the possibilities available to new you (representing the illicit handler of your identity, who might be inclined to do things that you have never done or would never do). Although each door roughly corresponds to the two John Schmidt scenarios previously outlined, offenders might not always have a choice between doors or be able to open both at the same time, depending upon the quality and type of information (or identity) in their possession.

Both doors—and everything that goes on behind them—lead back to you in the end, but owners are usually unaware (at least at first) that someone has invaded their life. Thus, the victims of identity theft usually have a passive role at this stage, only appearing toward the end after discovering that their identities have been misused. Victims of identity theft nevertheless remain the guardians of their own identities at all times. They are also expected (although not required) within U.S. society to maintain active surveillance behaviors or identity management in that regard, particularly if they have been put on notice at any previous time that the security of their identity information has been breached. The most centralized way for owners to monitor their identities in the United States (and perhaps many other countries as well) is through their national credit report, but even this financial accounting of an owner's life does not reflect all of the ways in which an identity can be misused. In the United States, there are also three main versions of your financial reality: Experian, Equifax, and TransUnion.

The Victims of Identity Fraud

When a misappropriated identity is transferred for any otherwise licit purpose, the new handler of that identity simultaneously becomes a victim of identity fraud, as might the co-owner of the identity information in some circumstances, such as when an owner's extant credit card account is misused. This process of identity fraud victimization encompasses all of the activities that take place during this stage of identity theft, as a given identity can be transferred once or many times, to a single victim or to several.

While there might be guardians who are not the direct handlers of identity information at this stage, the security failures that permit the misuse of identity information largely take place within the environs of the collective victims (or handlers) who erroneously validate the offender as being the owner of the identity presented during a transaction. Victims of identity fraud are therefore the primary or active guardians at this stage, and they are often the only ones in a position to detect or prevent identity fraud (and thereby identity theft) while it is occurring.

These collective guardians may include many of the same ones affected by the problem of information breaches, although the character of their victimization is much different here because it pertains to the misuse of identity information. The victims of identity fraud, however, comprise a group largely empowered with control over their routine dealings (i.e., the processes of identification and authentication). As such, very little information is commonly available regarding what occurs during this stage, and no estimate of the number of identity fraud victims (as herein defined) has visibly surfaced from any part of the world. This group nevertheless includes social collectives of all kinds (e.g., businesses, financial institutions, governing bodies), from the local to the national level. Wherever a real identity may go, identity fraud victims might therefore be found.

Because the act of misusing an identity is universally known as identity fraud (even within some parts of the United States, the birthplace of identity theft), answers to the related issues of how it occurs and what should be done about it are largely hidden behind the doors of various social collectives. Thus, the parties who must address this problem—identity fraud, the much larger mechanism behind identity theft—are the collectives themselves, particularly government in its status as a social collective and in its role as administrator over all others. The specific ways in which identity fraud can be accomplished nevertheless remain contingent upon different contexts and may not be committed in the same way across nations, even though identity fraud is a global offense.

Returning to the example of auto theft, the act of breaking into a car might be accomplished in different ways (e.g., with a stolen key, rock, or lock pick). There are additional factors that can either facilitate or hinder the accomplishment of theft concerning the location of the car (e.g., a public garage versus a private street) and any guardians or other deterrents that might be in the immediate vicinity (e.g., an alarm system, a camera surveillance system, a security guard, the owner, or other potential witnesses). The same types of contingencies hold true for identity fraud, but the specific threats involved with this offense are evolving alongside everything else that is techno-modern-global in this world; thus, what might work today may not work tomorrow, and what works in one country might not work in another.

Being in possession of the keys to someone's car is not necessarily evidence of having driven it or having the intention to drive it, but this is really the heart of the matter separating identity theft from identity fraud. Needing an identity and misusing an identity are therefore two completely different problems that must be addressed separately, but also in combination as they apply to the overall commission of identity theft (as defined in relation to identity owners). The social conditions that allow either problem to exist or persist must also be considered alone and in combination, particularly as the activities of identity fraud may be accomplished globally, whether through some traditional or otherwise techno-modern-global means.

Given the dislocation of an identity from its owner at this stage, the different qualities of identities involved, the countless convergences of potential offenders and targets across space and time, and the equally incalculable number of security measures adopted by various identity handlers within society, there is certainly much left to learn about the global problem of identity fraud. The bulk of what is known about identity theft, however, begins with the discovery of victimization.

RECOVERING IDENTITIES

Almost everything currently known about identity theft comes from its victims (i.e., identity theft is victimcentric in more ways than one), but identity theft victims as a group are only as homogenous as this title implies—the identities or good names of these owners have been abused in some way. The lived realities of victimization are another matter, with many important consequences based on whether an offender has had access to old you or new you. Because the personal affairs of old you are more likely to be monitored or utilized by you, the damages that an offender can cause are often more limited than what he or she can accomplish as the new you. Let's rejoin Mr. Schmidt for two more examples of how his identity can be misused.

SCENARIO #3: THE OLD MR. SCHMIDT

John Schmidt (in addition to having a car) also has one credit card (a MasterCard), which he uses on a regular basis. While reviewing his latest account statement, he notices several strange and expensive charges made within the past 30-day period. Since he knows for a fact that he did not engage in these particular transactions, Mr. Schmidt calls his credit card company to resolve the matter.

SCENARIO #4: THE NEW MR. SCHMIDT

Mr. Schmidt (with his car and his MasterCard) is busy living his life. One day he receives a call to discuss his outstanding debt from an unpaid Visa bill. John Schmidt's response: "What on earth are you talking about? I don't have a Visa card."

Before identity theft had a name, it had victims. Perhaps not as many victims as there are today, but their collective cry was finally heard and answered within American society and several others as well. The message of that call for help—not me—is the essence of Mr. Schmidt's reaction in both of these scenarios, but his recovery process as a victim will likely be much different in Scenario #3 than in Scenario #4. While the same is not necessarily true regarding his recovery from Scenarios #1 and #2 (related to John Schmidt's car), his MasterCard account can be hijacked in the same way as his car (Scenario #1). The takeover described in Scenario #1 is nevertheless a much different type of victimization than the one described in Scenario #3, which is more of a joyride than a carjacking.

Because of the close-knit circumstances surrounding the abuse of old you, the chances for early detection are greater, which in turn strengthens the ability of affected parties to respond quickly and mitigate their damages. While the personal costs associated with this type of misuse can be extensive at times, they are also confined to the value or worth of an identity. Thus, if old you cannot afford to buy a cup of coffee on credit, neither can new you. The fraud liability of owners can further be restricted under law or the terms of the contract held with the company that issued the account, so many owners may have no responsibility to reimburse parties for any associated losses, especially when it comes to existing credit.

Something very different happens when an offender truly becomes the new you. Since such activities can be tangential to the reality of an owner's existence, the chances for detecting new types of misuse are generally smaller than those for detecting existing types of misuse. The resulting damages and costs associated with new you are therefore often more extensive for all parties involved, in part because they can go on unabated for an extensive period of time. How could Mr. Schmidt be expected to know about the activities being committed under his name in Scenarios #2 and #4? In the United States, the general answer to that question is identity management, but the specific answer is credit report monitoring. The real John Schmidt has an implicit responsibility to engage in both practices as a citizen, if not simply due to his own concerns about the safety of his identity.

Scenarios #3 and #4 can generally be referred to as credit card fraud, just as Scenarios #1 and #2 were described as auto theft, but credit card fraud comprises the bulk of what today is known as identity theft, whether related to old you or new you. Generally speaking, however, the sole victimization of old you (whether through a credit card or some other means) accounts for approximately two-thirds of the identity theft problem overall. Why should this matter? Because there is a tremendous amount of difference between the experiences of these two sets of victims.

The substance of identity theft victimization can be described in different ways, but it mainly consists of two problems: (1) a great quantity of victims that experience a small degree of harm (primarily old you); and (2) a small quantity of victims that experience a great deal of harm (primarily new you). When you put them all together, you get identity theft victims, but there is a price for that convenience—even more so than when the problem is dichotomized as either old you or new you. In reality, an offender can cross over both thresholds in relation to a single owner-victim. There is also another level of the problem to be considered. What if Scenarios #1–4 all happened to Mr. Schmidt? Poor John Schmidt is now a repeat, multiple victim as well, which adds entirely different dimensions of quantity and quality to his experience that are not uncommon to the overall experience of identity theft victimization.

Imagine that John Schmidt is now a victim of classic auto theft—his car has disappeared, stolen right out of his driveway. When its absence is discovered, he immediately calls the police and his insurance company to report the theft. Two days later, Mr. Schmidt receives a call informing him that his car has been found, abandoned a few miles away, with a flat tire but otherwise undamaged. John Schmidt now has his car back, sitting in his driveway and as good as new. Is he still a victim of auto theft? Yes, but perhaps not to the same degree as if his car had not been recovered.

An identity might be recovered in the sense that the misuse of an identity stops, but can an identity truly be restored in the same sense as Mr. Schmidt's stolen car? Since the contents of stolen identities are often unknown in their particulars, their ultimate fate is somewhat unclear. Some serial numbers, like those associated with a credit card, can easily be changed in comparison to something akin to the social security number. The misuse of an identity can also continue past the point of discovery, however, and despite active steps on the part of victims to prevent further misuse. Thus, it may not be possible to recover an identity in a full sense if the original target (i.e., the identity information involved) cannot be secured, thereby neutralizing all remaining threats.

For individual victims, the process of recovery can vary greatly depending upon the activities that are committed under the guise of either old you or new you; the time elapsed between the onset of misuse and its discovery (e.g., one day versus one month versus one year); and the resources or assistance available to them. While identity restoration may not be completely possible in many cases, old you tends to come out unscathed relative to new you, whose old life may now be a thing of the past.

The Pains of Victimization

The costs of identity theft victimization are often viewed in monetary terms, but the pains of victimization extend far beyond dollar signs, particularly for the individuals whose identities are misused.[10] Although these costs are not distributed evenly between individual and collective victims, they are shared nonetheless. These consequences are also reciprocal among victims and extend to society at large: the primarily economic costs of identity fraud victimization are shifted onto consumers (identity theft victims and nonvictims alike); the pains of identity theft victimization are then directed back at social collectives (identity fraud victims and nonvictims alike). Thus, everyman shoulders the burdens of identity theft and identity fraud together.

Economic

Hard costs are the actual monetary losses resulting from identity theft, which are distributed between identity owners and collectives. Although these costs should be the easiest to calculate, practice tells a different story. Victims of old you and new you may walk away with both their identities and pocketbooks intact, even though this is less likely to occur in the case of new you. The out-of-pocket expenses for victims can also range from a few dollars to a few thousand, again with victims of new you being the most likely to pay for their victimization.

While the collective victims of identity fraud routinely absorb the losses associated with some forms of activity (particularly within the realm of credit), they can also pass them along to others in the form of higher prices for goods and services, or otherwise offset them, such as through the marketing of preventative services or the commercial sale of personal information. The hard costs for nations may be even greater given the extent of what is involved, yet these too are likely recouped in the form of higher taxes or other social premiums.

Soft costs are also monetary costs, but they cannot be fully estimated given certain future contingencies. These expenses might reasonably be encountered at some point down the road, but may or may not be incurred. One example would be the ongoing but unforeseeable costs associated with maintaining, upgrading, or repairing various technologies used in the detection or prevention of identity theft.

Human

The human costs of identity theft are the lived realities of victimization, minus the money, but it can be difficult to draw the line between human and economic costs in some cases. If you were to lose your job as the result of identity theft victimization, would you view it more as a personal (human) loss or an economic one? What about losing your job and your home because you were wrongly arrested? Although such events may result in economic consequences at times, the human costs of identity theft are largely intangible. In terms of individual victimization for example, there may be an overall sense of violation and confusion, lost time in dealing with the aftermath of an offender's activities, and an assortment of other frustrations derived from contact with the responders of society (such as the collective victims of identity fraud or the police) who all have a role in helping victims to recover their identities, if not their sanity after discovering the mess that someone else has made of their lives.

Opportunity

Opportunity costs arise when social doors (once open to you) have been shut, such as those leading to a mortgage or a new job. These are somewhat like the soft human costs of identity theft, given the difficulty of calculating what might have been if you had not been victimized. Although often discussed in relation to identity owners, collective entities may suffer opportunity costs as well. A company that loses customers as the result of an information breach, for example, may also have difficulty finding new ones later on.

Societal

The social costs of identity theft are mainly the threats posed to national or pubic security (e.g., in its relation to other social problems such as tax evasion, immigration offenses, welfare fraud, or terrorism). There may also be threats to national or public stability if the issue of identity theft touches upon the foundations of a society, just as it has in the United States over the rights and responsibilities of identity ownership within the general constitutional arena of privacy. Like any other social collective, however, a government may lose face with the public as the result of a breach or some other relevant point of contention, which may in turn lead to instability or insecurity within society as a whole.

The Universal Script

ONE PLUS ONE will always equal two, but the sum of the identity theft equation in chapter 2 depends upon a number of factors that are not as easily definable in mathematical terms. The functional level of this equation can nevertheless be understood through a different (albeit equally rational) analogy. A script is a basic map of rational action that resembles a theatrical script in many ways. A situational script is often used for the purposes of crime prevention, which requires detailed information to deconstruct how a specific type of behavior is carried out from beginning to end. In order to fully understand identity theft in the context of today's world, however, it is necessary to consider some additional levels of the problem with the assistance of a universal script. Using this device, identity theft can therefore be viewed as a contemporary social drama that unfolds in three acts.

The criminal portion of the identity theft equation can be viewed in Figure 3.1 as a series of three stages or acts: Acquiring Identities (Act I), Misusing Identities (Act II), and Recovering Identities (Act III). As a popular rule of thumb, the term *identity theft* can be applied to any one of these three phases (acquiring or misusing or recovering), to the entire process of victimization (acquiring + misusing + recovering), or to some combination thereof. The term identity fraud generally applies only to the second area (misusing identities), as well as to the collective victims present during Acts II and III.

Figure 3.1 also represents identity theft as a system of linked events related to a minimal cast of actors: one IDT victim, one offender, one IDF victim, and one responder (an agent or agency called for help in response to IDT victimization). The social positions of these characters are shown relative to one another in terms of their centrality to each act, but the entire play is premised on the IDT victim's point of view. Given that identity theft can be committed in many different ways and within many different contexts, interactional connectors between actors cannot be supplied for this process overall. In order to represent the lived experience of individual victims, however, two points delineate the transition between acts: (1) the onset of identity theft victimization, or the initial transfer of an individual's personal information; and (2) the discovery of identity theft victimization.

Figure 3.1 Identity Theft in Three Acts

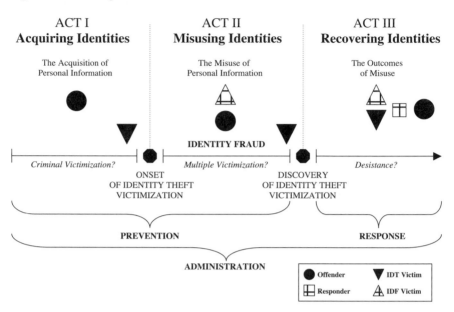

Acts I and II deal with the acquisition and misuse of personal information, which as previously discussed, alternately consists of an individual's name; contact information such as their address, e-mail address, or telephone number; social security number or other government identifier such as a driver's license number or passport; common private industry identifiers such as account numbers, credit cards, ATM cards, and associated passwords; and biometric identifiers such as fingerprints or DNA. Such information may also be physical and/or virtual, but it often exists in multiple forms under the control of various parties.

Given this diversity, an individual's personal information can be obtained and manipulated (Act I) in a variety of ways before it is actually misused. For example, a driver's license (or its number) may be stolen directly from an individual or another guardian (e.g., the Department of Motor Vehicles), or a new driver's license might be manufactured or otherwise legitimately acquired using someone else's personal information. The act of obtaining personal information may also be a criminal act in itself, depending on where or how it occurs.

Despite common differences in the use of related terminology, identity theft is conceptualized to occur in Figure 3.1 at the point of a transaction intended to defraud a third party (the beginning of Act II). Using the previous examples, identity theft occurs when a stolen or counterfeited driver's license is used, or when someone's information is presented to obtain a real driver's license from a state agency. Once the first fraudulent transfer of personal information has taken place, the activities of the offender have become linked to the owner of the identity in question. The span of time that occurs before an individual can discover the misuse of their identity therefore depends on a number of factors, including the type of personal information that is involved and the types of misdeeds being attempted or committed under their name.

The misuse of an individual's personal information may also continue well past the point of initial discovery, and in some cases even after the activities have been reported to an authority. Once an individual becomes aware that his or her personal information has been compromised (i.e., the discovery of IDT victimization), and/or collective entities realize that they have been defrauded (i.e., the discovery of IDF victimization, which might occur during Act II or somewhere alongside individual victims), the overall process of recovery begins (Act III).

Further represented in Figure 3.1 are the jurisdictions of prevention (covering Acts I and II), response (Act III), and administration (Acts I–III). Generally speaking, there are only two chances to prevent identity theft victimization: by protecting personal information in all of its locations, and by securing the social transactions requiring the exchange of identity information. Although opportunities for preventing the act of identity theft technically end when an offender crosses over the threshold of misuse, there may still be chances left to deter additional misuse.

The primary social response to identity theft occurs after the misuse has been detected, but other types of responses (ones not wholly describable in terms of being preventative) might also be necessary at different stages of the process leading to discovery; for example, contacting identity owners after a breach of their information has occurred in Act I. The areas of prevention and response are similarly governed by different layers of administration (e.g., within the organizational levels of a collective or as superceded by law), which add yet another level of response to both sides of this equation insofar as procedural rules apply to the social collectives involved in preventing and responding to the totality of identity theft.

While Figure 3.1 only lays out the basic (or universal) components of a single instance of identity theft, more detailed scripting within and between each act is possible.[1] In the context of understanding identity theft as a global crime, this framework can also be expanded to include the social networks that bring offenders and targets into contact with one another. At a different level of universal abstraction, identity theft can therefore be understood overall as a series of criminal, personal, social, and global problems that intersect and systematically function side by side in today's world.

THE CRIMINAL MECHANICS OF IDENTITY THEFT

Identity theft begins with an offender who is motivated by some personal desire, but otherwise in need of another identity to achieve his or her goal.

Regardless of whether that *need* is premised on convenience (e.g., because other means are either unavailable or unappealing) or necessity (i.e., because their goal is only achievable through a new or better identity), filling this deficit represents a universal motivation for identity theft. The criminal problem is nevertheless made possible through a combination of several personal, social, and global conditions that differentially converge to produce identity theft.

Offenders accomplish identity theft via a series of linked criminal processes, which are variously comprised of different interactional sequences between people, tools, and targets over time and across space. In its entirety, identity theft works by acquiring and misusing suitable identities, and thus occurs within various social contexts requiring the exchange of identity information and/or at the locations where identity information can be found. As a criminal act, however, identity theft is experienced locally—relative to the positions of offenders, victims, and targets, which may be physically distant from one other. Understanding the proximal mechanics of identity theft outlined in Figure 3.1 therefore requires specific, contextual knowledge regarding the circumstances under which different instances of identity theft occur.

THE PERSONAL MECHANICS OF IDENTITY THEFT

The personal threat posed by identity theft is universal to some degree, given that almost everybody has an identity and the fact that identity theft has been accomplished successfully for centuries (i.e., long before the development of many techno-modern-global advancements). Even if everyone did have an identity deemed suitable for the purposes of identity theft, everyone in the world does not universally share in the dangers of personal exposure. As such, the personal problem of identity theft is just that—personal. Identity theft works at this level as a general threat of harm and as the personal experience of harm. Owners are also responsible for their identities in many ways, so while they may play a direct role in their own victimization at times in terms of losing their identities, they are stuck with the task of responding to any harm that might result from the subsequent misuse of their identities.

THE SOCIAL MECHANICS OF IDENTITY THEFT

As the setting for personal interaction, societies can be responsible for identity theft in many direct and indirect ways. Criminal activity typically falls under the domain of public justice systems, but additional authorities (such as security personnel or administrative officials) have power over the problem of identity theft as it occurs locally within a society. Thus, there are intricate jurisdictional mechanics behind the social problem of identity theft that vary from place to place, and from culture to culture. At the social level, there is also an ongoing interaction between individuals and collectives with regard to identity ownership. This is not a zero-sum game, with compromises on both sides leading to the push-and-pull dynamics between the need to have an identity and the need to have the right identity, which propels the social problem of identity theft in many different directions.

THE GLOBAL MECHANICS OF IDENTITY THEFT

The global mechanics of identity theft are the linkages between social systems, particularly those regarding the transnational dynamics of offending and victimization. These linkages are both physical and virtual insofar as they connect people across cultures. There are also several international justice organizations (such as Interpol and the International Criminal Court) and political organizations (such as the European Union and the United Nations) that are currently dealing with the problem of identity theft—however defined or acknowledged—as it occurs within or threatens their own realms of influence.

ALL THE WORLD'S A STAGE

Since the criminal, personal, and social realities of identity theft are all global to some degree, the situational interactions represented in Figure 3.1 must also be situated within the world at large. Each actor represents a point or location within time and space, someplace within the universe of lived existence. The complexities of understanding the overall mechanics of identity theft are therefore compounded exponentially on the global level, particularly in the absence of data regarding the actual locations of actors involved in a single instance of identity theft. The lived reality of these mechanics might therefore be like playing an international game of Clue,[2] where you start with a victim but have to figure out whodunit, with what type of information, and where. In order to solve the mystery of identity theft, however, we need a conceptual model big enough to incorporate everyone and everything in today's world.

In scientific terms, what we need is a systems approach to identity theft in which this concept can properly be viewed as the outcome of a functioning whole.[3] If identity theft can rightly be called a social plague, it is one manufactured by civilization—not sent somewhere from above. Rational thinking dictates that if we want to solve the identity theft equation, then we need to do so one piece at a time. The networked realities of identity theft nevertheless require that many functions be examined simultaneously as well. Since the system of life is really what makes identity theft possible, the particular systems approach suggested here starts with you.

You are the center of your own universe, phenomenologically speaking. You are also at the center of the identity theft universe, but there you are just one among billions. You may be an offender or a victim (or according to lore, a little of both), but you exist in the social world and you live your own life. That life is centered at home but extends outward to society and the world, even if you personally never step foot off your own front porch. That is the reality of life in today's world, and the criminal threat of identity theft cuts right through the middle of it all.

Although you are the alpha and the omega of identity theft, this linked series of events is played out on a global stage. If an image of Earth were superimposed over Figure 3.2, we could begin to map out the social networks (or smaller systems of people and things) that globally contribute to identity theft and its prevention.[4] Within this larger context, identity theft therefore includes:

Everything: Every area of social life that deals with identity can be affected by identity theft, but not all are affected equally within or across cultures.

Everyone: Identity theft does not discriminate like humans do, but everyone who has an identity is differentially threatened by identity theft.

Everywhere: Many societies are known to experience identity theft, whether it is called such or whether any official attempt has been made to measure it. Most (if not all) societies are also extensively linked together in today's techno-modern-global world, even the ones that might not be considered "modern" by today's standards.

All the Time: The Earth spins 24 hours a day, 7 days a week, and so does the world of identity theft.

Figure 3.2 The Identity Theft Universe

The global dimensions of identity theft have in part been made possible by a world shaped through various techno-modern-global advancements, but there is currently no solid evidence regarding the extent to which transnational violations are occurring in relation to identity theft.[5] This is true whether defined as the unauthorized access to personal information or as an act of identity misuse, let alone in terms of the methods used to successfully complete either. The complexities of international offending include more than just the Internet, however, as national borders are standard sites for determining the identity of the people who wish to cross over them. International crimes of all kinds are therefore investigated through many traditional means (such as cooperation or agreements between nations), as well as through technological means (such as telephones[6] and the Internet). The same can also be said for the methods used to commit identity theft, as will be discussed further in Part II.

In an overall sense, the commission of identity theft can be understood as the networks that bring offenders into contact with targets and victims across space and over time. Identities are measured and tracked by societies for a variety of reasons, however, with some of the most central to identity theft being security, management, and profit. Data to understand the problem of identity theft therefore exists, but not all in one place or under the control of any one party. In other words, there is no single eye (human or electronic) watching everyone all the time. At least, there's not supposed to be. Information about identity theft is thus routinely (but not equally) shared within and among social sectors around the world, and all of it—in one way or another—has to do with you.

An identity was previously defined as Body + Name, and both are important within the context of surveillance. At a minimum, most societies keep records of their law-abiding citizens, as well as the physical bodies of some who are not (i.e., prisoners). If there were a single eye that could see everyone and everything, mankind might have to share it like the Graeae—three sister witches from Greek mythology who had one eye and one tooth among them. If all the information of the world were similarly stored in one computer instead of one eye, however, life might get a lot easier or a lot harder, depending on who you are.

While there is a universal demand for identification that must be fulfilled by the identities of this world, the requirements of the exchange between an identity and some other item of value can vary greatly within different contexts. If anyone is interested in "doing something" about identity theft, it will therefore be necessary to take a closer look at the situations in which it arises. This can be done to some extent for the American context using available data, but many of the processes underlying identity theft (and moral panics) are rational, and therefore universal. In other words, crime, societies, and people are inherently the same wherever you go.

A systems perspective can be used to broadly understand how the world fits together, and as a way for promoting three-dimensional thinking about

Figure 3.3 The Black Box of Identity Fraud/Theft

the problem of identity theft. As factual matters stand with regard to this universe of identity theft, however, the bigger picture can be viewed as a million-piece jigsaw puzzle with about 999,500 pieces missing. When viewed as a universal process, identity theft is similarly a black box (within the larger black box of identity fraud) where identities go in and victims come out. Although this process can be summarized as the acquisition and misuse of identities, and a few things can be said about how identity theft works in the United States, the quality of available information about the problem of identity theft is deficient across the board: personally, locally, nationally, and globally. Thus, the offending process as a whole remains somewhat of a mystery for both the United States and the world at large.

PART II

Identity Theft in an Irrational Society

A Matter of Perspective

THIS CHAPTER INTRODUCES the moral panics perspective as a vehicle for better understanding identity theft, as well as ourselves as rational beings. Moral panics are likely misunderstood by everyone to some degree because the academic concept behind this popular term is not clearly definable, even after several decades of attempts. While this perspective remains the best available for understanding society's creation of and reaction to the problem of identity theft, alas, it is not a theory. Nothing can really be expected or disproven in the world of moral panics except the characteristically exaggerated or irrational claims that surface during this near-mythical period of social crisis.

The term *moral panic* first appeared in an article written by Jock Young in 1971, but Stanley Cohen was the first to develop this idea in his 1972 work, *Folk Devils and Moral Panics: The Creation of the Mods and Rockers.* In the introduction to its third edition (2002), Cohen noted that both he and Young probably picked up the term from Marshall McLuhan's 1964 book, *Understanding Media,*[1] but that concept similarly did not "spring full-blown from the head of its creator. Rather, it developed from earlier concepts, most notably the moral crusade."[2] While moral crusades are associated with Joseph Gusfield's (1963) research on symbolic crusades, moral panics are more closely linked to Howard Becker's (1963) work on moral enterprise.[3] Regardless of when the notion of a moral panic specifically began though, this line of inquiry has examined many historical events that are the ancestors of the modern-day moral panic: for example, the Salem witch trials of the 1690s and McCarthyism in the 1950s. Since its "discovery" in the 1970s, however, the moral panics tradition has been a patchwork of ideas and disciplines that evolved into something less than a unified whole, much like the concept of identity theft today.

The opening paragraph of *Folk Devils* has been repeatedly cited as the rather cumbersome definition of a moral panic, but these words are the traditional starting point for understanding this phenomenon:

> Societies appear to be subject, every now and then, to periods of moral panic. A condition, episode, person or group of persons emerges to become defined as a threat to societal values and interests; its nature is presented in a stylized and stereotypical fashion by the mass media; the moral barricades are manned by

editors, bishops, politicians and other right-thinking people; socially accredited experts pronounce their diagnoses and solutions; ways of coping are evolved or (more often) resorted to; the condition then disappears, submerges or deteriorates and becomes more visible. Sometimes the object of panic is quite novel and at other times it is something which has been in existence long enough, but suddenly appears in the limelight. Sometimes the panic passes over and is forgotten, except in folklore and collective memory; at other times it has more serious and long-lasting repercussions and might produce such changes as those in legal and social policy or even in the way society conceives itself.[4]

While it may be true that "Cohen's first paragraph need no longer be cited as indicating, without further discussion, what a moral panic is,"[5] very little attention has actually been given to this issue. There have only been two major attempts to revise and reorganize this perspective over the past three decades (the first by Erich Goode and Nachman Ben-Yehuda in 1994 and the second by Chas Critcher in 2003), but neither provided a more succinct or alternative definition for the moral panics concept. In fact, both attempts expanded Cohen's description through models intended to capture different features inherent to a moral panic.

Folk Devils is a case study of society's reaction toward two British youth groups: the Mods and the Rockers. While Cohen's analysis was later used as the basis for similar research, it was not originally presented in a format conducive for systematic replication. Subsequent studies have therefore been criticized for either misrepresenting Cohen's intentions or being "ritualistic reproductions" of his work.[6] The best-known example of the first category is *Policing the Crisis* (1978),[7] which has been heavily faulted over the years for its Marxist undertones. This study of mugging was also the focus of one of the best-known critiques of the moral panics concept in general.[8] Although its insights were later incorporated into the entire perspective as one avenue through which moral panics might develop,[9] it has been argued that the authors' political transformation of the moral panics concept in this case constitutes a separate perspective.[10]

As one critic of moral panics remarked, however, its fundamental difficulty "is not the concept itself, but the way that it has been embraced by the generations of writers, researchers, journalists and students who have been applying it uncritically ever since its inception in 1971."[11] While this author nevertheless points out a number of additional difficulties with the perspective, this is the most poignant flaw of the moral panics tradition in two senses. First, countless actors over the past 30 years (academics and nonacademics alike) have used the term *moral panic* as a type of haphazard conclusion. Although evident even in its first use by Young, this term has become a label for anything remotely alluding to the idea of irrational, hysterical, or immoral behavior, and "its application [is] used as proof that little more need be said."[12] In many ways, this brand of popularity has kept the concept alive over the past few decades, but it has also undermined the importance of moral panics as an object of empirical research and potential intervention.

Second, many valid attempts to apply the perspective have merely reproduced it (rather unconvincingly by some standards) without contributing much toward its development or standing within academic communities. This universe of literature is much smaller, but it is also scattered across various disciplines that have used different approaches to examine a wide range of problems under the rubric of moral panics. While a few have attempted to follow some type of construct derived from Cohen's original work or the variant later proposed by Goode and Ben-Yehuda,[13] others have drawn from or referred to Cohen's work in a less systematic fashion.[14] As a result, the case studies that have been performed in this tradition are not firmly anchored in a shared understanding of what constitutes a moral panic, or how it should be studied. This area of research also seems to be driven by the thought that a case might fit the mold of a moral panic, so its processes and results are particularly vulnerable to producing evidence in favor of a foregone conclusion.

While the proponents of moral panics have addressed many of the specific criticisms leveled against this perspective over the past three decades, very little progress has actually been made toward clarifying its terminology, its premises, or its structure.[15] Recent work has also disputed the displacement of moral panics in light of more contemporary perspectives—particularly that of the risk society proposed by Ulrich Beck in 1992, which foretells the coming of a society characterized by heightened anxiety caused by the unintended consequences of modernization (perhaps one just like identity theft). Despite its popular reputation then, several fundamental issues continue to cast doubt on the issue of whether a moral panic is a valid academic construct. Even so, this perspective helped to make sense of the identity theft phenomenon in the United States when nothing else could.

To describe this proposed association between identity theft and moral panics in the words of *Policing the Crisis*:

> When the official reaction to a person, groups of persons or series of events is *out of proportion* to the actual threat offered, when "experts," in the form of police chiefs, the judiciary, politicians and editors *perceive* the threat in all but identical terms, and appear to talk "with one voice" of rates, diagnoses, prognoses and solutions, when the media representations universally stress "sudden and dramatic" increases (in numbers involved or events) and "novelty," above and beyond that which a sober, realistic appraisal could sustain, then we believe it is appropriate to speak of the beginnings of a *moral panic*.[16] (italics in original)

This excerpt simply resonated with what seemed to be happening across the United States, while it was happening (ca. 2005). It was later discovered that others in the United States and the United Kingdom shared this impression as well,[17] but the idea that any nation's response to identity theft could be a moral panic had never been systematically examined. While this investigation has since been performed,[18] it remains unclear whether identity theft is an appropriate topic for research in the moral panics tradition.

The threats inherent to a moral panic have often been contrasted against those found in nature, but there are at least three different types of threats that might evoke panic. First, there are naturally occurring threats over which people have little or no control (natural threats). This category includes the dangers posed by the elements, Earth, and its nonhuman inhabitants. Second, there are accidental threats that result from human behavior (unintended threats), which encompass the types of dangers faced in a risk society as described by Beck. This term is used here more broadly, however, to describe those risks resulting from a range of human actions that were not specifically intended to cause harm (i.e., accidents; e.g., transportation disasters, global warming, food/water contamination, and preapproved credit card offers in the case of identity theft). Finally, there are threats posed by purposive human behavior (moral threats) in the sense that they are intended to cause harm or are known to have the potential to cause harm. These can generally be understood as the threats posed by criminal or deviant behavior, which are really just different degrees on a continuum of good and bad.

While there may be some type of outrage or blame expressed in relation to the actors behind unintended threats, these are unlikely to generate the same type of reaction as a moral threat unless the behavior causing it is considered to be intentional or blatantly irresponsible (i.e., something a little more or less than unintended). The objects of moral panics are therefore found within this third category of threats, but many acts of crime and deviance are generally considered to be immoral, and thus a potential threat to the well-being of society. Prior research has nevertheless focused on a seemingly limited but predictable set of crime and deviance topics that otherwise have very few similarities between them. As such, it is necessary to consider whether all types of moral threats have the potential for panic.

Cohen noted that "[t]he objects of moral panic belong to seven familiar clusters of *social identity*" (italics added):[19] young, working-class, violent males; school violence; drugs used by the wrong people in the wrong places; child abuse, satanic rituals, and pedophile registers; sex, violence, and blaming the media; welfare cheats and single mothers; and refugees and asylum seekers.[20] Children seem to play a pivotal role as victims in many moral panics, but at the same time young people have been featured as the folk devils in quite a few.[21] There also seems to be a general emphasis on victimless or consensual crimes grounded in a disapproval of hedonistic pursuits (e.g., drug use, media consumption, sexual deviance), yet also a separate thread of violence that runs throughout several areas.

Some topics therefore epitomize actions that are *mala in se* (i.e., intrinsically bad, such as child abuse), while there is less agreement over the inherent immorality of others (e.g., drug use, single mothers). None of these characterizations adequately describe a category such as refugees and asylum seekers, however, which is further tied into the much larger issue of immigration. As such, there appears to be a mix of foci within and between these clusters regarding the victims, offenders, and activities typically thought to incite moral panic, but there may also be many different types of panic dictated by the circumstances surrounding different types of moral threats, falling somewhere on a continuum between bad and worse.

Although moral panics research has tended to examine a rather discrete set of crime and deviance topics, this may be due to a number of factors. One question that has been asked, for example, is why moral panics do not form around other types of issues such as white-collar crime. One common explanation is the lack of general prejudice or discrimination against this category of offender—a feature that is often present within the moral panics tradition. The stereotypical white-collar offender has a lot of power in relation to his position and class within society, however, which is not true of the stereotypes typically at the heart of a panic.

This particular issue might be explained through Angela McRobbie's[22] discussion regarding the increased ability of marginalized groups to "fight back" against the label of folk devil in more recent times. In this sense, white-collar offenders have always hailed from a social group with access to a greater range of resources, which can help to win this type of battle if indeed they have ever been confronted with this label. White-collar offenders, however, are not a marginalized group relative to other classes of offenders.

At the same time, it is possible that the furor over some white-collar scandals was either a failed moral panic, or an actual moral panic differentially tempered by the circumstances surrounding this category of offenses. On their own, acts of theft and fraud are unlikely to generate the same type of emotivism associated with violent acts, racial/ethnic prejudice, or the victimization of vulnerable persons (e.g., children, the elderly). If any one of these hot-button issues is present, which all of them are in both direct and implied senses with identity theft, the social reaction to the problem might more closely resemble moral outrage, and thus a moral panic.

White-collar crimes also tend to be hidden from public view, and they have a relatively low ranking on the totem pole of public fear and concern about crime. Perhaps the largest reason to explain why an incident such as Enron was not the subject of even a failed moral panic, however, is that it was never examined as such.[23] This would seem to result from the selectivity of researchers and perhaps some preconceived notions regarding what moral panics can or should entail. The more appropriate question may therefore be why moral panics research has focused on particular types of threats, rather than on why certain problems appear to be immune from moral panics.

The examination of identity theft as a topic of moral panics research challenges a variety of traditional assumptions to some degree. As argued, identity theft may be an appropriate issue merely because it falls into the category of purposive human behavior, but it still seems very far removed from those examined by prior research—especially since identity theft is often characterized as a white-collar crime. The topic of identity theft also seems to fall more in line with the mugging research reported in *Policing the Crisis* (1978), even though this work was later criticized for its radicalization of the perspective. This particular work has nevertheless been used to highlight the links between economic panics (e.g., during the U.S. stock market crash of 1929) and moral panics, which in itself is a prominent component of the identity theft phenomenon.[24]

On the other hand, identity theft is concerned with a very specific form of social identity (i.e., the absence of one, or anonymity), and this appears to generally fit with Cohen's above-mentioned description regarding the typical objects of panic. Cohen also offered some additional insights regarding the predictable objects of moral panics (shown below in three parts,[25] which provide further justification for the application of this perspective to the case of identity theft, as well as a further introduction to what it entails.

> The objects of panic are new (lying dormant perhaps, but hard to recognize; deceptively ordinary and routine, but invisibly creeping up the moral horizon)—but also old (camouflaged versions of traditional and well-known evils).

Whereas the term *identity theft* is relatively new, the activities that comprise it are *mala antiqua*; that is, *mala in se* activities that have "been recognized as criminal for a very long time."[26] The perception of identity theft's novelty largely stems from various technologies that are now available to commit very old, very traditional, and very well-known offenses. In the case of identity theft, this equates to various forms of fraud and theft. As such, the means to commit such offenses may have evolved, but the ends for which they are committed have not.

> The objects of panic are damaging in themselves—but also merely warning signs of the real, much deeper and more prevalent condition.

All forms of identity theft are damaging to some degree, but the underlying problem is society's continued reliance on information; hence, a recurring prediction in the U.S. narrative that the problem will only get worse as time goes on. This relates to privacy issues as well as individual and collective security issues, evidenced by a definitional shift in the meaning of identity theft from the misuse of personal information (ca. 1990s, but ever-present throughout), to the illicit acquisition of personal information (ca. 2005), which is a much more prevalent and problematic condition contributing to its occurrence.

> The objects of panic are transparent (anyone can see what's happening)—but also opaque: accredited experts must explain the perils hidden behind the superficially harmless.

Some dangers now collectively known as identity theft have been anticipated since the dawn of the information-technology age (ca. 1960), even though the full extent to which technology has aided in the commission or detection of related offenses is less clear. Experts were therefore already in place to deal with some issues (i.e., privacy, technology, security) while others rose to the occasion, but the purpose of some "identity theft experts" was to explain the largely innocuous albeit routine and annoying occurrence of existing credit card fraud.

TWO WAYS TO PANIC

In the early 1990s, Erich Goode and Nachman Ben-Yehuda made the first attempt to reorganize thinking about moral panics within a social constructionist framework. In particular, they distilled five elements from Cohen's original work, which have since been used intermittently within moral panics research. Although their model was an improvement at that time, it was not able to resolve all of the problems associated with this perspective. Chas Critcher, one of the researchers involved with the study of mugging published in *Policing the Crisis*, later revisited the concept of moral panics to see "whether it had stood the test of time, required revision or ought to be abandoned."[27] The research informing this volume adopted Critcher's approach, which compared the model of moral panics developed by Goode and Ben-Yehuda (an "attributional model" comprised of five traits, plus one that Critcher added) with one he personally derived from Cohen's work (a "processual model" comprised of seven stages). These two models are summarized in Box 4.1.

There are many similarities between these models since Cohen's work was used as the basis for both, but there are also several differences. The element of disproportionality is similar in both models, for example, as it is the most fundamental characteristic of a moral panic. Cohen nevertheless placed greater importance on the role of the media in this process, while Goode and Ben-Yehuda contributed a great deal toward outlining what this element entails. Further, although the term *folk devils* appears in the title of Cohen's work, only Goode and Ben-Yehuda viewed them as essential to a moral panic. Aside from the fact that this term does not appear in Cohen's opening paragraph, his inclusion of "conditions and episodes" implies that people (or the most obvious folk devils) are not always the object of a moral panic. The terms *claims maker*, *expert*, and *moral entrepreneur* are also not synonymous, but all are used to express somewhat similar ideas between these models. *Policing the Crisis* further used the term *primary definer* in the context of their study, which is particularly applicable to the case of identity theft. One of the largest differences, however, lies in the nature of the models themselves.

The processual model is best described as a narrative case study, with questions designed by Critcher to shape the direction of research. Goode and Ben-Yehuda prepared their model to act as a type of checklist for the attributes of a moral panic (hence, Critcher's use of the term *attributional*), but

Box 4.1 Two Models of Moral Panics[1]

The Processual Model	The Attributional Model
Description of Stage	**Description of Element**

Stage 1: Emergence
A form of behavior comes to be perceived as a threat, which may be new or long established.

Element 1: Concern
There is a heightened level of concern over the behavior of a certain group and/or its consequences for the rest of society. This concern must be manifested or measurable in concrete ways, which include public opinion polls, public commentary in the form of media attention, proposed legislation, and social movement activity.

Stage 2: Media Inventory
A preliminary explanation of the nature of this threat, and those who pose it, is articulated primarily through the media. Three strategies are involved: exaggeration/distortion (the seriousness of events, the numbers involved or the extent of damage is skewed), prediction (such events are expected to recur), and symbolization through language (a word or phrase comes to stand for or symbolize a group and its deviant status). The media also become sensitized to apparently similar events.

Element 2: Hostility
There is increased moral outrage toward those who engage in this behavior. This group is collectively designated as the enemy (folk devils) of respectable society, and their behaviors are seen as harmful or threatening to the values, the interests, and even the existence of society.

Stage 3: Moral Entrepreneurs
Groups or organizations take it upon themselves to assert the nature of the problem and its best remedies. They also offer emotional and intellectual responses, images of the deviants, and their own causal explanations.

Element 3: Consensus
Concern and hostility must resonate so that there is a certain minimal consensus in society as a whole (or within designated segments of the society) that the threat is real, serious, and caused by the wrongdoing of a certain group or its members.

Stage 4: Experts
Socially accredited experts pronounce their diagnoses and solutions.

Element 4: Disproportionality
Public concern is not proportional to the objective harm posed or caused by the threat. Statistics may be exaggerated or fabricated, the existence of other equally or more harmful activities may be denied, or concern may be demonstrably out of line with measures of actual trends in allegedly deviant behavior.

(Continued)

Box 4.1 (*Continued*)

The Processual Model	The Attributional Model
Description of Stage	Description of Element

Stage 5: Coping and Resolution
The reactions of the media, moral entrepreneurs, and experts contain ideas about the required measures. Current powers are exploited, but if deemed inefficient, demands for legal reform will follow.

Element 5: Volatility
Moral panics erupt fairly quickly, but may lie dormant or latent for long periods of time and reappear from time to time.

Stage 6: Fade Away
The moral panic ends, but may reeemerge.

Element 6: Claims Makers
Claims makers are those who seek to establish ownership over a given problem. They give the problem a name, establish the problem as a threat, and advocate solutions for response. While Goode and Ben-Yehuda did not specifically delineate this aspect within their original model, Critcher added it as an attribute due to its importance in social constructionist research. Critcher also noted that Goode and Ben-Yehuda implicitly concentrate on claims makers and "are remarkably uninterested in other key actors," particularly the media.[2]

Stage 7: Legacy
The panic may have little long-lasting effect or may produce changes in social policy, the law, or society's view of itself.

---

[1] These descriptions were edited from different texts. For further discussion of these models, see chapter 3 in Goode and Ben-Yehuda (1994), chapters 1 and 2 in Critcher (2003), and the introductions in Cohen (2002).
[2] Critcher (2003): 26.

---

they never provided any guidance regarding the quantity or quality of evidence necessary to substantiate the presence of one. Neither of the models is empirical in nature, however, and this is primarily witnessed through the open-ended nature of the research questions involved with both.[28]

Cohen's case study of the Mods and Rockers phenomenon in Britain drew on a number of different sources, including media reports, criminal justice statistics, and firsthand observations of community reactions. Even at the risk of ritualistically reproducing his work, many of these avenues were not available for the purposes of a national identity theft case study. While Goode and Ben-Yehuda also attempted to provide some type of systematic guidance for moral panics research, their suggestions ultimately fall short in many respects. There are nevertheless many dangers in expecting any moral panics model to provide more than it was designed to deliver.

The proof presented to corroborate the occurrence of a moral panic under either model is often circumstantial at best. Moral panic investigations therefore mimic a criminal trial in that evidence can be presented or manipulated in favor of either the prosecution or defense. Trials are nevertheless governed by laws and procedures, which are currently lacking for the assessment of moral panics as a whole. The conclusions of all moral panics research thus stand on shaky empirical ground.

While Critcher ultimately considered how these models could be united, they were treated separately within the case study of identity theft in order to evaluate his conclusions. In his final assessment of both models, however, Critcher found that the "attributional model seems less satisfactory and can be abandoned, except for some important insights."[29] Critcher subsequently used these to improve the processual model, but the rigidity and linearity that it implies remains problematic. For example, the second stage (media inventory) suggests that the media are always first on the scene of a moral panic, while the moral entrepreneurs (stage 3) and experts (stage 4) follow suit. Despite Cohen's focus on media involvement in a moral panic, these stages give a false impression of the actual processes that are involved, and both Cohen and Critcher recognized this problem. One possible solution to this challenge is therefore outlined in the following section. This heuristic is not only proposed as a structure for future moral panics research, it is the main structure used to organize the discussion of identity theft in the remainder of Part II.

THE UNITED WAY

The moral panics perspective has incorrectly been called a theory at times, but it has not reached that level of maturity, if indeed it ever can. As Critcher reflected:

> At first I naively thought that my aim was to "prove" whether or not moral panics existed but came to realize that moral panic was not a thing but an abstract concept, a model of a process. The task then became to find if there were consistencies in the model when applied to quite different examples. Any moral panic model became not an end but a means. Its usefulness lay as much in what it did not reveal about a given example as what it did. In sociological parlance, this is called an heuristic device, more specifically an **ideal type**.[30] (bold in original)

An ideal type does not imply that a model of moral panics must be perfect or account for every variance that might occur. It also does not mean that improvements can never be made, which in essence encapsulates the process of theory building. While there is no way to tell whether the moral panics perspective will ever become a theory, the first step would be to develop the ideal type started by Critcher. The proposed framework attempts this by situating its elements within a more structured framework that is also flexible enough to incorporate the processual dynamics of moral panics.

Theater performances are undeniably dynamic and three-dimensional, whereas stories are more linear and two-dimensional by nature. Stories can nevertheless engage their audiences in a similar way through the narrator's ability to create a mental picture for the audience (in this case, a listener or reader). The real difference between stories and plays therefore lies in the method of presentation. This becomes important for understanding the parallels between a narrative approach, represented by the processual model, and a theatrical (or script) approach, which may ultimately be developed for use within the moral panics tradition.

Moral panics are particularly suited to both structures, and their associated terminologies have been used in different ways within all three of the major academic writings on this topic. Cohen used many theatrical references in *Folk Devils*, and describes the feeling of a public incident involving the Mods and Rockers as a "modern morality play, in which good (the police and courts) met evil (the aggressive delinquent)."[31] In his opening paragraph, he also equates the memory of a moral panic with folklore—an apt analogy for the largely retrospective nature of moral panics research. These themes are also reproduced by Goode and Ben-Yehuda, who for example describe the "actors in the drama of the moral panic";[32] and Critcher, who specifically employs narrative reconstruction, alludes to moral panics as "a kind of moral fable,"[33] and uses the term denouement to describe their ending.[34]

This type of narrative structure, or script, is also used with the field of criminal justice, as was illustrated in Figure 3.1. Therefore, in the terminology of the script approach, the continued development of an ideal type would be akin to a universal script in which the known elements of a moral panic could be situated. If a suitable universal script could be created, the next step would be to examine whether metascripts could be developed in relation to different types of moral panics, if indeed more than one type exists. As it stands, however, the moral panics perspective is a story about a story, and the proposed framework is merely a heuristic packaged within another heuristic.

The basic notion that every story has a beginning, a middle, and an end is attributed to Aristotle's *Poetics*. Gustav Freytag, a 19th-century novelist and playwright, later used this work in order to analyze the structure of Greek and Shakespearian dramas. The resulting structure, published in *Die Technik de Dramas* (1863), is known as Freytag's Pyramid, which includes five basic stages for a dramatic plot as illustrated in Figure 4.1: Exposition, Rising Action, Climax, Falling Action, and Denouement.

Freytag's Pyramid has been represented in a number of ways over the past 140 years, but these basic stages have remained intact. For example, the Exposition is sometimes pictured on the increasing slope before the Rising

Figure 4.1 Freytag's Pyramid of Moral Panics

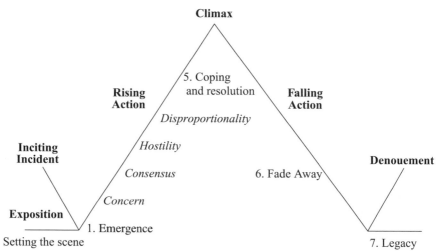

Note: Cohen's processual stages are denoted by numbers; the three missing stages (2. Media Inventory, 3. Moral Entrepreneurs, and 4. Experts) are treated as part of the "cast of characters." Goode and Ben-Yehuda's attributes are in italics; the shape of the diagram itself represents the missing element of Volatility.

Action, and the Denouement on the declining slope after the Falling Action. The Inciting Incident has also been considered as a separate point in the pyramid or as part of the Exposition, but it is used separately in Figure 4.1 to demarcate the discovery of a problem. Some license has therefore been taken to present the pyramid in a manner conducive for understanding the structure of moral panics, and the elements associated with the attributional and processual models are superimposed to illustrate their place within Freytag's narrative structure. Box 4.2 shows a different representation of the information presented in Figure 4.1 by outlining the components of both moral panics models in relation to one another and their place within the unified narrative. This information is helpful for understanding how Part II of this volume is structured, as well as how certain parts of the discussion were shaped.

Cast of Characters

Since the entire cast of identity theft is humanity, each individual (you) can be expected to operate within certain established parameters. You are a rational being, self-possessed of choice, and presumably the owner of some identity. You are also systematically motivated in the same way as them (being everybody else), albeit toward different ends at different times. As a lead character then, you can play a villain or a victim depending on the circumstances. You

Box 4.2 A Unified Model of Moral Panics

Unified Model	Processual Model	Attributional Model
Cast of Characters	Stage 2: Media Inventory Stage 3: Moral Entrepreneurs Stage 4: Experts	Element 6: Claims Makers
Exposition		
Inciting Incident	Stage 1: Emergence	Element 1: Concern Element 3: Consensus
Rising Action		Element 2: Hostility Element 4: Disproportionality
Climax	Stage 5: Coping & Resolution	
Falling Action		Element 5: Volatility
Denouement	Stage 6: Fade Away Stage 7: Legacy	

might also play one of many supporting roles in the drama of identity theft, alone or as part of a group.

Any of these individual or collective roles can similarly be characterized as a good guy, a bad guy, or one of those other guys in between. The usual collectives in the drama of a moral panic nevertheless conform to the typical classes of social life, as well as some classical theatrical elements if the case of identity theft is interpreted along the lines of *Policing the Crisis*: the Ruling Class (governments); the Producers (private industry); the Hoi Polloi (the public); and the Chorus,[35] which is comprised of the Defenders (grassroots organizations) and the Grapevine (media).

As a social extension of you, your identity (mini you) can be personified as a separate actor in the drama of identity theft. The initial crisis of identity theft therefore occurs when mini you is kidnapped (or infonapped) and later violated by some unscrupulous fiend(s). Although your identity can also be viewed as an important prop (or offender tool) in this drama, the issue of individual identity ownership generally seems to justify breathing life into this two-dimensional concept in the present context.

Exposition

The background of the story, representing the preemergence stage of a social problem, is particularly important in the context of identity theft and perhaps moral panics as well. With identity theft, it seemed necessary to examine how this term became the victor among competing labels during the period preceding its "discovery" in the United States. The particular question requiring an answer was this: Why identity theft all of a sudden? At the same time, the typical objects of panic witnessed thus far have been integral parts of societies for centuries, so every case of crisis might require some consideration of the depths from which it emerged. The exposition therefore provides a context for interpreting events, and prevents the problem from being regarded as some kind of spontaneous or magical occurrence by otherwise rational people. The term discovery is thus used loosely here, since much of what is "new" in the context of moral panics really seems to be the result of social rediscovery within the bigger scheme of life.

Inciting Incident

Moral panics are sometimes a reaction to a particular incident, but this is not always true and this was not the case with identity theft. This stage of the model nevertheless explains the immediate context in which the problem is discovered and related concerns are discussed, perhaps in an actual state of physical panic, depending upon the circumstances. Ultimately, a social consensus is formed about the problem. In other words, during this period of problem recognition, it is generally conceded that the issue is big enough or bad enough to warrant concern and additional attention.

Rising Action

Once a consensus has been reached about the object of concern, which may in some way be irrational on its own, the reaction to that problem (however defined) is usually out of proportion to the real threat involved. This stage of the model is therefore focused on evaluating the claims made by various social actors about the problem. While disproportionality is the key characteristic of a panic and the focus of most research evidence, this skewed thinking also extends to offenders—or the potential folk devils—of the moral panics narrative.

According to Cohen, the element of hostility consists of "moral outrage towards the actors (folk devils) who embody the problem and the agencies . . . who are 'ultimately' responsible (and may become folk devils themselves)."[36] While this sounds very similar to what might occur in a risk society, the main obstacle to employing this description in an empirical sense lies with the nature of morality itself. The boundaries of this concept have never been defined within the moral panics tradition, and no one has attempted to sketch out what something like "moral outrage" might entail in practice or theory.[37] Critcher sidestepped this issue until the very end of his work, and it was not a strong feature underlying the case study of identity theft, so it remains a dysfunctional part of the moral panics tradition overall. A very broad framework for understanding this issue can nevertheless be provided in the context of this volume.

As previously explained, rational choice means what it implies: choice that is rational, not rational choices. While the decision to violate any social norm (particularly law) may not appear rational on its surface to some people, the process through which that violation occurs is very rational indeed. People (being human) always need something, which in turn motivates the action geared toward acquiring whatever that is (food, security, luxury). The absolute value[38] of this dynamic therefore represents the basic variables of purposive, live action—means and ends. This idea simultaneously applies to identity theft and moral panics, however, as both are fairly standard deviations from acceptable behavior in any world.

Regardless of the roles that individuals play in life, the decision to knowingly pursue "bad" ends or use "bad" means typically invokes moral reasoning. While the internal act of weighing the positive and negative aspects of a contemplated action has been classically described as a hedonistic calculus, the actual process of choice is as complicated as this image suggests on both the individual and collective levels of decision making. The experience of moral choice is part of the human condition, however, one commonly portrayed as a tiny devil and angel oppositely perched upon the shoulders of everyman. *Good v. Bad* is therefore a classic case that can be decided with the guidance of ethical principles, whether whispered in your ear or bellowed in a courtroom.

Since the verdict of good or bad is not as important as the trial in the current context, it is only necessary to understand that such decisions are made within an ethical framework[39] that can broadly be geared toward relativism (i.e., determining what is good and bad as defined by an individual) or absolutism (i.e., what is good and bad in a universal sense). These frameworks are applicable to individual and collective decision making, whether related to weighing the pains and pleasures associated with engaging in a given course of action, or when considering the rightness or wrongness of a completed act. Decision making, moral or otherwise, is thus the product of an internal calculus (compounded at the collective level) that is usually directed at the most beneficial ends, however defined in context.

The means by which such ends are achieved, whether good or bad in themselves, is another matter to consider. In particular, there are four basic moral dichotomies of human behavior:

    Good Means + Good Ends
    Bad Means + Bad Ends
    Good Means + Bad Ends
    Bad Means + Good Ends

The first two equations represent the archetypal good guys and bad guys of this world, while the remaining two sets of guys might not really be much better or worse than the other overall. All four represent the rationality of moral decision making, which provides a basic lens for examining ethical behavior in a world that might be more relativistic than not. In sum then, the individual and collective calculations of these equations drive the offending behavior of the bad guys, and the rising action of a panic for the good guys. These vital dualistic concepts—means and ends, good and bad—are therefore highlighted in various places throughout the identity theft narrative that follows in this part of the volume.

Climax

The climax of a drama is also known as the crisis. In essence, the story is approaching its tipping point: something must be done about the problem and it must be done now. The "something" that is done at this point can vary (i.e., legislation is passed or proposed, offenders are sentenced, community groups are organized), but an essential feature of the moral panic is that such actions are usually symbolic. That is, something minimally appears to have been done but it is not likely to be effective or address the underlying problem.

Falling Action

Moral panics are reputed to erupt fairly quickly, and end just as suddenly. Although there are several caveats to this brief interpretation, once the crisis from the previous stage has been averted in the eyes of those concerned, attention toward the problem will be redirected.

Denouement

As the counterpoint to the inciting incident, the clamor surrounding an issue comes to an end, although it may be easily forgotten or never completely disappear. This concept is more abstract, however, in that it does not necessarily represent a specific moment or event that brings the panic to an end. Like the effect of throwing a stone into a pond, attention is likely to ripple throughout society before resembling something potentially close to its "pre-problem" state.[40] Deciding the point at which a story ends can therefore be extremely arbitrary, and this is captured by the final stage of the processual model.

The panic will eventually come to an end, but it may also leave a lasting impression of its former existence. The legislation passed as the result of a moral panic, for example, will undoubtedly continue to affect people's lives for good or bad. One set of researchers in particular has proposed adding misdirectedness as an element of Goode and Ben-Yehuda's model to better incorporate the idea that the actual response during a panic is disproportionate to the issue itself: "Standard reactions to a problem are not directed and/or can be known to be inadequate to solve the problem as it is defined by the majority of those who want to tackle it. The problem . . . may even disappear for a while, but it is clear that it will emerge again."[41] While Critcher did not discuss this issue directly, it is consistent with his conclusions regarding the element of disproportionality and the general importance of symbolic responses during a moral panic, particularly in the role that they might play in fueling serial panics.

Since symbolic responses are unlikely to address the problem, it is possible that another round of attention will be generated after discovering that the initial measures are ineffective, thus creating the need for "something else" to be done. In that case, the prior panic and its legacy would become the exposition for another moral panic, and the process just described would start again. Considering that very little new information has actually come to bear on the problem of identity theft over the past several years, the identity theft narrative is extremely suggestive of a serial panic. Thus, the legacy of identity theft may become the fodder for another round of attention at any time when some "new" crisis is identified.

The basic story of identity theft in the United States, as told forthwith, was reconstructed with the help of this unified model. While a theatrical play is still the confined systems model used for representing the situational dynamics (or dramas) acted out along the offending-victimization continuum, both in relation to identity theft and moral panics,[42] necessity dictated using a narrative structure with touches of theatrical flair. The earliest claims of the dominant narrative also set the stage for very specific claims later on, which are directly associated with the situational contexts (or acts) of identity theft represented in Figure 3.1. The need to examine different levels of claims therefore demanded some additional deviation from Freytag's structure, but this does affect the actual evidence of the case, only the order in which it is presented.

SOBERING THOUGHTS

Both of the models tested in the original research failed to certain degrees, and some of those failures remain in the unified model. It was nevertheless concluded that identity theft is an example of a modern-day moral panic by an overwhelming preponderance of circumstance. That conclusion was thus the starting point for this volume, but while this label was not arbitrarily or carelessly applied to the case of identity theft, its contemporary usage remains problematic.

Considering that moral panics develop around real social problems, there will always be room to criticize the methods used to draw this particular conclusion. The advantage of this type of analysis, however, does not lie in the ability to rightly call something a moral panic. Having enough evidence to suggest that a given social reaction is consistent with a moral panic is instead a valuable indicator that something might be seriously wrong with society's reasoning about a problem. Although this appears to be the case with identity theft in the final analysis, this is simply an unfortunate reality of American society rather than a triumph of the moral panics perspective.

Although the original research described here was also guilty to some degree of uncritically applying Critcher's approach to the case of identity theft, there were immediate benefits to replicating his work. In particular, no examples using this approach could be located and his conclusions could be evaluated in light of a somewhat unconventional topic for moral panics research in general. The term replicate, however, must be interpreted somewhat loosely in this context as well. Critcher largely relied on the research of others to assess each model through a series of case studies,[43] but each was conducted and reported by Critcher in slightly different ways. There is also a general vagueness surrounding the methods that have been used in previous moral panics research, so there was an additional need for the investigation to consider the implications of various methodological issues, which are reflected throughout this volume at different times.

As a final note pertinent to the global context of identity theft, Critcher provided international comparisons for each case study, which fell far beyond the scope of the original project and the current one. Although one analysis of the UK problem concluded that identity fraud was a moral panic using less stringent methods than the ones described herein, identity theft continues to dwell primarily in the United States.[44] Nevertheless, IDT is an international issue that has received a large share of attention, and additional case study comparisons should be the focus of future research in the moral panics tradition. This is particularly important given that almost everyone in today's world needs to become more discerning when it comes to applying the labels of moral panic *and* identity theft.

THE PERFECT PANIC

In academic terms, there really is no unequivocal answer to the question of whether identity theft is a moral panic because the conclusions of the original research largely cancelled each other out. Many features of the identity theft phenomenon were consistent with the presence of a moral panic, but the perspective itself remains flawed. These findings, however, do not completely negate the validity of the moral panics perspective or the value of approaching the case of identity theft with the type of focused skepticism that this tradition provides. In fact, the moral panics perspective appears to be stuck in the 20th century and is thereby ill-equipped to identify modern-day moral panics, of which the case of identity theft ostensibly qualifies. In popular terms, therefore, identity theft is not only a moral panic, it is the perfect storm of social panics.

Due to the enormity of this concept, identity theft has acted like a magnet for almost every other type of social problem imaginable—particularly two of those noted by Cohen regarding the typical objects of panic (drugs and immigrants), as well as terrorism, which is a more recent area examined by moral panics research. There were also a number of other conditions swept up in this reaction, notably information and technology, which may have been the real impetus driving concerns about identity theft. In particular, one possibility suggested by the investigation was that identity theft was on the periphery of another panic (or phanic) focused on the Internet—particularly new crimes such as phishing, pharming, and phreaking. Thus, identity theft may be uniquely situated in modern society as a point of convergence for several different types of traditional and contemporary panics. However, such a possibility would need to be examined through additional research specifically directed at these tangential objects of the identity theft panic.

RIDING THE STORM

As mentioned, identity theft may also be an example of a serial panic. Although this idea seems to contradict the traditional wisdom that moral panics are volatile—that is, "they erupt fairly suddenly (although they may lie dormant or latent for long periods of time, and may reappear from time to time) and, nearly as suddenly, subside"[45]—it is a possibility recognized within the academic tradition. In discussing one case, for example, Goode and Ben-Yehuda note:

> [T]he American drug panic, which at first glance appears to stretch back over a century, upon closer inspection, turns out to be relatively local and time-delimited. One of the most remarkable features of note about the many drug panics that have seized American society over the past century is that, typically, later ones have built upon earlier ones. That is, organizations and institutions are often established at one point in time and remain in place and help generate concern later on, at the appropriate time.[46]

If the phrase *identity theft* were substituted in the right places, this would be a fairly accurate description of this phenomenon's gradual transformation over the past century from an entertainment novelty into public enemy no. 1, as well as its projected course into the new century—and new countries—that lie ahead. This description also suggests another way to look at the hype surrounding identity theft, which is patterned to sound the same yet somehow different every time, as there is rarely anything new to report about identity theft aside from more victims. With over a decade of information to consider, however, it does in fact appear that the issue of identity theft developed along multiple trajectories.

The evidence as a whole suggests three main cycles of attention that were in some ways driven by the events of September 11, 2001. Unfortunately, there is no way to completely understand the impact that this tragedy has had on the issue of identity theft, or how its evolution would have progressed had 9/11 not occurred. These periods in the narrative are nevertheless delineated by other events that were evident along with a single unifying theme: the economic interests that underlie the collective problem of identity theft.

The first period of attention (the victim narrative) centered on the criminalization of identity theft and roughly began sometime during or slightly before 1996. If the progression of national criminalization can be any guide (see Table 6.1), this period seemed to reach its peak in 1999—the year in which 22 states passed this type of legislation—and then gradually tapered off through the end of 2005. This also seems true for the federal government in that the Federal Trade Commission began its work with identity theft at the end of 1999. Despite a succession of ongoing activities, these events showed concretely that something had been done to address the problem and assist victims, thus symbolically placing a period at the end of this first episode.

The second attention cycle (the national security narrative) roughly began in 2002 and ended in 2004. Although the potential links between identity theft and terrorism were understood before the events of September 11, identity theft became somewhat of an addendum to the nation's war on terror after this point. The issue of identity theft also served to bolster the nation's ongoing struggle with immigration policy, as well as its war on drugs and practically everything else. Identity theft initially received some attention from federal authorities who believed that the 9/11 hijackers had probably used some form of false identification to perpetrate the attacks, but this attention would later be refocused after it was discovered that at least one person suspected of training the hijackers to fly had been using the social security number of a New Jersey woman who had died in 1991.[47] Attention would then peak again in 2003 following the release of the Federal Trade Commission's survey report, which seemed to confirm all previous speculation that identity theft was indeed a national epidemic. At this point in the narrative then, the threat was national as well as personal.

The final and largest cycle of attention (the privacy narrative) began in 2005 after the ChoicePoint incident. This is primarily witnessed within media sources, however, perhaps because many other social actors were busy staring at the blunt end of a pointed finger during this phase of the crisis in terms of assigning responsibility for the insecurity of U.S. identity data. The original research period ended in 2005, so it is unknown whether or when the American privacy narrative ended, but the dominant identity theft narrative is still going strong.[48]

One of the most astonishing features of this panic overall, however, is how a very limited (yet completely erroneous) set of core claims about identity theft were continually recycled through some new association with one of its same old tired faces. Completely unquestioned, these claims were then parroted and mutilated like a rotten grapevine, over and over and over again—by pretty much every sector of society for more than a decade. These particular claims will be considered in detail later on, but such claims helped to fuel these internal narrative cycles, as well as breed confusion and general outrage over the problem of identity theft in the United States.

EVERYMAN'S DILEMMA

As a final level of perspective on the moral problem involved with identity theft, the American saga can be viewed as a modern-day morality play regarding how we live our social lives (from beginning to end, and ever after), just as *Everyman*, a 15th-century morality play, was concerned with how we (humankind) manage our spiritual ones. Identity theft is a contemporary harbinger of social death, with victimization representing the moment at which we are asked to account for our lives, or at least for the lives of our identities. The universal moral of the identity theft story therefore pertains to how we do social business in this world. Using this analogy, identity theft also becomes "everyman's crime." While this moniker is justified in the context of moral panics alone, it is particularly fitting when the dominant narrative maintains that everyone can be an offender and a victim. Although this point of view adds another layer to the discussion of identity theft that follows, much of this implied moral analysis will be left to the reader's imagination and judgment.

A MATTER OF RESEARCH

The phenomenon of identity theft was born in the United States, which was the geographical focus of the research underpinning this volume on global crime. As just described, that project examined the question of whether identity theft was a modern-day moral panic. The nature of that research was exploratory because no standard methodological structure exists for conducting traditional moral panics research,[49] and very little is actually known about identity theft in objective terms. Since much of the content herein is the result of that research process, a brief explanation of its two largest methods will now be provided.[50]

Literature Review

The research for this project first began in the fall of 2004 as part of a literature review conducted on behalf of the U.S. National Institute of Justice.[51] Several methods were later used to expand the scope of this initial review and include literature published through mid-2007. A concentrated effort was also made to uncover literature published prior to the year 2000, including attempts to identify the origins of such terms as identity theft, identity thief, and identity fraud. Searches using these terms were first conducted using relevant databases including Lexis-Nexis, Access World News (NewsBank), Factiva, and the ProQuest New York Times historical database. Beth Givens, the director of Privacy Rights Clearinghouse and an early pioneer of this issue, later offered access to her library, which housed a number of early documents that could not have otherwise been obtained.

There was a dearth of information published prior to 1999, and at first this appeared to be due to the fact that very little attention had actually been paid to the issue. It was also possible that identity theft had simply been referred to by some other name or alias (e.g., stolen identity, assumed identity, name theft), but systematic searches for alternate terms were prohibited by the various constructions that could be used for a single concept (i.e., assumed identity, assuming the identity, identity was assumed) and the commonality of the terms involved (impersonation, assumption, name, identity). An examination of this possibility nevertheless confirmed that concern for identity theft existed prior to 1999; it was just not being called such on a regular basis.

The Internet search engine Google was used extensively to identify and access information from a broad range of sources, particularly international ones as they apply to the present context. Additional search engines were also used at various times (e.g., Yahoo, Ask.com) to see if different results could be obtained. While some of these searches were dictated by the topic of the research at hand (e.g., specific searches for statistics regarding the offense or related consumer behaviors), many were guided by a snowball effect in which one source would lead to the investigation of others. Several hundred documents were ultimately reviewed to shape the content of that research, but only a portion was used to construct the narrative presented in this volume.

The original literature review by Newman and McNally (2005) concluded that there were very few sources of good information about identity theft in the United States, despite the sheer amount of information that was available at that time. Since the original case study built upon the results of that review, it should be noted that this assessment remains essentially unaltered after several years of additional research. International data about the problem are also virtually nonexistent, but information about the global problem of identity theft might be suffering in some instances from the same disease responsible for the U.S. crisis (i.e., panic).

Newspaper Sample

A dataset of newspaper stories was also compiled in the tradition of moral panics research. Identity theft, identity fraud, and identity thief coverage were examined in six daily newspapers, selected to roughly correspond with the progression of identity theft criminalization in the United States.

While the *New York Times* is a quintessential newspaper for media analysis within many research traditions, examining this range of newspapers was desirable for at least two reasons. First, it had been suggested that moral

Table 4.1 Identity Theft

State	Year IDT criminalized	Regional newspaper
Arizona	1996	*Arizona Republic*
Massachusetts	1998	*Boston Globe*
Virginia	2000	*USA Today*
New York	2001	*New York Times*
Washington, D.C.	2003	*Washington Post*
Colorado	2005	*Rocky Mountain News*

panics are likely to end with legislative action, or more broadly when something "appears to have been done."[52] It was therefore expected that the attention given to identity theft would be greater prior to its criminalization, or any similarly focused effort that occurred on a local or national level. Second, the importance of examining variation within and between media outlets and markets had been noted by prior moral panics research.[53] While this investigation focused on only one type of media outlet, each newspaper reflected a different type of market, with some being distributed and read on a national level (e.g., *New York Times*, *USA Today*). The selection of these particular newspapers was further affected by their circulation size and full-text availability, with each representing one of the largest in circulation for its respective area and the nation as a whole.

The original intention was to examine a period of at least 10 years (1996–2005) within the newspaper sample, but consistent data were not available prior to 1999. The reason for this was related to the process of retrieving articles, which was performed using two standardized archives: Lexis-Nexis and Access World News (also known as NewsBank).[54] Although these archives have been used in similar research, the decision to use both was necessitated by the absence of daily Arizona news source coverage within Lexis-Nexis. Articles from the *Arizona Republic* were therefore retrieved from Access World News, but none of those published prior to January 1, 1999, were available for analysis.[55]

Data collection began in early 2006. In order to distinguish coverage of identity theft from identity fraud, as well as reporting about the offense (identity theft) from its associated offenders (identity thieves), three discrete samples of newspaper references were compiled using rather extensive procedures. The Identity Theft Sample (n = 1,839) comprised all references in which this term appeared, regardless of whether the terms identity fraud and identity thief also appeared. The Identity Fraud Sample (n = 181) consisted of all such references, regardless of whether the term identity thief also appeared. The Identity Thief Sample (n = 86) contained only references with the term identity thief. Inappropriate items were also removed from the original

Table 4.2 Final Sample of Newspaper References

Newspaper	All references		Total	1999–2005*		Total
Arizona Republic	Theft	339	369	Theft	339	369 (0)
	Fraud	17		Fraud	17	
	Thief	13		Thief	13	
Boston Globe	Theft	204	262	Theft	200 (4)	258 (4)
	Fraud	46		Fraud	46	
	Thief	12		Thief	12	
USA Today	Theft	198	215	Theft	195 (3)	211 (4)
	Fraud	8		Fraud	7 (1)	
	Thief	9		Thief	9	
New York Times	Theft	394	452	Theft	382 (12)	435 (17)
	Fraud	30		Fraud	26 (4)	
	Thief	28		Thief	27 (1)	
Washington Post	Theft	558	648	Theft	541 (17)	630 (18)
	Fraud	68		Fraud	67 (1)	
	Thief	22		Thief	22	
Rocky Mountain News	Theft	146	160	Theft	143 (3)	157 (3)
	Fraud	12		Fraud	12	
	Thief	2		Thief	2	
			2,106			2,060 (46)

*Figures in parentheses represent the number of references that were removed because they were published prior to January 1, 1999.

sample (e.g., duplicates, false hits, teasers), and a further decision was made to exclude articles retrieved with only comparative terms, such as assumed identity and stolen identity, due to the difficulties previously described. Table 4.2 shows the characteristics of the final sample of references, including the reduced sample for the period between 1999 and 2005 for which comparisons could be made.

References were then coded for a number of standard elements (e.g., author, date, length), as well as for the presence of key terms (identity theft/fraud/thief) and any alternate terms. An emergent coding scheme was also developed in order to examine different themes, but since the importance of these codes relates to the presentation of evidence, they will only be discussed in context when necessary.

The Life and Times of IDT

WHILE IDENTITY THEFT can be understood in mathematical terms, the U.S. computation has shown that the resulting product can be much greater than the sum of its parts. In particular, identity theft can be personified as a trickster in the U.S. tradition, which according to legend is a being (not necessarily human) who "plays tricks or otherwise disobeys normal rules and conventional behavior."[1] Identity theft reflects any face, speaks every language, and the realm of social norms is its stomping ground. Identity theft, however, is a being of our own creation. The images we see and the voices we hear are our own, all victims and offenders together in the wonderful world of identity theft. But when trying to explain identity theft, how does one account for everything and everyone? Let us start by taking a closer look at some of these faces of identity theft—the ones that are being projected out into the world.

Identity theft has a conceptual relationship with many different types of crime, and thus it can been described in relation to many specific forms of criminal offending: for example, organized crime, white-collar crime, financial crime, street crime, drug crime, Internet/online crime, computer crime, immigration crime, terrorism. Although identity theft can be discussed in relation to each of these offenses, it cannot be classified on the whole as being one more so than another, at least not without proper data about the problem. As things stand, however, the concept of identity theft is not properly described as being any one of these acts alone (e.g., identity theft is a white-collar crime, identity theft is an online crime), even though it is commonly described in such absolute terms and statements based on the importance or placement of these other crimes on a society's agenda at any given moment.

Identity theft is like a pizza with everything on it that is only being offered to the public one slice at a time (by governments, industries, media, police). Maybe one slice has no mushrooms or too much pepperoni relative to other slices, but the consumer does not necessarily know that his piece has too much or too little of some topping. What he sees may be all that he gets—a slice of mainly pepperoni pizza—but those engaged in distributing slices of identity theft to the public do not always take the time to explain what exactly they are putting on the plate or what might be missing.

HIGH IN THE STREETS

As an example of this, consider two often-used portrayals of this offense: identity theft is a white-collar crime and identity theft is a drug crime. These categories of crime are not mutually exclusive, but each one reflects a very different image of what identity theft is supposedly all about. They also suggest what classes of offending we might be dealing with, and that particular dichotomy is not easy to reconcile. Have you ever heard of a white-collar drug offender? Probably not, as stated in those terms, because drugs are often associated with the streets and white-collar offenders generally commit their crimes well above them. How then can identity theft be both?

Although these characterizations are based on very specific viewpoints (or foci) within law enforcement, each one is really just a different slice of the pie, and everybody's got a piece of it. In the earliest account that could be located (1995), the claim that identity theft is a form of white-collar crime was attributed to a representative of TRW—a U.S. credit bureau (not law enforcement agency), now known as Experian.[2] The U.S. Attorney General's Council on White Collar Crime was in fact working with the Federal Trade Commission (FTC) on the problem of identity theft from a very early point in the history of this issue.[3] This particular idea is also connected to the work of the Federal Bureau of Investigation and similar entities that routinely investigate white-collar offenses around the globe.[4] The claim itself therefore regards identity theft as seen through the eyes of these beholders, not necessarily TRW.

Identity theft is both a means and an end of white-collar crime, but state and local officials also view a strong link between drugs (particularly methamphetamine) and identity theft. According to one police officer, however, identity theft offenders were "[t]raditionally and initially . . . the white collar guy; now it is the guys that used to be in narcotics."[5] There is a lot being said here, but how should such a statement be interpreted? Identity theft used to be a white-collar crime but isn't anymore? If so, the white-collar agencies just mentioned never got that message. Neither apparently did white-collar identity thieves. In the words of Lawrence, convicted of identity theft and sentenced to three years: "I ain't knew they'd give me this much time. I thought because of a white-collar crime I'd get a slap on the wrist and like probation or something."[6] These sentiments of unproportionality are shared by many of his fellow inmates, whose stereotypes about white-collar crime may have been factored into their own deterrence equation (i.e., weighing the certainty, severity, and celerity[7] of engaging in identity theft)—the sum of which somehow landed them all in federal prison.

A more localized example of the meth-IDT nexus took place in Arizona, which was engaged in a specific debate during the mid-2000s over proposed legislation to block access to prescription medications for the purpose of manufacturing methamphetamine. Consider the following three claims involving the links between meth and identity theft in this state:

> Meth use is currently a factor in over 85 percent of property and identity theft crimes in Arizona.[8]

This first statement by Pinal County Sheriff Chris Vasquez indirectly pins most of the responsibility for property crime and identity theft on meth users. Being a meth user is not a crime, but meth users certainly appear to be thieves. What does this statistic tell us however? That over 85 percent of the identity theft in Arizona is motivated by the need for drugs? Or that 85 percent of identity theft is committed because offenders are high on meth?

> Last year, Arizona led the nation in identity theft per capita, largely because of the state's "tweaker" population.[9]

This second statement, which can only be attributed to the journalist since no other source was mentioned, says much the same thing as Vasquez, albeit with a more direct and derogatory tone. Meth users (aka tweakers) are still responsible in this example, but we still don't know what their actual role is in identity theft. It might also leave readers with the erroneous impression that meth is the leading cause of identity theft in the country, not just Arizona.

> In addition to wrecking lives, meth is closely tied to a laundry list of serious crimes, including domestic abuse, burglary, assault, auto theft and identity theft.[10]

This final statement, made by Arizona Attorney General Terry Goddard, merely implies the culpability of meth users in identity theft but broadens the scope of their wrongdoing from property crime to violent crime. While his laundry list may be a little short, the underlying target of derision in all three of these references is meth—not identity theft. The guilt of meth users seems to be a foregone conclusion, but so is their complicity in identity theft (at least in Arizona). Cooking, dealing, or shooting meth is not identity theft, however, stealing identities is.

In a similar way, such contrary labels as high-tech crime and low-tech crime cannot be applied wholesale to the problem of identity theft without excluding the other. In other words, identity theft is neither a high-tech crime nor a low-tech crime; it is both to different degrees and within different contexts. As just one example of the difficulties associated with applying such labels in general to the topic of identity theft, consider the difference between the descriptors computer crime and online crime. Both are related since computers are the vehicles to the Internet, but the Internet provides a virtual connection to other people and places, while a computer on its own does not.

A computer, unconnected to the Internet, represents one set of security risks. When connected to the Internet, a computer creates an open door between the online universe and the computer itself, thus representing an entirely different set of risks for users and their computers. If we only look at the face of Internet crime, however, then we ignore an entire host of security concerns and perhaps reinforce certain stereotypes about identity theft that will not ultimately aid in the goals of criminal deterrence or prevention.

ANYTHING GOES

As reflected by its many faces, identity theft means many different things to many people. The term itself seems to have been coined in the United States (ca. 1964[11]) and is still primarily used there. Most of the world and even some parts of the United States continue to use the broader and more established term *identity fraud*, which occurs when a party is defrauded via the receipt of false identity information. Identity theft in contrast only occurs when that identifying information belongs to an actual individual (living or dead), as opposed to a purely or even partly fictitious one (the latter sometimes being known as synthetic fraud). A real identity may be as valuable as a fake identity in the context of social interaction, assuming that the requirements of identification and authentication can still be met. Fabricated (or synthetic) identities nevertheless add another level of complexity to the distinction between identity fraud and identity theft.

As noted by the Federal Deposit Insurance Corporation, "[u]nlike typical identity fraud where a fraudster steals the identity of a real person and uses it to commit a fraud, a synthetic identity is a completely fabricated identity that does not correspond to any actual person."[12] Although this description would seem to imply that synthetic fraud is very different from identity theft, this is really not the case. For example, one study of the topic found that "synthetic identities are more commonly used to commit identity fraud than true-name identities,"[13] but related press releases continued to give the impression that the information involved in synthetic fraud was completely fabricated (i.e., fake).[14] A press release from an earlier version of this study also reported that "the majority of applications contain actual, valid identity information."[15] So which is it—completely fake or only partly fake? Mike Cook, a cofounder of ID Analytics (the firm that conducted this research), subsequently provided a more comprehensive description of synthetic fraud:

> It may contain identity elements that are valid and accurate by themselves, such as a Social Security number, a name or an address . . . [b]ut since the combination of the name, address and Social Security number do not correspond to one particular consumer, the fraud is unreported and often goes undetected.[16]

In other words then, the criminal problem of identity theft gets even worse. There appears to be an entire category of unresolved and/or undiscovered fraud in which a single case may simultaneously be associated with the personal information of several, very real individuals. Synthetic fraud therefore seems to hover somewhere in the middle between identity theft and identity fraud, at least until these identities begin to find their way home.

Identity theft and identity fraud can also be thought of as constituent elements of an even broader category, identity crime. Considering the relationship between identity theft and identity fraud, however, identity fraud is a much larger offense category because it includes the victimization of all entities that receive both real and fake information with the intent to defraud. In this way, every instance of identity theft can be conceptualized as an instance of identity fraud, but the reverse is not true.

One man's identity theft is literally another man's identity fraud, but these terms are also used interchangeably within and across many parts of the world. Javelin Strategy & Research, for example, is a private company that has conducted some of the largest U.S. victimization studies to date. While this research replicates a national study of identity theft conducted on behalf of the FTC, Javelin uses the term *identity fraud* instead. Specifically, Javelin defines identity fraud as "the unauthorized use of another's personal information to achieve illicit financial gain"[17] (i.e., misusing identities), and identity theft as "the unauthorized access to personal information" (i.e., acquiring identities).[18] These definitions are particularly problematic given Javelin's eminence in the world of identity theft and the true substance of what their research measures, which in popular terms is known as identity theft.

An individual's personal information must be acquired before it can be misused, but the issue arises as to whether the illicit acquisition of such information constitutes an act of identity theft in itself. In particular, Javelin asserts that identity theft can occur without identity fraud; for example, as the result of a large-scale data breach.[19] If this sentiment is true, then the problem of identity theft just got much worse once again. Remember the 500 million breached records to date? Those are just the tip of this particular iceberg.

While one company has recently suggested that the chances of identity theft victimization following a data breach are very small,[20] there are actually many different kinds of data breaches and not all carry the same risk, depending upon the type of personal information that is involved. The idea of "unauthorized access" promoted by Javelin might also include almost any type of information mishandling up until the point that an individual's personal information is fraudulently transferred to another party.

While a laptop might be stolen with the intention of obtaining the personal information that it stores, it might also be the only intended target of a theft if the offender has no knowledge of the computer's contents. Someone who achieves unauthorized access to personal information in this manner may therefore have no intention or ability to misuse it, but this possibility does not negate the owner's responsibility with regard to the safety of either the laptop or its contents.

Contrast this with an example of personal information that is legitimately given in good faith, for instance, to a store clerk during a transaction. While certain personal information must be exchanged in this context (e.g., a credit card number), the clerk may intend to use it in an unauthorized manner at a later time. In effect, the employee's authorized access to this information ends with the decision to use it for illicit purposes, regardless of whether the information itself is ever actually misused. Legal definitions of identity theft do not add much clarity to this issue, however, since many include the possession of personal information with the requisite intent to defraud. The intention of the parties involved nevertheless appears to be an integral part of the relationship between the unauthorized acquisition of personal information and its misuse.

On its own, the illicit acquisition of personal information is an enormous privacy issue and a larger-than-life factor contributing to identity theft victimization. It is not identity theft however; that problem is unmercifully bad enough already. Individuals are not always criminally harmed as the result of unauthorized access to their personal information, but this does not mean that such access is acceptable or that personal information should not be protected. The previous discussion is therefore not meant to downplay these considerations, but to illustrate the difficulties associated with calling the acquisition of personal information identity theft regardless of the intention to misuse it or whether this information is ever in fact misused.

A similar set of problematic definitions centered on the misuse of information is illustrated by LifeLock cofounder, Todd Davis: identity fraud occurs "when someone gets hold of your credit card and uses it" and identity theft occurs "when someone assumes your identity to open a new line of credit."[21] While these descriptions are misleading insofar as they imply that both identity theft and identity fraud are only related to the credit card industry, the idea behind both can be summarized as follows: Identity fraud is committed through the violation of old you, and identity theft is committed through the violation of new you. Once again, the main problem with this type of division is that both are parts of a whole. In this case, however, the separation is premised on the experience of individual victims, which is really what identity theft is all about.

Society knew that identity theft occurred before it was called such, but the emergence of this term as a predominant label reflects an important shift in perception. Until the 1990s, individuals (in the United States at least) were not considered to be the victims of these activities—collective entities were the only victims of identity fraud. As such, a number of industry terms were initially used to describe what was occurring when a case of identity fraud involved a real person. One of the first terms to surface during the mid-1980s was *real person fraud*,[22] soon followed by *true name fraud*[23]—a moniker that initially competed with identity theft for distinction, but ultimately lost the race. The phrase *true name fraud* is nevertheless more consistent with the fact that concern about identity theft victimization, at least in the beginning, was focused on new you rather than old you.

One of the first articles on identity theft from 1989 focused on the "not me" files handled by the Broward County (Florida) State Attorney's Office, which largely referred to cases of criminal record fraud (i.e., offenses noted under the motivational category of anonymity).[24] A similar story from 1991 recounted victims' frustration over the failure of authorities to act on the problem of social security number misuse in Massachusetts.[25] There are hundreds of examples like this within newspapers that all have one thing in common—new you. Although concerns about plain old you can often be found alongside those for new you, and despite the fact that existing account victimization represents the majority of identity theft, one of the most prominently displayed faces of identity theft has been that of new you victimization—or the worst case scenario of what can happen when your identity is stolen.

At a minimum, lumping all of these victims together under the heading of identity theft seems to be perpetuating a disservice to the victims who endure the worst of the problem, including the original victims who fought to have their status recognized under U.S. law. Even worse perhaps is that the regrettable truths that can be uttered about the horrors of new you have been publicly generalized to apply to the collective whole. Thus, the problem of identity theft in popular terms is comprised of a massive amount of victims whose lives are devastated, but this is simply untrue. The whole truth, unfortunately, is lost within the label of identity theft and the complexities of its occurrence. When it comes to understanding identity theft in today's world then, all of its reflections should really be considered. The meaning of any term related to identity theft is therefore best interpreted in context, whenever or wherever one might be encountered, and recognizing the essence of identity theft can help in that regard.

AD-LIB

Identity theft is a(n) _____ problem. Identity theft is a problem all right, but what kind of problem exactly? We have already seen some examples of how to render this statement false (e.g., identity theft is a white-collar problem [period, end of story]), so now let's fill in the blank with some adjectives that allow this statement to retain a little more of its underlying truth.

Identity Theft Is an Old Problem

The only thing new about identity theft is its name, and some of the methods that are used to accomplish this time-honored tradition of social chicanery.

Identity theft may seem new depending on which face you see, and relative to who you are, but it's really just another plain old face of identity theft somewhere underneath.

Identity Theft Is a Real Problem

The problem of identity theft is very real. It exists, and it too has a body and a name. Its reputation in the United States is only one rather skewed version of that reality, however, which may have preceded identity theft's formal introduction to the rest of the world. That in itself is a problem with the potential to develop into a full-blown and equally real global crisis.

Identity Theft Is a Serious Problem

The problem of identity theft is not only real, it is extremely serious. It affects billions of people and victimizes millions of identities from all over the world. Its practice in general also disrupts the normal ebb and flow of social life. Identity theft is a particularly serious problem for all of its victims, however, who must clean up the mess someone else has made of life in general, even if it is just a small one.

Identity Theft Is a Criminal Problem

Identity theft is a criminal problem and threat that traverses the personal, social, and global domains of life. It is not a crime everywhere in the specific legal sense of this word, but it is accomplished through a universally criminal process, and its commission generally falls under the heading of identity fraud within international law. Even if this statement was not completely true for all nations, the laws of every society prohibit the basic acts underlying identity theft—theft and fraud. While the harm experienced by a victim results from the physical act of an offender, this act may also be accomplished across different points in space and time; thus, the criminal problem of identity theft is everybody's problem, and it can be discussed and understood in standardized terms regarding offenders, victims, tools, and targets, as they interact across contexts and jurisdictions over time.

Identity Theft Is a Personal Problem

For most people, the problem of identity theft is the threat posed to personal security via the breach of identity information, but this threat does not apply equally to everyone. Identity management is nevertheless a basic requirement of social existence, thus many people have engaged in the protection of their personal identities for centuries, and for very different reasons other than the specific fear of identity theft victimization. A second problem occurs when individuals are victimized via the misuse of their identities, which requires additional management and response activities on the part of owners. Identity theft is therefore always a personal problem when all is said and done.

Identity Theft Is a Social Problem

Societies—being the collective embodiments of people—must deal with the criminal realities of identity theft (i.e., offending and victimization), but they must also deal with the social opportunities that make identity theft possible. Generally speaking, the need for identity ownership is premised on the social contract between a society and its people, which creates the primary condition necessary for identity theft, as well as the social substance of personal identity. As this need translates into practice, the routine and related social processes of identification and authentication combine to form the more specific context in which the exchange of personal information can result in harm. The social problem of identity theft can therefore be described in relation to owners (people) and co-owners (collectives), as well as in terms of the relationships between them (e.g., government-citizen; employer-employee; acquaintance-stranger; friend-enemy). Although societies have a collective role to play in the problem of identity theft, whether as causes or responders, a given society simply represents the general setting in which identity theft occurs.

Identity Theft Is a Global Problem

Identity theft is a global problem if only by virtue of being a predominantly U.S. crime that knows no borders. The many acts that comprise identity theft are nevertheless global in spirit, and the impact of their occurrence is continually felt within many other nations. The world, however, represents a much larger context for the commission of identity theft, involving even larger jurisdictions than those encountered at the social level. Thus, the global problem is a sum of national experiences with all things resembling identity theft at the conceptual level.

Identity Theft Is a Techno-Modern-Global Problem

The world is forever changing, physically and socially. This dynamic process is part of evolution, but the concept of identity theft has also evolved alongside societies. Technology has often been blamed for the problem of identity theft as we know it today, but so have a lot of other things such as personal information, credit, the Internet, and terrorists. Everything listed here (including terrorists at times) is a tool, which in itself is neither inherently good nor bad and can only be described in such terms in relation to how it is used or what might result. Although technology still plays a large role in the contemporary problem of identity theft, the conditions that make identity theft possible are universally social, but not universally technological.

If another culprit had to be named in lieu of technology (or any of the other candidates named for similar reasons), it would boil down to a tie between modernization and globalization. However, since both processes are intimately related and both have certainly felt the impact of technological progress over the years, the matter of choosing among any of them becomes rather chicken-and-egg. This resultant technology-modernization-globalization nexus can therefore be held responsible for making the world feel like a smaller place (by bringing people and cultures closer together across the world), as well as a bigger one (by physically isolating people and making them vulnerable to new threats).

This nexus of power is also accountable to no small degree for the problem of identity theft (née fraud), but there are still many people—by choice or otherwise—who do not enjoy the many benefits or suffer the many headaches derived from various techno-modern-global advancements. While the world might therefore spin at a constant rate, many parts of it are evolving differently, particularly with regard to identity theft.

Identity Theft Is a Complicated Problem

All of the above statements apply to identity theft, which on its own constitutes a particularly thorny problem. However, as a final point related to the meaning of identity theft, there are further sociological and psychological undercurrents related to the term identity that contribute a greater importance (and additional levels of complexity) to the phenomenon as a whole.

Regardless of an offender's specific motivation or the ultimate form of his or her fraudulent activity, the assumption of an identity—other than an individual's established identity within society—essentially provides immunity from identification, thereby threatening harm to its actual owner and society at large. As such, the crime of identity theft provides an array of offenders with a highly coveted anonymity regarding their own identities. While individual identities are not stolen in any real sense, the damages suffered through some forms of this offense can harm people in very powerful ways by robbing them of their sense of personal or social security and/or their access to institutionalized means within society.[26] When victims are truly robbed of their good name, it therefore amounts to a metaphorical social death that is premised upon the importance of certain types and exchanges of personal information within society.

Similar connotations of the term are also transmitted to the public in subtle and not-so-subtle ways. One example of the former is the way in which the term ID theft became shorthand for identity theft in U.S. society, the implicit message being identification (or ID) = identity. An example of the latter is the way in which the psychological concept of an identity crisis became the U.S. poster child for identity theft, the implicit message here being you—the best target and next victim of identity theft. Understanding the essence of identity theft, however incomplete its coverage herein has been, can therefore help everyone to translate such messages in context, and thus more effectively and completely whenever or wherever they are encountered.

THE MUG SHOT

Old (or existing) and new activities are commonly viewed within society as different forms of identity theft victimization. This offense was legally constructed at the federal level to include both types of victimization, and the largest national victimization studies have used a similar operational definition. The first study conducted on behalf of the FTC broke the offense into three categories, based on victim reports of the most serious type of misuse experienced:

> New Accounts and Other Frauds (the most serious)
> Misuse of Existing Non-Credit Card Account or Account Number (the middling)
> Misuse of Existing Credit Card or Credit Card Number (the least serious)

Javelin subsequently replicated the FTC's methodology, but combining all three categories inalterably skews our perception about these huddled masses of identity theft victims. The results of the 2003 FTC identity theft study will therefore be used to illustrate this point in further detail.

Table 5.1 shows the percentage of identity theft victims identified for each of the FTC's categories within the entire sample of survey respondents (N = 4,057). The second column represents the percentage of individuals who reported identity theft victimization during the year prior to the survey (March/April 2002 through March/April 2003). The third column represents the percentage of individuals who reported identity theft victimization during the five-year period prior to the survey (March/April 1998 through March/April 2003).

Based on population estimates from the U.S. Census, these figures were reported to represent approximately 27.3 million adults (12.7%) who had discovered some form of identity theft victimization over the five-year period, 9.91 million (4.6%) of which had discovered some form of identity theft victimization during only the previous year (referred to herein as The 9.9 Million).[27] A basic visual inspection of Table 5.1 immediately reveals higher overall percentages in the category of Misuse of Existing Credit Card or Account Number, whether based on one-year or five-year totals. Aside from sheer numbers, however, there are more substantial differences among the experiences of these identity theft victims.

Table 5.1 Summary of FTC Identity Theft Survey Results

	Discovery of victimization only within past year (%)	All discovery of victimization within past five years (%)
New accounts and other fraud	1.5	4.7
Misuse of existing non–credit card account or number	0.7	2.0
Misuse of existing credit card or account number	2.4	6.0
Total % of identity theft victims	4.6	12.7

Source: Synovate (2003: 5), N = 4,057.

In general, there are two main forms of identity theft: old you and new you. Table 5.2 illustrates that when the categories of Misuse of Existing Credit Card Account or Number and Misuse of Existing Non-Credit Card Account or Number (as discussed in relation to Table 5.1) are combined into a single category of Existing Account Misuse (or old you), the total percentage of victims greatly exceeds that of New Accounts and Other Fraud (or new you).

Some victims of new you in the FTC's study also experienced misuse related to old you. Further, some victims within the category of Existing Non-Credit Card experienced the misuse of an Existing Credit Card, while victims in this last category only experienced the misuse of an existing credit card account. As such, none of the victims in the combined category of Old You experienced any type of new activity. While this illustration is not meant to suggest that characterizing identity theft with even broader categories is preferable, depicting identity theft in this way is helpful for visualizing what each of these two distinct groups of activities contributes toward the problem of identity theft as a whole. In particular, Table 5.2 shows that victims of old you outnumber victims of new you by a ratio of approximately 2:1.

The key distinctions between these two main categories of identity theft are represented in Figure 5.1, which illustrates the range of activities commonly grouped under the label of identity theft. This continuum generally increases in severity from left to right, starting with Impersonation (old you) on the extreme left and ending with Assumption (new you) on the extreme right. Existing credit card fraud is the least serious form of identity theft, followed by various types of existing non-credit card misuse. Bank fraud, for example, would fall just to the left of Assimilation.

As discussed in relation to John Schmidt Scenario #1, account takeover is the worst-case scenario of old you. This can be accomplished, for example, by gaining access to an existing account and changing pertinent information such as an account number, billing address, or password/PIN. Some part of

Table 5.2 Old versus New IDT Activities

	Discovered victimization within past year*	Discovered victimization within past five years
New you (Accounts and other fraud)	1.5% (3.23 million)	4.7% (10.1 million)
Old you (Existing account misuse)	3.1% (6.67 million)	8.0% (17.2 million)
Total	4.6% (9.91 million)	12.7% (27.3 million)

Note: Percentages represent the number of identity theft victims identified in the FTC's study (Table 5.1). Synovate estimated whole numbers from these percentages on the basis of the U.S. adult population, which were recalculated for the categories in this table.
* Whole numbers in this column do not equal 9.91 million because they were not rounded.

Figure 5.1 The Continuum of Identity Theft Victimization

old you is therefore assimilated by evil you for his exclusive designs. An existing resource will eventually be depleted when the money runs out or a credit limit is reached; thus, the assumption of your identity represents the worst-case scenario of identity theft victimization overall.[28]

ENCORE

None of the victim categories introduced so far has reflected the issues of multiple or repeated victimization, multiple in the sense that more than one type of activity may be occurring, and repeated in the sense that any given activity may be occurring more than once. While these considerations are integral to understanding identity theft from a criminological point of view, they are also helpful for pointing out the potential relationship between new you and old you in the commission of identity theft. This issue is again illustrated with results from the FTC's 2003 survey.

Among existing non-credit card victims, 40 percent also experienced the misuse of an existing credit card account. Among victims of new accounts, 65 percent of victims also experienced some type of existing account misuse: 22 percent were victimized by the misuse of an existing credit card account;

26 percent were victimized by the misuse of an existing non-credit card account; and 16 percent were victimized by the misuse of both an existing credit card and some other type of existing non–credit card account.[29]

When all of these figures are taken into consideration, approximately 14 percent of all identity theft victims within the FTC's study only experienced some form of new activity (or new you), and 23 percent experienced new you and some type of old you. The remaining 63 percent of victims experienced one type of existing account fraud, or some combination of old you therein. Table 5.3 reflects these patterns of multiple victimization among the victims identified over a five-year period within the FTC's survey (12.7% of the entire sample of respondents). The most important information conveyed by the third column of Table 5.3 is the mix of existing and new activities experienced by victims of new you, although the realities of multiple and repeated victimization are much more complex.

As will be discussed further in relation to the costs of this offense, victims of new you are the least likely to discover their victimization in a timely manner, and the most likely to suffer severe consequences as a result. Individuals who experience both types of misuse (old and new) may therefore have different opportunities to respond to their victimization since uncovering one type of misuse may lead to the discovery of another.[30] In other words, because new activities are the most difficult to detect, identity theft victims who only experienced new you (1.75% in column 2 of Table 5.3) are likely to encounter the most serious problems. However, the information provided in Table 5.3 does not reflect other dimensions of this issue that further impact the severity of a given victimization.

Table 5.3 Multiple Identity Theft Victimizations by Type

	Single type of victimization (%)		Two or more types of victimization (%)		Total (%)
Old you	Credit card	6.0	Credit card		8.0
	Non–credit card	1.2	and Non-credit card	0.8	
New you	New you fraud	1.75	New you and credit card	1.0	4.7
			New you and non–credit card	1.2	
			New you, credit card and non–credit card	0.75	
Total		8.95		3.75	12.7

Source: Calculations for this table were based on information provided by Synovate (2003: 5, footnote 2) regarding multiple victimizations among all identity theft victims (n = 515; 12.7%) identified over a five-year period within the entire sample of respondents (N = 4,057).

In particular, the label of new you masks several different types of activities that are facilitated through the misuse of someone else's personal information; for example, the creation of new financial accounts, obtaining employment or housing, and criminal record fraud. The label of non-credit card similarly extends to all types of accounts, from bank accounts to utility accounts (basically everything except for a credit card), and reflects the dominance of credit card fraud in everything identity theft. All of these considerations are further complicated by the fact that any one of these activities, however labeled, may occur repeatedly or in combination with one another.

The Michele Brown story is a classic and famous case of IDT that will be discussed further in the next chapter, but it will be used here to summarize how this process works. According to her testimony (also presented in chapter 6), Ms. Brown's thief acquired approximately $50,000 worth of goods and services using her identity over a 1-1/2-year period. Although the precise order of events is unknown based on her retelling, there is a basic pattern to the multiple/repeated victimization activities she speaks of—it's called life:

Identification:	Duplicate driver's license
Communication:	Cell phone service, telephone service
Home Base:	Leased property, utility accounts
Transportation:	$32,000 truck
Employment:	Fake Brown activity led to warrant and arrest for the real Michele Brown
The Good Things:	$5,000 on liposuction, attempted time-share financing and department store credit

The Talented Mr. Schmidt[31]

Fake Michele Brown (Heddi Larae Ille) was eventually caught and sentenced to prison: 2 years state and 73 months federal (6.08 years).[32] The fate of fake Mr. Schmidt (the offender from Scenarios #1–4 who represents the archetypal identity thief) is somewhat of a mystery however, in part because Mr. Schmidt's name still acts to protect the real identity of the man wearing his mask. In other words, this offender is nameless, and perhaps faceless as well, for the purpose of identification preceding criminal apprehension. Fake Schmidt may in fact be different offenders across scenarios, or he may be a repeat offender and thus responsible for victimizing Mr. Schmidt several times, along with several collective victims (e.g., the auto dealership, the credit card company). All identity theft offenders are guilty of multiple victimization by virtue of the two-sided nature of this act, which again adds another level of complexity to analyzing the dynamics of identity theft. The repeated victimization of John Schmidt may nevertheless represent the sum of this offender's criminal career, or only one linked sequence within it. Fake Schmidt also has his own name and a life outside of victimizing Mr. Schmidt. He may therefore be captured at any point during his Schmidt-related activities, his criminal or routine activities in general, or another act of identity theft involving some victim other than John Schmidt.

We have assumed thus far that this offender is a man because he was able to impersonate Mr. John Schmidt at the car dealership (Scenario #2). Although the issue of gender is often lost within the techno-modern-global face of identity theft, this in is fact one of the most basic requirements of personal identification that is not easily altered.[33] In Scenario #2, gender happened to be a requirement of the exchange, but perhaps not for any of the other scenarios outlined depending on the particulars of how each was committed. Fake Schmidt may therefore represent a mixed group of male and female offenders, who may also have connections between them insofar as the real Mr. Schmidt is concerned (e.g., through the sharing of his personal information within an offending band of thieves).

If one man—fake Schmidt—were truly capable of committing all four scenarios plus the physical theft of Mr. Schmidt's car, all without being apprehended, then he might be a very talented (or else very lucky) person indeed. Based on available international information, however, the problem of credit card fraud (especially the misuse of an existing credit card) constitutes a large part of the problem experienced in the United States and Canada, as well as the United Kingdom. This problem might in fact be common to all countries due to the universality of credit, and the ease with which old you can be committed relative to new you. At a minimum, the world appears to be filled with opportunities for credit card fraud, which may require more nerve than skill to accomplish overall.

Maybe most fake Schmidts are not really as talented as they appear. Some of them are however, so where are they hiding aside from behind the real John Schmidts of this world? Because one offender (or a band of offenders) can victimize multiple people during Acts I and II, the number of offenders in the United States cannot be expected to rival The 9.9 Million (or The 9.3 Million after that, or The 8.9 Million after that, and so on). These are still a lot of victims to account for though, so where are any of the offenders to match? On a national level, the information necessary to answer this question has not been forthcoming because identity theft is still a work in progress. The offenders that have been apprehended to date are therefore chalked up somewhere within the U.S. justice machine, and it is just not clear how many or where right now, or whether they are even identity thieves.

EXTRA, EXTRA

As discussed by Goode and Ben-Yehuda in relation to the attributional model of moral panics, one indicator of disproportionality is a disproportionate amount of attention toward a problem compared to the amount given to a larger or more serious problem over time. This particular issue was examined within the newspaper sample using two topics that preexisted IDT—identity fraud and credit card fraud.

The amount of attention given to the problem of identity fraud was first considered using the number of references within the Fraud Sample, which was selected on the presence of the term identity fraud (or a variant term such as ID fraud) but not the term identity theft.[34] Fraud references (n = 181) accounted for 8.59 percent of the total sample (N = 2,106), and their percentage within each newspaper was similarly small in all but one: *Arizona Republic* (17/369 = 4.60%); *Boston Globe* (46/262 = 17.55%); *USA Today* (8/215 = 3.72%); *New York Times* (30/452 = 6.63%); *Washington Post* (68/648 = 10.49%); *Rocky Mountain News* (12/160 = 7.50%).

References to identity fraud were then removed from the Theft Sample and added to the Fraud Sample in order to see how this impacted the total number of fraud references within each newspaper. While the total number of identity fraud references increased along with their respective percentages within each newspaper, the topic of identity theft still received a greater amount of attention overall. Based on the total number of references from the Theft and Fraud Samples,[35] the percentage of all fraud references within each newspaper were as follows: *Arizona Republic* (25/356 = 7.02%); *Boston Globe* (71/250 = 28.40%); *USA Today* (17/206 = 8.25%); *New York Times* (41/424 = 9.66%); *Washington Post* (95/626 = 15.17%); *Rocky Mountain News* (13/158 = 8.22%).

Prior to the emergence of identity theft, the problem of credit card fraud had also received its own share of negative attention as a growing but neglected problem,[36] an epidemic,[37] and a menace.[38] An additional search for all references to credit card fraud, which was conducted for each of the six newspapers, revealed that the issue of identity theft received considerably more attention across the board after this term had begun to appear. A search for credit card fraud was then conducted within the Theft Sample and very few instances were found overall.

Figure 5.2 shows rather graphic representations of how credit card fraud was treated relative to identity theft within the *New York Times* and *Washington Post* for as long as coverage could be located. The other four newspapers within the sample showed similar patterns, but these two had some of the oldest references to credit card fraud. These comparisons are based solely on the number of references to these terms, with the Credit Card Fraud Sample including all references to this phrase that appeared within the Theft Sample.

Considering the more extensive procedures used to collect the Theft Sample, the comparisons in Figure 5.2 are not completely accurate. Because more references were removed from the original search results than were later added to the final sample, the trend lines for identity theft might have been somewhat different if the representations in Figure 5.2 had been produced using the original hits from each search.[39] In a similar way, there may have

Figure 5.2 Comparison of Identity Theft and Credit Card Fraud References

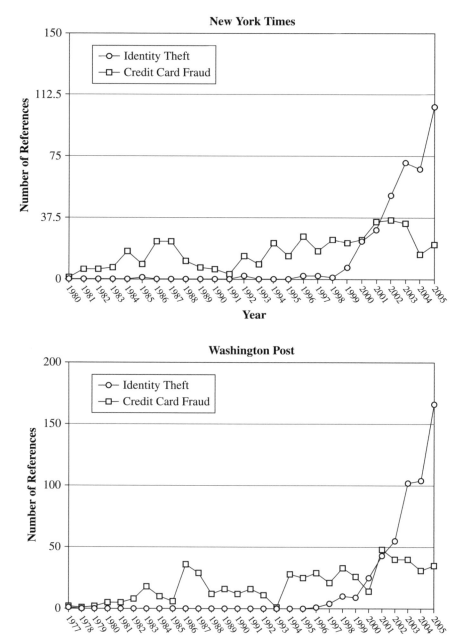

been false hits within the search for credit card fraud. Further, no attempt was made to search for alternate terms that describe this particularly old and well-known offense (e.g., credit card theft, credit fraud). By way of illustration, however, these results are rather dramatic.

The oldest identity theft reference was from 1985 within the *New York Times*, and 1977 within the *Washington Post*.[40] A few were also scattered about in the years leading up to 1997–1999, which is when identity theft starts to appear more frequently within both newspapers. Within the *New York Times*, these two sets of terms were neck and neck between 2000 and 2001. Identity theft first passed credit card fraud in 2002, and remained ahead thereafter. Something very similar happened in the *Washington Post*, with identity theft ahead in 2000 but then slightly behind in 2001, then once again by 2002, identity theft consistently surpassed credit card fraud. From a moral panics perspective, however, the trend lines for credit card fraud more closely resemble the volatility expected to surround an object of panic, with the complete opposite being suggested by those for identity theft.

Taken together, the media's usage of the terms identity theft, identity fraud, and credit card fraud provide mounting circumstantial evidence regarding disproportionality. First, the attention paid toward identity theft was much greater than that paid toward identity fraud. This is true although identity fraud is a much more extensive problem, and potentially more serious given that it includes identity theft by most definitions. The same also appears to be true for credit card fraud, which contributes a great deal toward the problem of identity theft. Second, the attention paid to the issue of identity theft mainly begins to increase after most locations had already criminalized it. Newspaper reporting on identity theft also increased rather steadily over time, and much more dramatically in relation to its rivals, even though the status of that particular problem has not really changed.

Around the Beginning

CALL IT WHAT you will, identity theft is not a 20th century invention. It is, very plainly, one of the oldest tricks in the book. Some of the earliest examples of identity theft are supranatural, such as Bible stories in which mere mortals falsely claimed to be God, and stories about the Greek Olympians who are said to have experienced similar problems thousands of years before that. Comparable accounts have also been recorded over the centuries regarding attempts to usurp various human rulers and other significant figures,[1] and similar examples can be found in literature with one of the most poignant being *The Prince and the Pauper* by Mark Twain (1881). These types of tales are ancient history, however, as they portray identity theft more as it was or might have been, not as it is today. Identity theft has its very own rags-to-riches story though, which further embodies almost everyman's dream in life: trading in your own identity for one that is bigger, better or richer.

Although the contemporary story of identity theft begins during the mid-20th century, newspaper reports provide a more consistent view of what identity theft was before it became such. They also contain real-life stories of identity theft, the kind that are somewhat more likely to happen to everyman, rather than the king of Siam. Newspapers, in fact, contain a gold mine of information about identity theft hidden beneath its many aliases and dating back long before the 1950s.

An 1864 editorial from the *New York Times* discusses a case of voting fraud during the Civil War in which ballots were forged in the names of dead soldiers as well as those who were still alive.[2] In an example from the mid-1920s, a 17-year-old clerk impersonated his employer's son to forge checks and travel across Europe.[3] Then, in the late 1940s, a Canadian man, after having been deported for entering the United States illegally, reentered the country using an assumed identity and was caught attempting to rob a New York bank.[4]

These are all true stories, big enough to make the news in their respective eras, and each one represents a different face of identity theft today: voting fraud, financial fraud (which happens to be the modern face of identity theft), and illegal immigration. Identity theft can therefore be found whenever and wherever one chooses to look. The story of identity theft, as told within the next few chapters, is structured upon America's discovery of this fact and the crisis that ensued.

THE GREAT IMPOSTERED

In the beginning (pre-IDT; ca. 1950), there was fraud, but part of this basic concept evolved to become what is known today as identity theft. The act of stealing someone's identity was perhaps less commonplace back then, given the face-to-face nature of most social interaction and the slower pace of life in general, yet identity theft may have happened more frequently than we realize, as suggested by the crimes of Ferdinand Waldo Demara Jr. (otherwise known as the Great Imposter) and others like him.

Ferdinand Demara was not your average criminal, although he appears to be the first person dubbed an "identity thief" after his death in 1982.[5] Demara was an extremely intelligent and arguably likable man whose failed dream in life was to become a Trappist monk. While Demara posed as a Catholic brother more than once, he also assumed the identities of several individuals—with very different credentials—between the 1930s and 1950s. During this time, for example, Demara was employed as a college dean, a deputy prison warden, a cancer researcher, and a surgeon in the Canadian navy.

While Demara's service in the navy was his most disturbing charade, due to the operations he reluctantly (yet successfully) performed, this "Gentle Masquerader"[6] suffered from a Dirty Harry complex[7] in which the ends became more important than the means. As Demara's biographer noted, "[s]ince his aim was to do good, anything he did to do it was justified."[8] The U.S. public seemed to agree with this sentiment as the exploits of this self-proclaimed rascal were subsequently well received in the form of two books, which chronicled the "triumphs of a man who . . . is enthusiastically defying every law of human identity,"[9] and a 1961 movie in which Tony Curtis played this legendary thief. Demara committed many serious crimes, however, and this progenitor of identity theft was arrested several times throughout his life and ultimately captured by authorities in the 1950s.

The Great Imposter was not the first of his kind, nor would he be the last, but he was not typical by any standard—then or now. He was a full-blooded identity thief, however, having stolen many real lives for the sake of his own. Although Demara's fame diminished over the years as others stepped up to replace him, his legacy—the romanticized image of the mischievous thief who's "sticking it to the man"—nevertheless lives on somewhere in the shadow of identity theft, which is more commonly associated today with bad ends rather than good ends.[10]

The earliest reference in which the term identity theft appears, at least the earliest found to date, is the headline from a 1964 article in the *Billings* (Montana) *Gazette*.[11] The next known reference is from a 1989 headline in the *Sun*

Sentinel (Florida),[12] which represents a gap in coverage of 25 years, but also a migration of approximately 2,500 miles. By the 1990s, identity theft was starting to catch on and the term was being used more often. For this reason, 1989 appears to be the year in which identity theft was born, although the identity thief was born in 1982 with the death of the greatest imposter. Usage of identity theft did not become more consistent as time went on, however, and its history is therefore mingled with that of its brethren (e.g., identity fraud, credit card fraud) and further confused by its aliases (e.g., stolen identity, assumed identity). It is nevertheless possible to sketch out some of its earliest beginnings from available information.

The first book on identity theft was published in 1995 (one year prior to its initial criminalization in America),[13] and the first known television news segment on identity theft aired a few years earlier in 1991.[14] In terms of entertainment media, identity theft had been touted as a favorite theme within Hollywood movies as early as 1992.[15] Private industries were nevertheless well versed in the topic by this time. In 1986, for example, one U.S. credit bureau produced a short video detailing how easy it was to commit real person fraud.[16] Credit monitoring services were also available to the public in the early 1990s,[17] but would soon be marketed as a specific tool for detecting identity theft.[18] Identity theft insurance also made its debut in 1999,[19] even though identity theft insurance scams had begun to appear in 1997.[20] The idea behind identity theft had therefore been brewing in the United States for several years, but its discovery appears to have been precipitated by the "original victims of identity theft":[21] Bob and JoAnn Hartle.

In 1994, Bob Hartle discovered that his identity had been stolen back in 1988, but he and his wife JoAnn later realized that the prosecution of his case would be difficult because he was not considered a victim under any extant state or federal laws. Although Hartle's identity thief was eventually convicted of other charges related to this case, Bob and JoAnn began advocating for the creation of new legislation to address this problem. With the help of State Senator Tom Smith, their efforts led to the first criminalization of identity theft by Arizona in 1996: Taking [the] identity of another person or entity (Ariz. Rev. Stat. § 13–2008; notice the absence of the term *identity theft* here). The Hartles then worked with Representative John Shadegg and Senator Jon Kyl to draft a federal version of this legislation—the Identity Theft and Assumption Deterrence Act (Public Law 105–318), which was enacted in 1998.

Although identity theft was legally defined at both levels to include various types of misuse (i.e., new you and old you), the stated impetus behind criminalization at that time was the need to recognize the individual victims of identity fraud. As such, the term identity theft was eventually used to differentiate individual from collective victims of this already established offense. This was viewed as particularly necessary for victims of new you like Bob Hartle, whose lives were essentially ruined through the actions of their assumptors. The early or classic[22] victims of identity theft also embodied the serious threat posed to the social and economic order of U.S. society: Law-abiding citizens, faithfully engaged in the institutionalized means of social life, could ultimately be denied access to the American Dream despite all their hard work and through no fault of their own.

Michele Brown is one of the more famous victims of identity theft given that her story was featured in a made-for-TV movie that aired on the Lifetime cable network in 2004, and Brown recounted the details of her victimization during a U.S. Senate Committee hearing, as previously outlined in chapter 5:

> I believe that I strongly represent any average, respectable citizen of the United States. However, there is one clear-cut issue that separates me from nearly the rest of the population: I have lived and breathed the nightmare of identity theft. I will tell you firsthand, this is a devastation beyond any outsiders' comprehension, a nearly unbearable burden that no one should ever have to suffer. Imagine establishing credit at age 17, and building a perfect credit profile over the next 11 years. Imagine working consistently since age 15, helping to finance your education at an accredited University to advance your future success in life. Imagine never having been in trouble with the law. Imagine the violation you would internalize as you realize some vile individual you have never met nor wronged, has taken everything you have built-up from scratch to grossly use and abuse your good name and unblemished credit profile. That's precisely what happened to me. . . . To summarize, over a year and a half from January 1998 through July 1999, one individual impersonated me to procure over $50,000 in goods and services. Not only did she damage my credit, but she escalated her crimes to a level that I never truly expected: she engaged in drug trafficking. The crime resulted in my erroneous arrest record, a warrant out for my arrest, and eventually, a prison record when she was booked under my name as an inmate in the Chicago Federal Prison. The impersonation began with the perpetrator's theft of my rental application from my landlord's property management office in January 1998. Immediately, the perpetrator set up cellular service, followed by residential telephone and other utility services, attempted to obtain timeshare financing and department store credit cards, purchased a $32,000 truck, had nearly $5,000 worth of liposuction performed to her body, and even rented properties in my name including signing a year lease. Not only did this person defraud the Department of Motor Vehicles in obtaining a duplicate drivers' license (with my name and number) in October 1998, but she even presented herself as me with this identification to the DEA and before a federal judge when she was caught trafficking 3,000 pounds of marijuana in May 1999.[23]

The experience of Michelle Brown is not representative of all or even most identity theft victims since it epitomizes new you victimization. The most devastating consequences of this offense have nevertheless been unceasingly co-opted to describe the plight of identity theft victims as a whole, which is simply untrue and counterproductive to the purposes of education and prevention. Victims of all kinds, however, were intended to benefit from the criminalization of identity theft in the United States.

THE GREAT CONCURRENCE

Table 6.1 shows a basic visual representation of state legislative activity that appears to peak in 1999, but actual trends in the criminalization of identity theft as an independent offense are much more complex. Many states simply amended existing legislation, while others drafted separate statutes. Some U.S. legislation does not use the term identity theft at all, just like the first law in Arizona where the problem was "discovered." The last two states to criminalize identity theft both provide examples of some additional difficulties associated with interpreting this particular bell curve.

By the beginning of 2005, only two states were believed not to have specific identity theft legislation: Colorado and Vermont. The Federal Trade Commission (FTC) initially reported this information in 2003, but subsequent research had been unable to locate any evidence that either state had enacted this type of legislation by the end of 2004.[24] Vermont had nevertheless signed legislation that created the crime of identity theft in 2003 and this legislation did not take effect until June 2004 (13 VSA § 2030). Colorado passed legislation in 2005 that made identity theft a felony, which was signed by the governor the following year.[25] Similar legislation was previously proposed in this state but never passed,[26] and this was reportedly due to issues with the state's budget.[27] However, other types of legislation had been passed in Colorado prior to this time; for example, in June 2002 the governor signed HB 1258 related to increased protections for the victims of identity theft.

Although few in number, some sources reflected the idea that identity theft was not an offense in Colorado until the 2005 legislation had been signed. Instead, it appears that identity theft was simply not a felony, and this was somehow transformed into the claim that this state had no identity theft legislation at all. While this is suggested by the fact that Colorado had specifically been attempting to pass felony legislation since the year 2000, there was also an editorial published in the *Rocky Mountain News* that supports this interpretation of events:[28]

> The [Denver] Post announced, "Identity thieves are drawn to Colorado because it is one of two states that do not have an identity-theft law." The headline claimed, "Colorado's lax laws attract ID thieves." Supposedly buttressing this claim was the fact that Colorado ranked 14th in ID theft in 2001, and 11th in 2002. The article correctly stated that the District of Columbia and Vermont also lack an ID theft law. Yet the article reported no data from those jurisdictions. According to the FTC, the District of Columbia is the No. 1 jurisdiction for ID theft while Vermont ranks 49th. So although the Post made the factual assertion that "lax laws" attract ID thieves, Vermont's experience is completely to the contrary. Deep in the article, the 22nd paragraph acknowledged that Colorado already has ID theft laws, since "laws on forgery, criminal impersonation and theft have been tweaked to include identity theft." The article quoted an expert sheriff's investigator who said that Colorado laws have not caught up to the burgeoning problem. But the

Table 6.1 The National Criminalization of Identity Theft

1996	1997	1998	1999	2000	2001	2002	2003	2004	2005
			Arkansas						
			Connecticut						
			Florida						
			Idaho						
			Illinois						
			Iowa						
			Louisiana						
			Maryland						
			Minnesota						
			Missouri						
			Nevada						
			New Hampshire						
			New Jersey						
			North Carolina	Delaware					
			North Dakota	Kentucky					
			Ohio	Michigan					
		(Federal)	Oklahoma	Pennsylvania	Alabama				
		Georgia	Oregon	Rhode Island	Alaska				
		Kansas	Tennessee	South Carolina	Indiana				
		Massachusetts	Texas	South Dakota	Montana	Hawaii			
	California	Mississippi	Washington	Utah	New Mexico	Maine			
Arizona	Wisconsin	West Virginia	Wyoming	**Virginia**	**New York**	Nebraska	**(D.C.)**	Vermont	**Colorado**
1	2	5	22	9	6	3		1	1

Note: States are listed alphabetically. Bold items indicate the areas represented by the newspaper sample used in the original research.

article included no explanation of precisely why Colorado's current laws are supposedly inadequate.[29]

Despite the detailed realities of legislative events, the information provided in Table 6.1 represents the popular version of what happened with regard to the national criminalization of identity theft. It also shows that more than half of the states had criminalized identity theft by the end of 1999, and all but Vermont and Colorado had followed suit by the end of 2002. Aside from the question surrounding whether either of these holdout states had actually addressed the problem of identity theft through legislation by this time, the fact that all of the other states had done so is particularly important in the context of national events.

FRAMING THE CRISIS

As directed by the Identity Theft and Assumption Deterrence Act, the FTC began collecting complaint data and providing information about identity theft to the public in November 1999 through its newly established Identity Theft Clearinghouse.[30] The first published report on these data contained the only concrete victimization figure available at that time. During its first year of operation, the clearinghouse received 31,103 complaints.[31] Although this was much less than an original guesstimate (approximately 350,000 victims in 1997),[32] the FTC's data somehow confirmed suspicions that the problem was enormous, as illustrated through the following headline: "ID Theft Becoming Public Fear No. 1; Federal Hot Lines Clogged With Calls."[33]

This headline appeared in the year 2000, when more than 30 states had already criminalized identity theft and the FTC itself was framing the problem as a crisis.[34] This was also a few years before the arrival of The 9.9 Million, honest-to-goodness victims who do not appear until a little later in the story. In hindsight then, all of this was really just a prelude to the crisis that had yet to come.

The emotive connotations traditionally associated with the term *identity* reach beyond the immediate social context of identity theft to incorporate fundamental aspects of the individual (i.e., you), which is best witnessed through the usurpation of the phrase *identity crisis* to frame the contemporary problem of identity theft. This concept was first developed by psychologist Erik Erikson to describe "a turning point in the development of personality that commonly occurs during adolescence and young adulthood, wherein a decisive turn is taken either toward establishing a sense of identity or toward identity confusion."[35] Although this turning point in relation to identity theft generally refers to victimization, it also symbolizes an ongoing struggle within U.S. society to balance the rights of individuals against those of the social collectives that rely on personal information as part of their day-to-day operations. While such considerations have little to do with stealing identities in a practical sense, they do speak to the manner in which identity theft has been portrayed—and specifically marketed—to the U.S. public.

Like what happened with our friends, the Arizona identity tweakers, the U.S. identity crisis was a foregone conclusion. This makes many—if not all—things about the episode suspect, yet everyone eagerly hopped aboard the identity crisis bandwagon. Box 6.1 lists a selection of headlines and titles from a range of sources to illustrate the persistence and prominence of this theme, as well as its changing associations over time. Please keep in mind, however, that these are the big examples. This identity crisis frame did not always make the front page or the headlines.

Like identity theft, this identity crisis frame is not really new at all as it has been used before to capture the tensions between individual and national identity, particularly within the context of immigration reform. For example, a 1977 article titled "An Identity Crisis" discussed problems related to immigration and fraud,[36] concluding, "it would be rash to launch any new government program that depends too much on any single ID to prove who's who." Although debates regarding a national identity card have been ongoing in the United States for decades, arguments for and against this measure were renewed following 9/11 and framed—once again—as an identity crisis.[37]

The identity theft crisis in the United States was a moral panic, however, and this country may have seen the like of it before. Traveling back in history for a moment, let's take a closer look at the Civil War frauds through the eyes of this anonymous 1864 author:

> The frauds in reference to the soldiers' votes continue to occasion great excitement and discussion—and well they may, for their extent is likely to be enormous. The parties were proved to have forged large numbers of ballots before their detection, and one of them said that there were twenty men at Washington engaged in the business. This statement is enough to awaken a very painful apprehension everywhere, for no one knows where the fraudulent ballots may make their appearance . . . though this one factory of fraud has been stopped, it by no means follows that the others will not keep at work. . . . They are bold, desperate men, or they would never have undertaken the business, and they will not be easily deterred from its prosecution. . . . Whatever is done, must be done at once, or it will be too late.[38]

These excerpts mirror statements that might be expected if the nation (or an individual) were in the throes of a moral panic. This "great excitement and discussion" is seemingly fueled by concern over a serious social problem—the extent of which (though unverified) "is likely to be enormous." In particular, the people caught forging ballots represent only the tip of the iceberg because there is an organized group of at least 20 others that will not be deterred by the law in continuing their desperate work. There is also a looming threat posed by these falsified ballots: In addition to the damage that has already been done, more may surface at any time or in any place. It certainly has all

Box 6.1 Look Out—It's a Crisis!

Year	Headline	Source
1983	Identity Crisis/Mystery Professor's Repertoire Grows: Investigators Find 14 Sets of ID	Philadelphia Daily News[1]
1996	Identity Crisis: Thieves Get Credit, You Get Bills	Miami Herald[2]
	Identity Crisis: When a Criminal's Got Your Number	New York Times[3]
	Identity Crisis: The Theft That's Tough to Thwart	Washington Post[4]
1997	The New Identity Crisis: Can You Stop A Thief From Stealing Your Good Name?	Palm Beach Post[5]
1998	Identity Crisis: Theft of Names on the Rise	Columbus Dispatch[6]
	Name Theft a Real Identity Crisis for the Victim; About 500,000 Yearly Undergo Long, Costly Ordeal of Trying to Regain Reputations	Pittsburgh Post-Gazette[7]
1999	Identity Crisis: Fraud Victims Have Hard Time Getting Back Their Good Name	Florida Times-Union[8]
	Identity Crisis in the Information Age	State Legislatures Magazine[9]
	Identity Crisis—ID Theft Can Rob You of Your Money—And Your Sanity	Chicago Tribune[10]
	Identity Crisis: Act Quickly to Recover Financial Good Name If It's Stolen—But Expect a Long Road	Dallas Morning News[11]
2000	Identity crisis. . . What to do if your identity is stolen	Federal Trade Commission[12]
	The Internet Identity Crisis	Government Executive[13]
	Money Matters/Identity Crisis; The Imposters, More People Seeing Their Good Names Sullied by Thieves	Boston Globe[14]
	Identity Crisis—With a Few Pieces of Personal Data, Identity Thieves Can Wreck Victims' Financial Standing	Fresno Bee[15]
2001	How to Avoid an Identity Crisis	Security Management[16]
	Avoid an Identity Crisis	Washington Post[17]
	Identity Crisis	Bank Marketing[18]
	Identity Crisis; Cyberthieves Are Taking Credit for Your Good Name—And All They Need Is Nine Numbers	Buffalo News[19]

2002	America's Identity Crisis: Document Fraud Is Pervasive and Pernicious	Center for Immigration Studies[20]
	America's Real Identity Crisis	Newsweek[21]
	A Major Identity Crisis; Info Stolen from Motor Vehicles Offices Has Residents Worried	Rocky Mountain News[22]
	Identity Crisis: Thief's Use of Your Social Security Number Can Create Financial Havoc	Indianapolis Star[23]
2003	Operation Identity Crisis: Making the Mail Even Safer	U.S. Postal Service[24]
	Identity Crisis—Thievery Creates Mystery Bills, Tax Mess for Single Mother	Grand Rapids Press[25]
	Identity Crisis; Technology and the Web Make IDs Easier to Produce and Harder to Spot	San Diego Union-Tribune[26]
2004	Identity Crisis: Credit Scams are Exploding Across the Nation, With Sophisticated ID Thieves Finding Victims Among the Most Careful and Savvy Consumers	St. Paul Pioneer Press[27]
2005	Identity Crisis: Theft of Private Data Grows	Sacramento Bee[28]
	ID Theft: The New Identity Crisis	Macon Telegraph[29]
	Identity Crisis: New Yorkers' Personal Information Needs Protection	The Council of New York City[30]
	Preventing an Identity Crisis: Rutgers Officials Protect Students, Strengthen Data Security	Rutgers University[31]
2006	Biometric Science Seeks To Avert Identity Crisis	Physorg.com[32]
	Identity Crisis in the Workplace	IdentityTheft911[33]
	Identity Crisis; An Epidemic of High-Profile Laptop Heists Shows How Vulnerable Americans' Personal Information Is	Washington Post[34]
2007	Identity Crisis—246,000 Hit in Theft Epidemic	New York Post[35]

(Continued)

[1] Sheehan & Preston (1983).
[2] O'Connor (1996b).
[3] Hansell (1996).
[4] Crenshaw (1996).

Box 6.1 (*Continued*)

5 Koenenn (1997).
6 Nirode (1998).
7 Klein (1998).
8 "Identity Crisis: Fraud Victims . . ." (1999).
9 Boulard (1999).
10 Schwanhausser (1999).
11 Yip (1999).
12 Federal Trade Commission (2000a).
13 Dean (2000).
14 Nelson (2000).
15 Correa (2000).
16 Del Grosso (2001).
17 Oldenburg (2001).
18 Bernstel (2001).
19 Stanley (2001).
20 Dinerstein (2002).
21 Alter (2002).
22 Huntley (2002).
23 Aamidor (2002).
24 U.S. Postal Service (2003).
25 White (2003).
26 Balint (2003).
27 Suzukamo (2004).
28 Kollars (2005).
29 Fulton (2005).
30 Allen & Choi (2005).
31 Alvarez (2005).
32 Jain (2006).
33 IdentityTheft911 (2006).
34 "Identity Crisis; An Epidemic. . ." (2006).
35 Singer (2007).

the earmarkings of a crisis (i.e., a moral panic), and something—whatever it is—must be done now because it can only be expected to get worse, and by then all hope may be gone.

Compare this description now with the first known book published about identity theft in 1995 (pre-criminalization and pre-data), which refers to identity theft as a "crime wave" and describes financial losses as having "reached crisis levels."[39] The discussion in the first few pages also appeals to the audience through a personal crisis frame:

> Identity Thieves are costing every man, woman and child in America $240 a year. . . . This is *before* you become a *direct* victim of Identity Thieves. . . . **You,** a member of your family, or someone you know will become a *direct* victim of Identity Thieves unless the law is changed to stop it.[40] (italics and boldface in original)

In an early example from 1994, one woman's "identity crisis" began simply enough with a stolen purse, but this resulted in a seemingly never-ending nightmare of debt and legal problems.[41] While the crisis referred to here was an instance of new you victimization, the implication of the crisis frame is that this will one day happen to you. Many audiences have similarly been lured in over the years by a blatant frame of personal threat:

> 1995: Are you a victim of identity theft?[42]
> 1997: Are you a target for identity theft?[43]
> 2001: Will you be the next victim?[44]
> 2005: You've been sold.[45]

Going, going, going . . . your identity is just plain gone by 2005, but now we are getting ahead of the story. This personal crisis frame is nevertheless related to the issue of prediction—identity theft will undoubtedly happen, so it is just a matter of time before it will happen to you, and it will have, once it's too late. The most suggestive evidence regarding this frame, however, is that it has been repeatedly employed by different groups of social actors, both before and after any empirical attempt had been made to examine the extent of identity theft. In fact, the original version of the 1998 federal legislation, which was first proposed in 1997, included a provision to study the issue within 18 months after its enactment but this stipulation was excluded from the final version and it ultimately took five years before the FTC conducted its first victimization study in 2003.

All Aboard!

The U.S. General Accounting Office (GAO) published its first report on identity fraud in 1998, which attempted to assess the initial dimensions of the identity theft problem.[46] The GAO did not publish any reports titled identity theft, however, until the year 2002.[47] In addition to a general assessment of the issue through data furnished by members of private industry—including various banks and national banking associations, Visa and MasterCard, and the three largest national consumer reporting agencies (Equifax, Experian, and TransUnion)—these reports provided very vague information on the roles and activities of several federal actors as well. Two of these later reports indicated that both the prevalence and cost of identity theft "appeared to be growing," but neither was able to provide a systematic evaluation of the issue due to the lack of appropriate data.

The GAO originally reported that TransUnion received 522,922 consumer inquiries in 1997, but this figure does not distinguish victimization reports from other types of calls.[48] TransUnion also mentioned that approximately two-thirds of these inquiries involved identity fraud; although an exact number was never provided, this equals approximately 348,614 inquiries. One of the earliest articles to reinvent this figure claimed that TransUnion received approximately 350,000 calls to report identity theft in 1997.[49] A later article claimed this same number to be over 500,000,[50] but this statistic was soon retracted as representing the total number of calls received by TransUnion's fraud victim assistance department—not the total number of calls related to identity theft. Based on later credit bureau statistics, identity theft was expected to affect between 500,000 and 700,000 people in the year 2000,[51] but even this guesstimate would be misunderstood to represent the measured incidence of identity theft.

To be fair, even if an exact figure of victim reports had been available, it would have underestimated the true extent of the problem at that time because TransUnion was only one of the three largest national credit bureaus, and there were many other social institutions affected by the part of identity fraud that involves real people. The figures originally provided by TransUnion were nevertheless promoted as representing a measurement of victimization, which was simply not the case.

The most pervasive effect of this single piece of information seems to have begun with an early television broadcast. In 1999, CBS News reported that identity theft "happens every 79 seconds in this country. A thief steals someone's identity, opens accounts in the victim's name and goes on a buying spree."[52] This suggested rate roughly translates into 399,190 victims per year, and the idea that identity theft affects "about 400,000 victims each year" soon began to magically appear in other places.[53] While no source for this statistic was ever cited, no other estimates existed at that time, so this figure was likely calculated based on some variant of the information provided by TransUnion. It is possible that this particular statistic originated from some unknown source, but there were still no concrete statistics regarding victimization until the FTC published its first report in 2001, which revealed a total of 31,103 victims for the year 2000.[54] As such, it is clear that the estimate of 400,000 did not originate from those data.[55]

If the wording of this claim can be taken at face value in that a new account is opened every 79 seconds, this also implies that these are victims of new you as opposed to old you, but this difference was not specified in the GAO report. In spite of the fact that somewhat better information became available in 2003, this claim was also repeated for at least eight years (1999–2007), with one of the last known sightings being Equifax's website.[56]

This particular claim has also been manipulated within several advertisements in order to sell computer security products: "CBS News reported that **every 79 seconds** a thief *hacks into a computer*, steals a victim's identity, and then goes on a buying spree" (bold in original, italics added).[57] Given the popularity of this news blurb, this rate could have been reproduced in a more dramatic fashion after The 9.9 Million arrived in 2003. Although this was done at least once,[58] maybe by that time everyone just wanted to remember a world in which identity theft only happened once every 79 seconds. This particular rate is typically calculated using the number of crimes that are reported to the police, however, and such data still do not exist in relation to identity theft. The fact that this completely erroneous statistic has survived intact for almost a decade speaks to the power and persistence of media messages, as well as the irrationality of U.S. society as a whole.

Train Wreck

The crisis behind identity theft was not limited to what perhaps began as a simple misunderstanding. The problem remained enormous by any guess, but it was continually perceived to be getting worse as witnessed by one customized version of this claim from 2005: Identity theft is a growing crisis in Colorado.[59] Here are some similar and more common examples of this claim, all taken from U.S. Attorney General websites around the beginning of 2008:

Colorado: Identity theft is the fastest growing crime in America[60]
California: Identity theft is one of the fastest growing crimes in America[61]
Virginia: Identity theft is one of the fastest growing crimes in the United States[62]
New York: The fastest growing financial crime in the nation—"identity theft"[63]
New Mexico: The crime of identity theft is on the rise[64]

Within print media, the idea that identity theft was a growing problem began to appear as early as 1996.[65] Referring to one case or instance as just "the tip of the iceberg," which seems to be a catch phrase of panics in general, also began to appear around that time.[66] In the earliest reference that could be located (1997), an article on insider crimes (or employee-related theft) cites Robert W. Jones, then vice president of fraud prevention/detection for Keycorp, as saying that identity theft cases involving employees had become epidemic.[67] By March 1998, however, a headline declared:

Identity Theft Reaches Epidemic Proportions—SFPD [San Francisco Police Department][68]

While this idea is abundant within newspapers, there is no evidence to suggest that the media created this claim given the dearth of comparable published resources prior to 1999, and the wide range of sources to which it has been attributed. The excerpts in Box 6.2 represent the diversity of this claim and its reputed sources within the newspaper sample alone between 1998 and 2005.

Box 6.2 The Trouble with Tribbles[1]

Evan Hendricks, editor of *Privacy Times*, a newsletter based in Washington, said shredding documents was smart because "identity theft is a growing problem to the extent of becoming a national epidemic."[2] *New York Times*, 1998

"I'm not sure as a nation we recognize how devastating this can be to someone" (quote from County Chairman, Jim Estepp). Estepp called identity theft a growing problem. The U.S. Government Accounting Office found last year that such crimes increased sixteenfold from 1992 to 1997.[3] *Washington Post*, 1999

FTC officials said after the hearing that because of the growing problem and consumers' increased awareness the agency expects to handle 100,000 calls next year and 200,000 the following year.[4] *Washington Post*, 2000

Identity Theft: It's a growing problem because it doesn't require a crook to dupe you into revealing information about yourself.[5] *Boston Globe*, 2000

Michael B. Keating, president of the Boston Bar Association, said lawyers are especially vulnerable to the growing problem of identity fraud because much information about practicing attorneys, who have to register with the Board of Bar Overseers, is available to the public, often through online databases.[6] *Boston Globe*, 2002

Identity theft is a growing problem, but this incident was particularly shocking to law enforcement officials because it involved a victim of 9/11.[7] *USA Today*, 2002

Editor's note: On Dec. 14, burglars stole confidential computer records on more than 500,000 people from Phoenix-based TriWest Healthcare Alliance. Today, that company's CEO writes about the growing problem of identity theft.[8] *Arizona Republic*, 2003.

Computer identity theft has long been a fast-growing cybercrime. But increasingly, hackers are seeking profit rather than just fun.[9] *USA Today*, 2003

The new equipment and document checks are not only focused on thwarting terrorists but on curbing identity theft, a growing problem in Massachusetts and the nation.[10] *Boston Globe*, 2005

At least 130 reported breaches have exposed more than 55 million Americans to potential ID theft this year. Security experts warn that wayward personal data, such as Social Security and credit card numbers, could end up in the hands of criminals and feed a growing problem.[11] *USA Today*, 2005c

---

[1] "The Trouble With Tribbles" is an episode from the original *Star Trek* series, in which small, fuzzy and seemingly innocuous pet-like creatures (Tribbles) were later discovered to have aggressive breeding traits that can threaten other forms of life within their environment if not controlled. The claim that identity theft is growing has replicated itself in a similar way.

[2] Meece (1998).

[3] Spinner (1999). The U.S. GAO only had partial estimates in 1999, as will be discussed further in an upcoming section.

[4] Mayer & Schwartz (2000). As shown in an upcoming section (Figure 5), the FTC received 86,212 complaints in 2001, and 161,896 complaints in 2002. The most important feature of this quote is how these increased figures are attributed to the growing problem on one hand, and increased awareness about the problem on the other. This latter point is critically important for understanding why identity theft might appear to be growing during its first years of measurement, and applicable to the previous quote by Estepp in Spinner (1999).
[5] Jerome (2000). *Translation*: If identity theft required a crook to dupe you into revealing personal information, it wouldn't be growing.
[6] Cambanis (2002).
[7] Jones (2002).
[8] McIntyre (2003).
[9] Swartz (2003).
[10] Daniel (2005).
[11] Swartz (2005c).

Many different social actors have directly transmitted the claim that identity theft is growing, whether quickly or otherwise. In fact, one would be hard pressed to find a document/webpage related to identity theft that does not begin with (or at least include) some variant of this misguided idea—even today.[69] While its original source could not be identified, some of the earliest examples are from actors within the federal government:

[F]raud related to identity theft appears to be a growing risk for consumers and financial institutions, and the relatively easy access to personal information may expand the risk.[70] Board of Governors of the Federal Reserve System, 1997

Identity theft is an important and growing problem facing consumers.[71] David Medine, then associate director for credit practices within the Federal Trade Commission's Bureau of Consumer Protection, 1998

Jodie Bernstein (then director of the Bureau of Consumer Protection) later remarked in 1999 that "subsequent press coverage helped to educate the public about the growth of consumer identity theft and the problems it creates."[72] This theme was similarly included in the president's remarks at the signing of the Identity Theft Enhancement Act in 2004 when the United States still did not have the correct kind of data to corroborate this claim: "We're taking an important step today to combat the problem of identity theft, one of the fastest growing financial crimes in our nation."[73] Additional examples can be found among law enforcement agencies,[74] grassroots organizations,[75] and state political leaders.[76] As a small experiment on consensus regarding this claim, Google searches for "fastest growing crime," "nation's fastest growing crime," and "America's fastest growing crime" currently return identity theft webpages as their first result, and continue for several pages thereafter.

This particular claim has also been mutilated in a number of ways over the years; for example, identity theft is a growing epidemic/menace/plague; identity theft is a growing form of white-collar/financial/high-tech crime. These types of claims can be witnessed for related issues as well: "White-collar crime is a growing problem" (2001);[77] the problem of check fraud is "epidemic" (2001);[78] and in an early example (1994), law enforcement officials declare fraud a "growing menace" in California.[79] As will be illustrated a little later on, however, the measured incidence of identity theft actually tells a much different story.

No Survivors

Although identity theft was popularly reputed to be big and bad, both before and after we knew much about it, two other sets of claims were working in tandem as well. One of them was that it can happen to anyone, and like all of the others, this pronouncement was made at the very beginning (1997).[80] When combined with previous claims regarding the certainty and celerity of identity theft, anyone therefore equals everybody. . . . "No one is safe"[81] and "Everyone is fair game."[82] This idea also extends to the identity thief, whose reputation for anonymity and seeming invisibility preceded him as well (1997): "Anybody can take anybody's identity if you know the numbers."[83]

Although none of humanity might be left standing guilt-free when all is said and done, some of us are undoubtedly more responsible for the problem of identity theft than others. Even in the absence of clear data about identity theft offenders (in the United States or elsewhere), it stands to reason that these thieves can hail from all walks of life given the broad spectrum of activities included under this label. While this was the conclusion of a 2007 research project,[84] these data were for a sample of 59 federal offenders who may not be representative of the offender population in America as a whole. At least, if this group of 59 offenders was entirely responsible for the victimization of The 9.9 Million, more offenders would seem to exist somewhere that have not been deterred by the law in continuing their desperate work. Although that would seem to be the case, this does not mean that all people are motivated (or equally motivated) to commit identity theft in any form.

While the idea that "everybody's doing it" is preposterous to some degree, the fact that very little information is available regarding offenders at all has perhaps contributed to this idea more than anything else. Although we know a lot more about motivated offenders than identity theft offenders, we know even less about identity thieves, other than some of the claims made about this group as a deviled whole.

The Devil's Where?

An unresolved issue between the attributional and processual models of moral panics is whether a folk devil needs to be present. A particular problem encountered during the original research was the need to substantiate the presence of a single folk devil under the attributional model, and this could not be accomplished beyond all reasonable doubt in the case of identity theft.

This issue was first examined using the Thief Sample (n = 86), which was selected on the appearance of the term *identity thief*, but included neither of the terms identity theft or identity fraud. There were very few of these references within the entire sample (4.8%),[85] however, or within any of the newspapers themselves, ranging from 1.25 percent in the *Rocky Mountain News* to 6.19 percent in the *New York Times*.[86] The idea of the identity thief nevertheless appeared within 15.62 percent of the combined Theft and Thief Samples,[87] although its presence was again more pronounced within some of the newspapers, ranging from 5.4 percent in the *Rocky Mountain News* to 28.98 percent in *USA Today*.[88] The fact that this term appeared on its own (in the Thief Sample), without reference to the act (the term *identity theft*), nevertheless suggests the independent recognition of this label in popular terms. Does it suggest the presence of a folk devil however? Let us go to the details.

Devil making is reputedly led by moral outrage, which is tricky to spot whether in the heat of the moment or in hindsight. The problem with rooting out the devil-makers is that the moral panics tradition has never adequately defined the limits of morality, or how it specifically fits into the equation of a panic. The combined framework guiding the case study of identity theft did not delve heavily into the question of what is moral, but surprisingly, neither does the tradition as a whole. Morality is therefore left to the eye of the beholder, but such relativity does not aid in the goals of science, only market research.

One common explanation for the morality inherent to this phenomenon is that the rhetoric of moral panics is composed of very basic dichotomies—one example being the distinction between good and bad (or worse, evil). According to Goode and Ben-Yehuda, folk devils are "the personification of evil,"[89] which lends particular credence to the idea that identity thieves are the folk devils of this drama because they have specifically been portrayed as an "evil twin" out to steal your good name and good credit.[90] Although evil was not an altogether uncommon image in the identity theft narrative, the portrayal of people as good—and by extension, innocent—was far more prevalent.[91]

On the other hand, the term evil twin has also been applied to a type of scam involving fraudulent wireless networks intended to steal users' personal information.[92] As such, the object of evil derision in the identity theft narrative was not always human. In particular, identity thieves are the rational choice for a folk devil because they are the primary (or proximate) actors in this social drama. These bandits also seem to share their status with identity theft at times, however, which in urban myth has become larger than life:

Identity thieves in metropolitan Phoenix are particularly nasty. The impostors tend to run up higher tabs than their counterparts in other areas and do more collateral damage to their victims' credit.[93]

Arizona Republic (2005)

> Identity theft is a nasty crime with a catchy name too catchy for our own good. Identity theft, though important, isn't the root problem, and focusing on it may distract us from real solutions.[94]

Boston Globe (2005)

Both actor and act are described as "nasty" within two different newspapers during 2005. Perhaps this is some kind of coincidence, but the thief and the theft are often interchanged during the midst of the narrative as well. While this seems to be consistent with Cohen's original description in that a *"condition, episode, person or group of persons* emerges to become defined as a threat to societal values and interests" (italics added),[95] the folk devil must embody a person according to Goode and Ben-Yehuda's interpretation, and a similar impression is left through Cohen's work.

When looked at in light of identity theft's personification as a monsterlike creature that might appear at any time or in any place to claim its next victim, the problem remains as to whether identity theft itself might fit the label of folk devil. This is also reinforced by the fact that some of the most common images associated with identity theft are techno-modern-global in nature: for example, computers, data streams, plastic cards, fingerprints. In terms of a ghost (or devil) in the social machine, and perhaps marking the crest of a different panic altogether, identity theft quickly came to represent the worst consequences of progress:

> Identity theft is perhaps the most glaring symptom of the ills that have accompanied the data revolution of the 1990s. Bounced checks. Loan denials. Harassment from debt collectors. Victims of identity theft—and there are millions of them—are often haunted by the consequences for years.[96]

A report from the credit card industry specifically blames the media (and some other financial institutions) for making identity theft "the latest symbol of the dangerous nature of electronic commerce" and perpetuating the public's misunderstanding that it is "credit fraud."[97] That is not a misunderstanding, however, it is U.S. law and more than half of the problem. Many things techno-modern-global have similarly faced public resistance throughout history, both with and without the aid of the media, but identity theft is symbolic of many things. Other candidates for the label of folk devil must therefore be considered, but identity theft remains in the running for now as the dark horse.

While the identity thief might be the undisputed perpetrator of identity theft, everyman can be held accountable for the problem as well. This is witnessed by the fact that the label identity thief has been applied (directly or indirectly) to a wide range of actors, from terrorist to neighbor. As far as people go, the identity thief is therefore an identifiable (but not necessarily undisputable) folk devil within the identity theft narrative. Those engaged in the storage and transfer of personal information have also taken their share of blame in recent history, but this label has rarely been applied to social collectives, outside of any orderly criminal group.

Stanley Cohen described, as follows, a process of symbolization in which the word mod became linked to a delinquent or deviant status: "a word . . . becomes symbolic of a certain status . . .; objects . . . symbolize the word; the objects themselves become symbolic of the status (and the emotions attached to the status)."[98] The identity thief embodies the status of every criminal in society, with this phrase representing anonymity (anyone) as well as personal threat (you). Such images then became the faces for identity theft offending as a whole (i.e., offenders often either had a blank face or your face), and these images were further associated with particular objects, such as the Internet or what's in your wallet. With the force of everything and everyone behind it, identity theft then became a vortex for all emotions attendant to well-established social issues such as immigration (legal or otherwise) and national identification, as well as all things (and people) criminal.

Some of the best-known offender images associated with identity theft are the usual suspects, or the criminals you know, as witnessed within the newspaper sample. Offender subthemes within the narrative were often subtle and varied given the wide range of criminal behavior normally associated with identity theft. Three of the largest issues were immigration, terrorism, and drugs, which by extension referred to immigrants, terrorists, and drug offenders, and all of the drama (with perhaps some panic) thus entailed.

Although these themes were not a significant focus of most references, they were an important undertone of some discussions. As a primary focus within the Theft Sample (n = 1,839), these topics were generally more common than victim subthemes,[99] but all were more prominent as the secondary focus of a reference.[100] Table 6.2 shows these topics as a proportion of their coverage within each newspaper.

Table 6.2 Offender Subthemes within Theft Sample

	Immigration	Terrorism	Drugs
Arizona Republic	8 (2.35%)	3 (0.88%)	20 (5.89%)
Boston Globe	2 (0.98%)	9 (4.41%)	1 (0.49%)
USA Today	0	5 (2.52%)	3 (1.51%)
New York Times	5 (1.26%)	12 (3.04%)	2 (0.50%)
Washington Post	1 (0.17%)	8 (1.43%)	0
Rocky Mountain News	0	4 (2.73%)	2 (1.36%)

Note: Whole numbers represent the total number of references with a primary and secondary focus on these themes. Percentages reflect the proportion of these references within each Theft Sub-Sample: AR (339), BG (204), USA (198), NYT (394), WP (558), RMN (146).

While many of the words and objects often associated with identity theft are criminal in nature, another face of the identity thief was the devil you know—friend, relative, neighbor, acquaintance, coworker, employee. Identity theft can be committed by people known to the victim, but this represents a certain percentage of cases, not all cases. Portraying offenders with this single face therefore has the potential to breed social distrust between individuals and collectives, as well as families and communities.[101] This idea also implies that you, the victim, have some part to play in your own victimization.

Given the number of strong entries in this narrative's race for a folk devil, this label is perhaps best thought of like a first-place sash that can be placed over the various heads of identity theft as they misbehave. The identity thief, however, is a sash that can be worn by many actors in the drama of identity theft, and thus he or she may qualify as the most representative folk devil in the tradition of moral panics. Identity theft is a very close second, however, so this one is a photo finish.

The Bionic Criminal

Identity thieves largely represent traditional criminals as a group, with their collective face of lore being akin to the Invisible Man. At the same time, however, identity thieves appear to be a new breed of offender according to the narrative: better, stronger, faster than the average criminal—the Bionic Criminal. In particular, there were a number of repeated references regarding the intelligence and cleverness of identity thieves, as well as their hyperevolved modus operandi, as reflected in Box 6.3.

Identity thieves are not only smart, they can learn, and their repertoire is commonly perceived to be evolving over time. In other words, it is not simply the case that more sophisticated offenders might be hopping on board the identity theft train. The offenders themselves are attributed with consciously acquiring new skills, from shoulder surfing to the creation of computer viruses, in order to largely keep up with opportunities for obtaining personal information. According to the narrative, this description also applies to everybody—hackers, surfers, and tweakers alike. Such statements represent rational offending as a whole, however, not necessarily the evolutionary tract of identity thieves.

The good guys and bad guys of this world are forever in the grips of a techno-modern-global arms race, in which tactics on both sides of this dynamic are developed in reaction to one another. Thus, depending upon your perspective, it might appear that one side is far ahead of the other at any given time, as they well might be. According to many accounts, however, the identity thief is truly something to behold as far as criminals go, even in criminological terms. If identity thieves were truly one class of offender, their collective accomplishments would indeed be remarkable. Another interpretation is available however:

> Today, Social Security numbers are used in countless ways—on driver's licenses and military IDs, for instance, and to chase down deadbeat dads. And while this

Box 6.3 The Evolving Criminal

As the crime has gained in popularity, identity thieves have become ingenious.[1] *USA Today*, 2000

Worse, the criminals are getting more sophisticated. Computer-savvy identity thieves have created Internet sites that closely resemble legitimate retail sites. Identity thieves have created computer viruses designed to steal credit card numbers or personal identification numbers from your computer.[2] *USA Today*, 2003

As identity thieves have become more sophisticated, "No company has files so secure that somebody can't get to them," says Jay Foley of the Identity Theft Resource Center, a non-profit organization that helps victims.[3] *USA Today*, 2003

US Attorney Michael Sullivan, who has taken a personal interest in prosecuting local identity thieves, said the biggest challenge lies in identifying and locating thieves, including those who have graduated from stealing wallets and checks to looking over a person's shoulder as he or she enters ATM pin numbers, known as "shoulder surfing." "Identity thieves have expanded their horizons," Sullivan said. "Identity theft is one of "the most rapidly and evolving [sic] crimes in the country."[4] *Boston Globe*, 2004

The case, authorities say, exemplifies an all too common crime in Arizona, the identity theft capital of the nation. Often motivated by the need for money to buy methamphetamine, small-time operators have become more sophisticated.[5] *Arizona Republic*, 2005

---

[1] Block (2000).
[2] Block (2003a).
[3] Block (2003b).
[4] Encarnacao (2004).
[5] Crawford (2005).

---

has provided convenience and accuracy in all sorts of transactions—both in government and in private commerce—the haphazard evolution of the system has left it riddled with gaps through which clever and even not-so-clever crooks can grab a person's number.[102]

The examples in Box 6.3 also stem from very different perceptions about identity theft and identity thieves, but it was often very difficult to disentangle various strains of the same claim from one another or correctly identify their source. The first three articles, for example, were written by Sandra Block. While this particular *USA Today* reporter appeared to be prone to sensationalism in terms of her own reporting on identity theft, the media are not the only group responsible for stereotyping identity thieves. In fact, the similarity of ideas across these sources and others points to a type of institutionalized stereotyping (varying only in frequency) in which certain topics were commonly but not always reproduced in comparable form by the media and other groups of social actors. Such stereotyping, however, might also be expected when the imagination is left to its own devices in the absence of fact, as mainly appears to be the unfortunate case with identity thieves and identity theft.

Not Me!

While victims may play an active role in their own victimization, this can only be said for a handful of cases, not for the process of identity theft victimization as a whole. According to the narrative, however, identity theft is your

---

Box 6.4 Caution—Low-Hanging Fruit[1]

Protect Your Social Security Number; Don't Be a Victim of Identity Theft[2]
USA Today, 1999
 Precautions, Vigilance, Insurance Help Fight Identity Theft[3]
Arizona Republic, 2000
 Don't Fall Prey to Identity Thieves[4]
USA Today, 2000
 Victims of Identity Theft Often Unaware They've Been Stung[5]
USA Today, 2000
 Identity Theft: Your Money And Your Life[6]
Washington Post, 2001
 Act Now to Prevent Identity Thief from Stalking the True You[7]
USA Today, 2002
 Identity Theft: It Pays to Be Diligent[8]
Washington Post, 2003
 ID Theft Begins When You Share Sensitive Info[9]
Arizona Republic, 2003
 How to Protect Your Credit Card from Headaches of ID Theft[10]
USA Today, 2003a
 Protect Yourself from Identity Theft[11]
Washington Post, 2003
 Avoid Online ID Theft[12]
Washington Post, 2005
 Don't Make it Easy for ID Thieves[13]
Arizona Republic, 2005

---

[1] Being a "low-hanging fruit" means being an easy target. This title references Cole and Pontell (2006), who also noticed this theme directed at individuals.
[2] Dugas (1999).
[3] Wiles (2000).
[4] Block (2000).
[5] Fields (2000).
[6] Singletary (2001).
[7] Block (2002).
[8] Oldenburg (2003).
[9] Wiles (2003).
[10] Block (2003a).
[11] "Protect Yourself from Identity Theft" (2003).
[12] "Avoid Online ID Theft" (2005).
[13] Beckage (2005).

own fault. Something you did or could have done might have prevented your victimization, as witnessed by the headlines in Box 6.4. Even after Choice-Point, when all hope really was gone, individuals were still somehow left with the mess and most of the responsibility for identity theft. The motivation of victims applies not only to the process in which victimization occurs, however, but to how they respond as a result.

The idea that identity theft can happen to anyone comes in many shapes and sizes, and it has been attributed to a number of different sources, as illustrated in part by the examples in Box 6.5. This general statement has also been used in conjunction with more specific stereotypes regarding vulnerable victims, most notably children, students, and the elderly (also illustrated in Box 6.5), as well as within a generalized prevention frame directed at individuals with an accompanying message of personal threat, as shown within Box 6.4. In other words, the idea of anyone in the narrative was specifically linked to someone—you.

In terms of individuals, the claim that anyone can be a victim is oversimplified by the idea that everyone has an identity, which strictly speaking is not true. While even the assertion that everyone has an address is debatable when considering the homeless population, not all citizens of the world (or even all Americans) participate in the modern economy through the possession of things such as credit cards, insurance, mortgages, or bank accounts, which are all used to primarily define identity in the contemporary age.

Although no comprehensive statistics are available in relation to this point, the Gallup Poll reported in 2001 that 22 percent of Americans did not have a credit card.[103] In terms of those without a bank account, the U.S. Secretary of the Treasury once remarked, "The problem of the unbanked is widespread and, as figures suggest, is of critical concern."[104] While the seeming crisis behind this concern is somewhat of a mystery, both the unbanked and the uncredited still represent portions of the U.S. population today. Thus, there can be no doubt that the personal accounts of the unfinanced will never fall prey to identity thieves because they do not exist. However, a more recent report by Javelin noted that "42% of Generation Y consumers have applied for a credit card online in the last 12 months. . . . This percentage is nearly double that of all consumers."[105] As such, the margin of concern for these economic holdouts might be closing faster than humanity thinks in the 21st century.

Many cases of new you victimization also likely depend on the possession of a social security number in the United States, which might seem to be a more commonly held aspect of identity among this populace, but not all Americans may have one. This is a much more complicated issue to untangle, however, since citizens are required to have a social security number in order to receive certain benefits and obtain legal employment. Social security numbers are also issued to noncitizens for various reasons, and the laws regarding its use have changed much over the past 70 years, since the inception of the

Box 6.5 The Meaning of Anyone

Anyone = Everyone

Identity theft is an equal opportunity crime.
—D. Barry Connelly, president of Associated Credit Bureaus[1]
If it happened to us, it can happen to anyone else.
—Identity theft victim[2]
People just need to be aware that identity theft may well happen to all of us in our lives.
—Lisa Curtis, director of consumer services for the Denver District Attorney's Office[3]
Anyone can be a victim of the radioactive fallout from the credit culture: Identity theft.
—Bob Sullivan, author/journalist[4]
The reality is that anyone can be a victim of identity theft.
—National Cyber Security Alliance[5]

Anyone = Vulnerable Victim

Anyone can be a victim of identity theft, including young children.
—New York State Consumer Protection Board[6]
Order credit reports for your child, anyone can be a victim of Identity Theft!
—Newport Beach (California) Police Department[7]
While anyone can be a victim, college students have become a prime target.
—Author, BusinessWeek[8]
Anyone can be a victim of identity theft, but it is a particular threat to our senior citizens.
—Mike Freeman, Hennepin County (Minnesota) Attorney[9]

---

[1] Connelly (1999).
[2] Quoted in Ellement (2003).
[3] Quoted in Wolf (2004).
[4] Sullivan, B. (2005).
[5] National Cyber Security Alliance (n.d.).
[6] New York State Consumer Protection Board (2007): 2.
[7] Newport Beach Police Department (2007).
[8] Weicher (2007).
[9] Freeman (2007).

---

program. This is not to suggest that new you can only happen via a social security number, however, since the exact type of "personal information" used to commit identity theft is often unknown.

Some data specifically regarding victim characteristics became available through the 2003 study commissioned by the FTC,[106] as well as through a later report based on that data[107] and the research subsequently conducted by Javelin. While a comprehensive profile of identity theft victims has never been complied, these findings provide some indication that the likelihood of victimization varies according to certain sociodemographic characteristics. While these results first appeared rather late in the national progression of the issue, and long after the particular claim that "anyone can be a victim" began to take hold, the risk of criminal victimization in general is not evenly distributed across the population. It depends on a number of spatial and temporal variables, as well as various lifestyle decisions.

In relation to existing credit card misuse, for example, the likelihood of victimization is greater for those who possess more than one credit card; the frequency with which, or the purposes for which they are used further impact the chances of victimization in various ways. In the case of identity theft, this risk is also associated with the quality of the identity in question, particularly in financial terms. In other words, some identities have a greater economic value than others. Just as all people who live in a dwelling do not face the same risk for burglary victimization, all people with an "identity" (financial or otherwise) do not face the same risk for identity theft victimization. This theme has nevertheless persisted over time, pre- and postdata.

While this particular claim has also been extended to several vulnerable populations, not all of these assumptions can be directly assessed. Groups are rendered vulnerable for a variety of reasons, but it is not clear whether any respective members are at even more risk for identity theft. As one example, this can be witnessed in relation to efforts to protect and educate older adults, which stem from concerns about their susceptibility to fraud in general.

A special 2002 FTC report on seniors noted that "although consumers over 60 represent 16% of the population, they represent only 10% of our ID theft complaints."[108] This report also found that "persons over 60 . . . report the most common form of identity theft—credit card fraud—at a slightly higher level than the population under 60."[109] A later analysis based on the FTC's national victimization study nevertheless concluded that "older people may face a somewhat reduced risk."[110] Similar findings were later reported by Javelin: "Seniors are almost half as likely to be victims of fraud as other age groups and sustain the smallest average fraud amount."[111]

While none of this is meant to suggest that the world's elderly population should not be protected from or educated about this problem, there is no evidence to suggest in an overall way that they are specifically targeted for identity theft or disproportionately victimized by this offense in the United States.[112] As witnessed with other parts of this collective problem, specific concerns therefore seemed to underlie and dictate the ways in which concern for identity theft found expression over time.

With regard to victims, this subtheme about vulnerable or at-risk populations is consistent with thinking about crime as a whole, but this was not a strong focus within the newspaper sample itself. For example, there were only 9 references (9/1,839 = 0.48%) that specifically focused on the problem of identity theft in relation to older adults, but 33 (33/1,839 = 1.79%) in which this issue was a strong undercurrent of the discussion. This topic also did not receive equal treatment within each of the newspapers, as shown in Table 6.3.

Although many of these references were announcements for prevention workshops devoted to educating seniors about identity theft prevention, some were more ominous in their tone, such as this 2003 headline from the *Washington Post*: "Identity Thieves Preying on Seniors."[113] Each of the newspapers therefore picked up on this particular theme at one point or another, but some reporting was driven by community concerns in the form of educational seminars rather than the result of active fear mongering on the part of the media. The fact that this theme was more often a secondary focus nevertheless suggests its minimalized importance within reporting overall. Other victim subthemes about children (particularly students) and members of the military were even less pronounced within the entire sample.[114] These references may nevertheless be reflecting smaller community-specific panics taking place within society at large, since vulnerable victim populations of any kind can often be found at their center.

A final example of exaggeration and distortion in relation to individuals relates to statements about the average identity theft victim. As mentioned before, but now illustrated in Box 6.6, the experience of new you came to represent the horrors of identity theft victimization in general. While sensationalistic reporting about crime is not altogether uncommon in today's world, this idea once again seemed to be reproduced within—rather than produced by—most media sources. Such claims about the average identity theft victim directly stem from the research conducted by the FTC and Javelin, however, as will be explained shortly in further detail.

The crisis frame considered here has been a common thread within the moral panics tradition (e.g., *Policing the Crisis*), as well as other forms of media research (e.g., *Creating Fear: News and the Construction of Crisis*[115]). Critcher also specifically discussed the media's use of this frame as a means

Table 6.3 Focus on Seniors as Victims within the Theft Sample

	Primary focus	Secondary focus
Arizona Republic	2 (0.58%)	8 (2.35%)
Boston Globe	1 (0.49%)	8 (3.92%)
USA Today	0	1 (0.50%)
New York Times	0	1 (0.25%)
Washington Post	5 (0.89%)	14 (2.50%)
Rocky Mountain News	1 (0.68%)	1 (0.68%)

Note: Whole numbers represent the number of references for each category. Percentages reflect the proportion of references within each Theft Sub-Sample: AR (339), BG (204), USA (198), NYT (394), WP (558), RMN (146).

Box 6.6 When IDT Strikes

"Identity theft isn't a violent crime in the traditional sense, but it's a highly invasive crime, said Bruce Townsend, director of the financial crimes division of the Secret Service. "Victims show the same kind of [psychological] signs as those who have been through violent crime."[1]

"The real hell of I.D. theft," Consumer Reports noted, "comes from nondollar damages: Your credit rating is ruined, you risk being rejected for everything from a college loan to a mortgage, and it's up to you to fix it all."[2]

Lynn Gates is taking seriously Colorado Attorney General Ken Salazar's warning to be on watch for identity thieves. The unfortunate thing, Salazar said, is that consumers targeted by identity thieves usually don't know they have been victimized until collection agencies begin calling them for unpaid accounts or they're denied credit because of unpaid debts rung up by criminals.[3]

Many people don't know they've been victimized [by identity theft] until their credit report is so damaged that they're rejected for a credit card, car loan or home mortgage. It can take months, even years, to repair. One of the most unsettling aspects of identity theft is that it can haunt you for years after the crime occurred.[4]

Clearing up your files after identity theft can take months of frustrating calls to credit bureaus and merchants.[5]

"You can't really protect yourself," says Martha Steimel, president of Washington-based Victim's Assistance of America, which focuses on identity theft. You can be totally mutilated financially by an identity theft perpetrator. It's scary."[6]

Identity theft is the fastest growing form of financial fraud in the U.S. and ruins the credit of millions of Americans every year.[7]

[1] Nelson (2000).
[2] Fryburg (2000).
[3] Sanko (2002).
[4] Block (2002).
[5] Harney (2003).
[6] Armour (2003).
[7] Wilmouth, Grossman, and Hillebrand (2005).

for representing an issue "as symptomatic of a wider problem,"[116] which ultimately corresponds to the social conditions that facilitate the commission of identity theft in the United States. The blame for such representations of identity theft, however, cannot be laid solely at the media's feet.

Some of this frame's association with identity theft might be attributed to pure literary license, as the essence of this problem had been framed as an identity crisis as early as 1983, but more frequently starting in 1996. This particular crisis frame was nevertheless adopted by the federal government in 2000, and later formed the basis of an entire public information campaign (Operation Identity Crisis) that coincided with the arrival of The 9.9 Million. That particular message to the nation was received loud, but not clear.

Somewhere in the Middle

THE FIRST PHASE of the identity theft narrative in the United States focused on its victims, and took place during a time when society only knew that they existed and took turns guessing at their numbers. Although identity theft involved everything and everyone from the very beginning, by 2003 there was little room for doubt with regard to the dimensions of this problem:

Identity Theft Victimizes Millions, Costs Billions[1]

FTC Says Identity Theft Is Rampant; *10 Million* Cases In the Past Year, Survey Concludes[2] (italics added)

The nation's worst fears about identity theft were now realized in the form of 9.91 (*not* 10) million victims following the release of the FTC's national victimization study.[3] That was the same year the federal government began its national public identity theft awareness campaign—Operation Identity Crisis,[4] which included public service announcements by spokesperson Jerry Orbach[5] and the production of a short video entitled *Identity Crisis . . . A Story of Identity Theft.*[6] The U.S. Postal Inspection Service describes the content of this video as "the story of a couple whose credit is ruined and of the criminals who defrauded them." Also provided were "tips on how to protect yourself against *identity fraud*—and what to do if you become a victim" (italics added).[7] In short then, this is the part of the story where the crisis of identity theft hits the fan.

THE 9.9 MILLION

Although it might be difficult to ignore the suffering of millions of people under normal circumstances (as America apparently had), it was rather hard to miss the 9.91 million identity theft victims that literally appeared in the United States overnight: *Poof!* This first actual figure of identity theft victimization, released by the FTC toward the end of 2003, was a complete shock to the nation but also somewhat of a mystery. The sheer numbers behind identity theft are problematic for several reasons, however, and need to be approached with caution—even today, close to a decade after the arrival of The 9.9 Million.[8]

During the early years before hard data, it had been mistakenly rumored (based on partial fact) that identity theft "victimized" between 350,000 and 400,000 people per year. There was actually much debate over this initial range, which was later reported to be as high as 500,000 people, but even this figure was too high for some and not high enough for others. Nevertheless, the consensus seemed to be that one of these proffered figures was bad enough—hence, the birth of identity theft as a national problem. Between the late 1990s and early 2000s, however, this problem was largely being represented by new you, or the absolute worst thing that could happen to the American identity—not plain old you, even though existing account fraud was always understood to be part of it. The assessment of the problem at that time was premised on considerations of quality, more so than quantity, which was all about to change with The 9.9 Million—or was it?

The problem of identity theft had already been framed as a crisis prior to 2003, when the victim count speciously stood at 500,000 and very few facts were available. Those involved with identity theft before The 9.9 Million also logically knew that the problem must be worse than expected because society had been ignoring it for decades. There was little proof of this before their arrival, except a few scattered voices across the country that were nevertheless chanting in unison at the doors of various social institutions: Not me! By 2003, however, the United States had a victim population larger than most of its individual states.

The immediate threat (or crisis) of identity theft was really twofold: It was gaining on us at the turn of the century, but then it finally caught up with us as the pace of our lives quickened and we became ever more complacent with our lives and our identities. This seemingly unintended consequence of everything techno-modern-global nevertheless qualifies as a result of negligence on our part, which is not as blameless as something truly inadvertent. The crisis of identity theft may therefore have been that we had nobody left to blame but ourselves; thus, the advent of identity theft may have occasioned great excitement and discussion like that surrounding the Civil War frauds. Identity theft is obviously a recurring threat, however, as the crisis of The 9.91 Million is now an annual event in the United States.

If 500,000 inquiries constitute a crisis, what words are left to describe the addition of a few million victims each year? Some of the terms that might immediately come to mind (menace, plague, epidemic) had already been used to describe the crisis of identity theft. In terms of national sentiment at the time of their arrival, however, The 9.9 Million were really just more-than-ample evidence in favor of a foregone conclusion: The problem of identity theft was enormous. The body of the problem after 2003 was monolithic, but its matching reputation actually preceded it (see Box 7.1).

The U.S. experience of identity theft might best be described as an information crisis, one involving risks to both personal information and identity theft information, but the problem of The 9.9 Million remains, compounding—but not necessarily growing—annually: 9.3 million victims in 2004, 8.9 million in 2005, 8.4 million in 2006, 8.1 million in 2007, 9.9 million in 2008, 11.1 million in 2009, and 8.1 million in 2010.[9] Those are a lot of victims, but they only represent a drop in the bucket of the U.S. population.

Based on these figures, the annual victimization rate in the United States has ranged between 3.5 percent and 4.8 percent of the adult population. That is certainly not everybody, but is that bad? Although one victim of any crime is really too many, there is no context for comparison even today. Identity theft is measured separately from the overall crime problem, which creates a palpable divide between crime victims and identity theft victims in the United States. As such, identity theft may be in a class by itself within U.S. society simply because there is only one class available: identity theft.

COUNTING BEANS AND IN-BETWEENS

The basic goal of science is to disprove. Although counting something tends to prove its existence, this is a necessary evil in the pursuit of knowledge; so, too, are statistics. True evil can therefore occur when statistics are used for bad ends, because they represent a good means when calculated correctly. Thus, who really knows what evil lurks in the hearts of men[10] when it comes to identity theft statistics?

The Dark Figure of Identity Theft

The dark figure of crime is like the Loch Ness Monster of criminal justice: both are large, scary beasts lurking within the shadowy recesses of some pretty big ponds. The dark figure is frightening to some extent because it represents an unknown universe of offending—unknown to society because these acts are not reported to the police, not because society is unaware of their existence. The dark figure is therefore one part of the crime problem that usually remains unseen, except for some blurry photographs and often-discreditable eyewitness reports that surface from time to time.[11] Identity theft is a dark figure itself, however, currently competing for the title of Biggest Fish in the Sea.

As sometimes occurs when a crime is discovered, the United States called upon its police to help solve the mystery of identity theft. IDT was like and unlike every crime the police had ever known, however, and everybody was a suspect. Although U.S. police forces had seen different faces of identity theft many times, they could tell us very little about the problem in official terms because identity theft was not recorded as such in the beginning, and may not be so in its entirety even today.

Box 7.1 Nessie Sightings[1]

2000: Identity theft, in fact, is fast becoming a bogeyman lurking in the shadows of mainstream America. And while identity thieves are still often low-tech con artists, the rise in cases, say observers, has roughly paralleled the proliferation of the Internet.[2]

2002: We have an underbelly of society wreaking havoc with our financial institutions, said Michelle Ahlmer, executive director of the Arizona Retailers Association.[3]

Horror movie fans know that the creepiest threats are the ones you cannot see. A big hairy monster in your dining room is unnerving, but at least you know what you are dealing with. A malevolent creature that lurks in the shadows is much scarier because you do not know when it will strike. That's why identity theft is so frightening.[4]

2003: These days, [David] Medine [former associate director for credit practices within the Federal Trade Commission's Bureau of Consumer Protection] says, almost everyone has a horror story to contribute to the conversation. "You have this seemingly low-level crime that, cumulatively, is a *national crisis*," Medine says. They are well aware that identity thieves are growing not only more numerous, but more menacing. Scam artists and grifters have been joined by criminal groups from abroad and street gangs that once specialized in robberies or extortion. And as September 11 made plain, identity theft also has become a favored technique of terrorists.[5] (italics added)

---

[1] Nessie is the nickname of the Loch Ness Monster.
[2] Nelson (2000).
[3] Sowers and Biggs (2002).
[4] Block (2002).
[5] O'Harrow (2003).

Despite the important role of local police forces in responding to victim complaints, many police agencies do not appear to be collecting identity theft statistics at all, or they may be recording them under another offense category. A newsletter published by the Utah Bureau of Criminal Identification in 2006, for example, notes that there is no classification for identity theft within the National Incident Based Reporting System and subsequently discusses strategies for reporting this offense under a variety of different headings (e.g., larceny, embezzlement, fraud). The National Strategy to Combat Identity Theft produced by the U.S. Office of Community Oriented Policing Services in 2006 similarly discusses recommendations for standardizing UCR reporting. While this state of affairs may explain states' reliance on the victimization figures annually produced by the FTC, it certainly complicates the prospect of understanding the true extent of victimization and the impact that identity theft has had on the routine work of police agencies around the country.

Table 7.1 U.S. Property Crime and Identity Theft Victimizations

Year	UCR property crime	NCVS property crime*	Identity theft
2003	10,442,862	18,626,380	10,100,000
2004	10,319,386	18,654,400	9,300,000
2005	10,166,159	18,039,930	8,900,000
2006	Not available	Not available	8,400,000

Sources by column: Federal Bureau of Investigation (2006), Catalano (2004, 2006), and Javelin Strategy & Research (2005, 2006, 2007a).
*These figures represent individual (not household) victimizations.

Since identity theft is a new offense category, where does it fit within the larger picture of crime in the United States? No official answer to this question has ever been provided, but given the strong economic undertones of identity theft within contemporary society, it might best be categorized as a property crime rather than a crime against the person. Although direct comparisons between identity theft and other crime categories cannot be performed due to various methodological issues, Table 7.1 attempts to place the estimated number of national identity theft victimizations within some type of context by viewing them alongside the reported (UCR, Uniform Crime Report) and estimated (NCVS, National Crime Victimization Survey) figures for property crime victimization within the United States.

All three sources of data in Table 7.1 (the UCR, the NCVS, and the Javelin studies) generally show a decrease in their respective columns over the four-year period considered. Each figure nevertheless represents something very different from the others. The UCR shows the number of crimes that were reported to the police each year, while the NCVS shows the number of people claiming to have been victimized by such offenses each year (some of which also reported calling the police). Although identity theft victimization would seem to be included within these categories of property crime somewhere, its incidence is measured like the NCVS and its results are treated with a reverence normally reserved for the UCR.

The overall crime rate in the United States has been declining steadily for many years, and the same is true for the property crime rate, whether measured by the NCVS or the UCR,[12] which together would appear to contradict the commonly reported claim that the incidence of identity theft is growing. This claim nevertheless stood in direct opposition to the largely declining estimates that were being reported by Javelin Strategy & Research after 2003, although other studies around that time were reporting increases in identity theft victimization.

Specifically, Gartner, Inc., is a research and consulting firm that has conducted two studies of identity theft victimization since 2003. The first was a mail survey of 2,445 U.S. households, and the second was an online survey of 5,000 U.S. adults. Both of these studies concluded that the incidence of identity theft was rising,[13] despite the substantial differences in their methodologies and the long lapse between when these surveys were conducted. While there is not enough available information to assess Gartner's categorization of identity theft or their findings, this company is involved with the development of identity scoring[14]—a new type of risk management solution for fraud detection that is perhaps likely to be in greater demand within a society rife with this particular type of criminal behavior.

Javelin is the only firm to have consistently examined this issue on a national scale, but this company is similarly involved in the development of approaches to fraud prevention. Three large private industry members also subsidize Javelin's research: CheckFree Services Corporation, Visa USA, and Wells Fargo Bank. Although their reports state that these "sponsors were not involved in the tabulation, analysis, or reporting of final results" in order to "preserve the project's independence and objectivity,"[15] Javelin's interpretation of some findings has been consistent with this group's interest in a cashless—and specifically paperless—society. These particular industry members might also have an interest in minimizing their own role in the occurrence of identity theft.

The purpose of Javelin's research most closely resembles that of the NCVS, the findings of which are consistently higher than those collected by the UCR because they measure the dark figure of crime. The scope of the NCVS is nevertheless much greater than those of other national identity theft victimization surveys. The NCVS is conducted with more than 70,000 households and 100,000 individuals each year, while Javelin's identity theft studies have been conducted with 4,000–5,000 individuals each year. The NCVS also estimates the victimization of U.S. residents aged 12 years and older, while the Javelin and FTC studies have only examined the victimization of U.S. adults aged 18 or older.

The NCVS began to measure identity theft in 2004, but its initial results were only available for a six-month period, and these were reported separately for identity theft. In other words, that report did not outline the relationship between identity theft and the other forms of victimization measured by the survey during that year. This information was also presented in terms of household (not individual) victimizations, so to present them in context: 12.1 percent of all U.S. households (14,032,570) were victimized by property crime in 2004;[16] 3.1 percent of all U.S. households (3,589,100) were victimized by identity theft during a six-month period in 2004.[17] The author of this report further notes: "It is likely that the 6-month prevalence estimate presented . . . would be somewhat more than half that of an annual estimate if a full year's data were available."[18] Thus, the annual estimate for 2004 should have been somewhat lower than 6.2 percent of all U.S. households (approximately 7,178,200).[19]

The addition of identity theft questions to the NCVS suggests that it was not previously measured by this survey. If identity theft is a separate offense category, one that is somehow different than either the property or violent crime victimizations measured by the NCVS, then it would seem to account for a very large portion of U.S. victimization that has heretofore gone unmeasured. This new category might also be remeasuring acts already counted in the NCVS, however, just as Javelin's results might overlap the NCVS estimates in many respects. Thus, for some inexplicable reason, identity theft stands alone in the world of American crime.

9+1+1

The figures reported by the UCR and Javelin measure different things, but the behaviors related to police reporting may be somewhat different than those witnessed for other types of property crime. While there is a sizeable portion of identity theft victims who do not report their victimization to anyone, available data suggest that some victims who contact the police are denied the chance to file an official report. According to the FTC survey, 38 percent of victims did not contact anyone with regard to their victimization; of those who did contact someone, 22 percent contacted a local police agency and a report was taken in 76 percent of these cases.[20] In order to examine the implications of these findings in more detail, Javelin's findings on this issue appear in Table 7.2.[21]

The second and third columns of Table 7.2 combined ("Didn't contact anyone" and "Contacted someone") are based on 100 percent of the victims within Javelin's samples for these years.[22] The fourth column ("Contacted someone, specifically police") is based on 100 percent of the victims who reported their victimization to someone. In 2003, for example, out of the 100 percent of the 77.4 percent of victims who contacted someone regarding their victimization in 2003, 33.2 percent contacted the police.[23] The final two columns combined ("Contacted police, report taken" and "Contacted police, report not taken") are based on 100 percent of the victims who reported their victimization to a police agency. Again in 2003, this means that out of the 100 percent of the 33.2 percent of victims who contacted the police, 76.1 percent were able to file a police report and 14.8 percent were not.[24]

Were you able to follow all of that? Many people were not, and with good reason. Considering that the relationship between these figures is largely lost through this common representation of the statistics derived from identity theft data, Table 7.3 presents a recalculation of these figures (and a translation in plain English) using available information for 2003 and 2004.

When the columns related to police reporting in Table 7.3 are added together (Contacted police, report taken + Contacted police, report not taken + Contacted police, report status unknown), approximately 25.65 percent of all victims in 2003 and 24.73 percent of all victims in 2004 reported contacting the police.[25] If considered in the context of how many victims contact the police to report a property crime victimization of any type, the percentage

Table 7.2 Identity Theft Victim Reporting Behavior, Javelin-Style

Year	Didn't contact anyone (%)	Contacted someone (%)	Contacted someone, specifically police (%)	Contacted police, report taken (%)	Contacted police, report not taken (%)
2003	22.3	77.4	33.2	76.1	14.8
2004	32.8	66.9	37.0	70.0[1]	27.1
2005	21.0	79.0	43.0	85.0	n/a[2]

Sources: Data for 2003 and 2004 were obtained from Javelin Strategy & Research (2005); data for 2005 were obtained from Javelin Strategy & Research (2006).
[1]In Javelin (2006), this figure was reported as 72 percent.
[2]Javelin did not report the percentage of cases in which a police report was not taken during 2005, but this figure may equal less than 15 percent due to missing responses.

Table 7.3 Identity Theft Victim Reporting Behavior, Everyman-Style

Year	Didn't contact anyone (%)	Contacted agency other than police (%)	Contacted police, report taken (%)	Contacted police, report not taken (%)	Contacted police, report status unknown (%)	Total % of all victims
2003	22.3	51.71	19.55	3.80	2.3	99.66
2004	32.8	42.15	17.32	6.70	0.71	99.68

The figures used to calculate Table 7.3 (shown in Table 7.2) did not equal 100 percent and an additional percentage was lost during the recalculation; thus, the "Total percentage of all victims" does not equal 100 percent for either year. Similar figures could not be calculated for 2005 due to the lack of necessary information.

of victims contacting the police to report identity theft is much lower: 25.65 percent compared to 38.4 percent in 2003, and 24.73 percent compared to 39 percent in 2004.[26]

There are nevertheless variations in reporting related to specific types of property victimization, and the two lowest percentages consistently reported for these years are for a "Completed Theft Totaling Less than $50" (18.4% and 18.8%, respectively, for 2003 and 2004) and a "Completed Theft Totaling Between $50 and $249" (26.2% and 27.4%, respectively).[27] The next highest percentage consistently reported is for a "Completed Theft of Any Amount" (31.7% and 32.1%, respectively). As such, the percentage of identity theft victims reporting to the police is not as high as the average rate for all types of property crimes, although it seems to fall somewhere in between the estimates for the two categories of theft in which losses totaled below $249.

While most identity theft victims experience no out-of-pocket expenses, it cannot be assumed that only those experiencing a financial loss contacted the police. However, the mean losses reported by Javelin are much higher than $249 ($536 in 2003 and $652 in 2004).[28] Part of the difference in identity theft reporting can also be attributed to other offense and demographic variables, although being under the age of 25 itself is associated with a decreased likelihood for reporting victimization to the police.[29]

The percentage of identity theft victims who did not receive a police report has yet to be taken into account, but the NCVS does not specify whether any victims who contacted the police were subsequently denied a police report. The NCVS also does not provide information regarding the number of victims who contacted another agency for help aside from the police. What these figures suggest, however, is that at least 19.55 percent of the estimated number of identity theft victims in 2003 (approximately 1,974,550) and 17.32 percent of the estimated number of identity theft victims in 2004 (approximately 1,610,760) contacted the police regarding their victimization and were able to file a police report. Since these figures represent what the UCR might have measured, they are probably closer to the incidence of identity theft according to traditional standards.

The criminalization of identity theft created a new offense category, but identity theft is not a new type of criminal behavior. Estimates of this problem, however, cannot be reconciled with the two most important sources of U.S. crime data. Although the UCR and the NCVS are flawed in their own respects and cannot be completely reconciled with one another, they also measure different things on purpose. The same cannot be said for the NCVS and the Javelin studies, since both now measure the dark figure of identity theft. The treatment of identity theft as a separate issue therefore makes it appear to rival all crime in the United States, which unduly elevates its role as part of the crime problem to that of its greatest crime problem.

And Then There Were Some[30]

While the preceding discussion has attempted to put the problem of identity theft into some kind of perspective using official statistics, there are several areas not addressed by available victimization estimates. In particular, there are valid reasons to believe that the problem of identity theft is overestimated (particularly because of the way it has been operationalized to include old you with a credit card) as well as underestimated. First, individuals under the age of 12 are not included in any current identity theft victimization surveys, although the FTC collects reports regarding victims of all ages. There are also no estimates regarding the misuse of a deceased person's identity, and this criminal afterlife is believed to be a rather substantial problem on its own. Finally, there is a possibility that extant surveys are underestimating victimization to some degree due to the prolonged periods of discovery that can often accompany cases of new you, but a number of factors have likely impacted this particular issue over the years as new reforms take effect and public awareness increases. Although these caveats further confound the measurement issues related to identity theft, they are all important considerations suggesting that the problem of identity theft does not begin or end with The 9.9 Million.

Javelin's research has more recently been criticized by one grassroots activist (Chris Hoofnagle) for not including synthetic fraud, defined as creating "an entirely new identity using information from many different victims."[31] Javelin acknowledged in one of its reports that it does not include synthetic identity fraud, which was therein vaguely defined as "a fictitious identity created in order to defraud an organization."[32] James Van Dyke (Javelin president and founder) nevertheless directly responded to this accusation by asserting that Javelin's survey does measure the type of synthetic identity fraud defined by Hoofnagle "since a real victim is quite often involved and therefore responds to our nationally representative phone survey."[33] This would be true if such fraud were eventually detected and linked to one particular consumer (or perhaps several), but this is the opposite of what is implied by the previous description of synthetic fraud given by Mike Cook, whose company examines this issue directly.

Van Dyke further distinguishes between three types of identity fraud: crimes that completely rely on a single person's identity, "pure synthetic fraud" that completely relies on an entirely fabricated identity, and crimes that use some combination of real and fabricated identities.[34] Whatever it is called, combining real and fictitious identity information in order to commit fraud is not a new phenomenon either, but categorizing identity theft as something completely separate from synthetic fraud adds little clarity to the issue as a whole if any innocent persons are ultimately held responsible for the fraudulent acts committed using any part of their identity.

It must also be emphasized within this discussion that the millions of victims already claimed to date[35] have seemingly failed to materialize or otherwise impact the national barometers for measuring criminal victimization. While anecdotal evidence consistently suggests an increase of identity theft cases on local levels, a number of issues are likely to have an impact in this regard: increased awareness about identity theft by victims and officials, the effects of state legislation or other types of regulation, changes in the way identity theft is recorded and/or dealt with by pertinent agencies, and a general lack of contextual information to assess various indicators in relation to their pre-IDT levels. This last issue is particularly important in light of the fact that the element of identity theft runs through many different types of crime, and these cases were already being handled by a variety of agencies and industries before it was independently criminalized as such.

Considering the current state of official statistics, the FTC's Identity Theft Clearinghouse (now part of the Consumer Sentinel) provides the next best estimate of identity theft victimization in the United States.[36] These figures represent the people who actually complain about identity theft when it happens, rather than the people who decide to cooperate with social research about their experience at some later time, but there are fewer of these victims overall. Partial data regarding the FTC's efforts are presented in Figure 7.1, which generally shows an increase in reporting through the end of 2005. All of the figures here nevertheless peak at around 250,000 complaints, which is less than half of the 500,000 victims expected before the arrival of The 9.9 Million. These data also show that the FTC was doing the job it was directed to do (collect victim complaints), so any crisis involved with these particular figures is not obvious either before or after 2003.

Individual reporting following a newly criminalized act can be affected by a number of factors, particularly increased public awareness regarding the offense following the roll-out of this type of national resource. Victimization reporting in general is also related to a number of individual and offense

Figure 7.1 Consumer Sentinel IDT Contacts

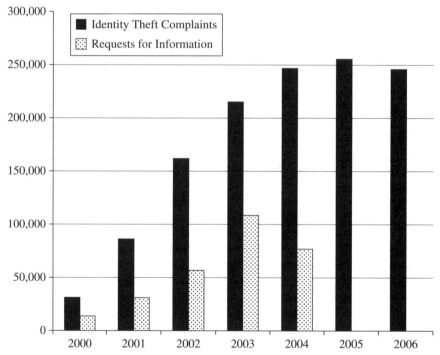

Note: The FTC Consumer Sentinel continually receives data and updates its statistics from previous years within each new annual report. Data regarding complaints were therefore taken from the most recent statistics available for each year as of 2008: 2004–2006 (FTC [2007a]), 2003 (FTC [2006]), 2002 (FTC [2005a]), 2001 (FTC [2004]), and 2000 (FTC [2003a]). Data regarding the number of requests for identity theft information were not reported by the FTC in 2006 or 2007, but these figures are provided for the years available: 2002–2004 (FTC [2005a]), 2001 (FTC [2004]), and 2000 (FTC [2003a]).

characteristics, but identity theft reporting is further fraught with difficulties that prevent comparisons even among the complaints received by the FTC. As such, it is difficult to interpret the precise meaning of these data as well.[37]

If the number of requests for information continued to decrease in 2005 and 2006 as potentially suggested by Figure 7.1, these figures might indicate that the public reached a certain level of saturation with regard to this issue in 2003. Identity theft information is nevertheless freely available on the FTC's website, along with many other locations on the web and elsewhere. The close proximity between the number of complaints received between 2004 and 2006 may also reflect a leveling-off of reporting rather than the beginning of an actual decline, but these figures do not reflect patterns in victimization per se. One Javelin analyst nevertheless interprets the 2006 drop in FTC complaints as making progress against identity fraud: "It is heartening to see that some headway is being gained in this battle,"[38] but this conclusion is completely unfounded on the basis of that information alone.

According to the results of national victimization surveys, it appears that only a small portion of victims contact the FTC to report identity theft victimization at all: 3 percent of all victims in the FTC's 2003 study,[39] and 4.2 percent of victims in 2003 and 3.3 percent in 2004 according to Javelin.[40] Based on corresponding victimization estimates for these years, however, these percentages suggest a higher number of reports than were actually received by the FTC: 215,177 actual complaints compared to an estimated 424,200 (4.2 percent of 10.1 million) in 2003; and 246,882 actual complaints compared to an estimated 306,900 (3.3 percent of 9.3 million) in 2004. The FTC's figures may also include victimization reports from other agencies or other countries, as will now be discussed, but the specific impact that this has on their reported identity theft statistics is unclear.

Information Isn't Free

As noted by another Javelin analyst: "The truth is, identity fraud is decreasing overall, and we're not the only ones advocating this reality—government agencies are saying the same thing."[41] The examples used to support this statement were decreases in the number of complaints received by the FTC and the FBI's Internet Crime Complaint Center (IC³). The IC³ is one of the leading contributors of fraud complaint data to the FTC's Consumer Sentinel Network, so these data sources are not independent of one another, but they do not contribute any identity theft reports—at least not according to the FTC.[42] This aspect nevertheless brings up an important point in that the federal government was strangely silent regarding the good news delivered by Javelin in the form of decreasing victimization estimates, particularly considering that the FTC initiated this annual survey in 2003.

In an attempt to obtain information regarding the federal government's assessment of Javelin's work, Hoofnagle requested related documentation under the Freedom of Information Act. Although 202 pages of information were located, his request was "partially" denied and 2 pages were released.[43] Neither contained any information regarding the government's position on Javelin's research. While this may not be that unusual on its own for a bureaucracy, the Federal Trade Commission has continuously reported identity theft to be its top consumer complaint for the past 11 years now,[44] which minimally suggests that this problem is larger or more often complained about than others. This particular claim therefore requires closer inspection.

The FTC's annual report includes data on the identity theft and fraud-related complaints that are received through the Consumer Sentinel Network, which also accepts a small percentage of reports from agencies outside the United States. Figure 7.2, which is reproduced as it appeared in the FTC's 2006 annual report, shows that the overall number of complaints received between 2003 and 2005 increased from 542,656 to 686,683, as did the corresponding figures reported for identity theft and fraud complaints. The total percentage of identity theft complaints decreased between these years, however, while the total percentage of fraud complaints increased. How then can identity theft be the top consumer complaint for any of these years, let alone 11 in a row?

Figure 7.2 Sentinel Complaints by Calendar Year

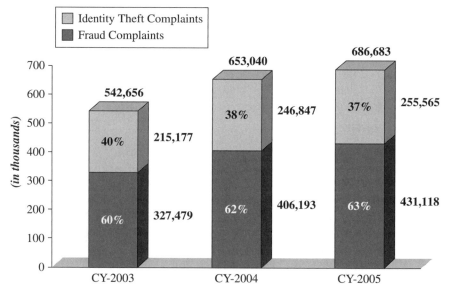

Source: Federal Trade Commission (2006). Percentages are based on the total number of complaints in the Identity Theft Data Clearinghouse for each calendar year: CY-2003 = 215,177; CY-2004 = 246,847; and CY-2005 = 255,565. Note that 20 percent of identity theft complaints include more than one type of identity theft in CY-2005, 19 percent and 20 percent for CY-2003 and CY-2004, respectively. The category of "Bank Fraud" includes fraud involving checking and savings accounts and electronic fund transfers.

The answer to this question can be found in Figure 7.3 (also reproduced as it appeared within the FTC's 2006 annual report), which shows the entire category of fraud-related complaints to be subdivided by type and compared against the entire category of identity theft complaints. The contrast necessary to substantiate this particular claim is indeed quite noticeable when viewed in this manner, and this representation has consistently provided the basis for the claim that identity theft is the top consumer complaint. Why, however, was Figure 7.2 included in the FTC's report at all if fraud complaints were not considered to be a homogeneous group? More to the point, why do identity theft complaints continue to be treated as a homogeneous group in Figure 7.3 and not the fraud complaints?

There is no obvious reason for the representation of data presented in Figure 7.3, as the FTC's annual reports actually contain a breakdown of identity theft complaints by subtype in their appendices, as shown in Figure 7.4. While these figures have never been used to produce a more accurate comparison of consumer complaint data similar to the representation of fraud complaints shown in Figure 7.3, the information provided in Figure 7.4 cannot currently be used to compare different categories of identity theft against those provided for fraud because the figures add up to more than 100 percent.

Figure 7.3 Sentinel Top Complaint Categories

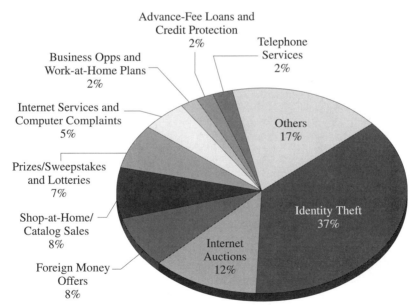

Source: Federal Trade Commission (2006). Percentages are based on the total number of Sentinel complaints (686,683) received between January 1 and December 31, 2005.

Figure 7.4 How Victims' Information Is Misused Calendar Years 2003 through 2005

Credit Card Fraud

Theft Subtype	Percentages CY-2003	Percentages CY-2004	Percentages CY-2005
New Accounts	19.3%	16.5%	15.6%
Existing Account	12.0%	11.9%	11.3%
Unspecified	1.4%	0.1%	0.2%
Total	32%	28%	26%

Phone or Utilities Fraud

Theft Subtype	Percentages CY-2003	Percentages CY-2004	Percentages CY-2005
Wireless - New Accounts	10.5%	10.0%	9.0%
Telephone - New Accounts	5.7%	6.0%	5.5%
Utilities - New Accounts	3.9%	4.3%	5.2%
Unauthorized Charges to Existing Accounts	0.6%	0.7%	0.7%
Unspecified	0.8%	0.3%	0.4%
Total	20%	19%	18%

Bank Fraud[2]

Theft Subtype	Percentages CY-2003	Percentages CY-2004	Percentages CY-2005
Electronic Fund Transfer	4.8%	6.6%	7.9%
Existing Accounts	8.3%	8.5%	7.4%
New Accounts	3.8%	3.6%	3.3%
Unspecified	0.5%	0.1%	0.1%
Total	17%	18%	17%

Employment-Related Fraud

Theft Subtype	Percentages CY-2003	Percentages CY-2004	Percentages CY-2005
Employment-Related Fraud	11%	13%	12%

Loan Fraud

Theft Subtype	Percentages CY-2003	Percentages CY-2004	Percentages CY-2005
Business / Personal / Student Loan	2.3%	2.6%	2.6%
Auto Loan / Lease	2.0%	1.9%	1.8%
Real Estate Loan	1.0%	1.2%	1.2%
Unspecified	0.3%	0.2%	0.2%
Total	5%	5%	5%

Other Identity Theft

Theft Subtype	Percentages CY-2003	Percentages CY-2004	Percentages CY-2005
Evasion of Legal Sanctions	2.1%	2.4%	2.2%
Internet / E-mail	1.6%	1.8%	1.9%
Medical	1.8%	1.8%	1.8%
Apartment / House Rented	0.9%	0.9%	0.9%
Insurance	0.3%	0.4%	0.4%
Property Rental Fraud	0.2%	0.3%	0.3%
Bankruptcy	0.3%	0.3%	0.3%
Child Support	0.2%	0.3%	0.2%
Magazines	0.1%	0.2%	0.2%
Securities / Other Investments	0.2%	0.1%	0.2%
Other	11.6%	14.4%	17.6%
Total	19%	22%	25%

Attempted Identity Theft

Theft Subtype	Percentages CY-2003	Percentages CY-2004	Percentages CY-2005
Attempted Identity Theft	8%	6%	6%

Government Documents or Benefits Fraud

Theft Subtype	Percentages CY-2003	Percentages CY-2004	Percentages CY-2005
Fraudulent Tax Return Filed	3.7%	3.9%	4.7%
Driver's License Issued / Forged	2.3%	2.3%	1.8%
Government Benefits Applied For / Received	1.3%	1.4%	1.5%
Other Government Documents Issued / Forged	0.4%	0.7%	0.6%
Social Security Card Issued / Forged	0.4%	0.5%	0.3%
Unspecified	<0.1%	<0.1%	<0.1%
Total	8%	8%	9%

Source: Federal Trade Commission (2006). Percentages are based on the total number of complaints in the Identity Theft Data Clearinghouse for each calendar year: CY-2003 = 215,177; CY-2004 = 246,847; and CY-2005 = 255,565. Note that 20 percent of identity theft complaints include more than one type of identity theft in CY-2005, 19 percent and 20 percent for CY-2003 and CY-2004, respectively. The category of "Bank Fraud" includes fraud involving checking and savings accounts and electronic fund transfers.

Figure 7.4 also illustrates that the FTC receives a large share of complaints regarding new accounts of various types (i.e., credit card, phone, utilities), even though the majority of identity theft measured by victimization surveys relates to existing account misuse. In other words, reporting to the FTC (as with other types of crime) seems to revolve around the most serious forms of this many-faceted offense. The Other Identity Theft category in Figure 7.4 is also interesting, not only because it includes the rather bizarre subcategory Magazines, but because more than half of it is comprised of *Other* Other Identity Theft over a three-year period.

Even more curious is the issue of why the FTC did not minimally present identity theft complaints in a manner consistent with its 2003 survey, which included three broad categories: New Accounts and Other Fraud, Existing Credit Card Account Misuse, and Existing Non–Credit Card Account Misuse. In spite of the problems associated with this breakdown of the offense, the use of these categories would at least have been a more accurate portrayal of the comparison presented in Figure 7.4. As it stands, therefore, the claim that identity theft is the FTC's top consumer complaint is extremely misleading, if not intentionally deceitful. This also represents a rather high price to pay for free information about identity theft, although Javelin's results are riddled with similar problems and are only available for a greater cost.[45]

What Goes Up . . .

Many claims of the U.S. identity theft panic are unsustainable because they are inherently illogical, despite all popular evidence to the contrary. It was just a matter of time, however, before dissension became noticeable in the ranks. One of the most significant counterclaims came from Javelin in the beginning, when it began to report a decrease in the incidence of "identity fraud" starting in 2003. These findings were largely unheeded in a society where identity theft was perceived to be growing, although even Javelin noted that "[n]otwithstanding the apparent decline in fraud, security experts say identity theft remains a big problem, as scammers try to stay one step ahead of consumers and businesses."[46] Javelin's findings have nevertheless resulted in a handful of heated comments in defense of the original claim. The following excerpt (sic), for example, was posted on the Javelin website in response to one of their blogs:

> ID theft is in no way in a decline. Im a retired NYPD Detective an expert in Financial Crimes and Teach and Lecture to Law enforcment Countrywide. Over half of ID theft crimes are probably not reported. You ask why? Becuase when someone makes a claim to thier bank that thier card or account has been compromised, the bank and Federal Regulation E does not require a police report. Hence, the claim is paid and the victim never makes a report. Also, when victims try to make a police report they are turned away over half the time becuase of cross jurisdictional issues or some other reasons requiring a note from the bank.

In my experience and I also have bank investiagtion experience with a major bank in NYC. This crime is way out of control and beyond epidemic proportions. Not to mention nobody goes to jail for this crime and so it sis the crime that pays.[47]

Javelin's research has similarly come under attack from Chris Hoofnagle (former senior counsel for the Electronic Privacy Information Center), who has openly challenged their findings in his web blog: "2007 brings another **identity theft survey** from Javelin Strategy. As usual, it strives to conclude that identity theft is on the decline and that most identity theft is the result of information being stolen from the victim. Both conclusions are dead wrong" (bold in original).[48]

Overall, it appears that the weight of Javelin's findings has made little headway with at least some members of the populace, but the idea that identity theft is a growing problem persists to this day because it was originally based on common sense—not statistics. Complaining about identity theft will do nothing to stop it, but neither will counting its victims apparently because the problem only promises to get worse using that method alone. Identity theft will therefore continue in its current course, growing or otherwise, for as long as we do nothing to effectively slow it down.

THE BILLIONS

Although some attempt was made to understand the international context of identity theft during the original research, as well as later on for this volume, data regarding the global problem are rare. When they can be located, all of the considerations discussed for the U.S. data apply, thus other national figures related to identity theft are equally problematic and incomparable. A 2008 Canadian survey, for example, found that 6.5 percent of the adult population had been victimized over a one-year period, representing approximately 1.7 million people: "More than half of these frauds involved nothing more than unauthorized purchases made with credit cards. Consumers rarely pay the costs of such frauds. If we eliminate credit card fraud from the incidence rate . . . the number of victims is reduced to 700,000" (herein known as The Canadian 700,000).[49]

Based on this description, it certainly sounds like the U.S. and Canadian problems might be two peas in a pod. In fact, if the U.S. problem were similarly pared down to its essentials (i.e., new you), its official incidence might be reduced to about one-third of its current size. If these rates can be taken at face value, however, the Canadian problem is worse: 6.5 percent versus 4.3 percent for America (being the reported figure for 2008).[50] This type of conclusion usually does not sit well because 9.91 million is obviously greater than 1.7 million, but that is the reality of math. While these rates are not in fact directly comparable due to some methodological considerations,[51] the Canadian example provides at least some reason to doubt the Americanness of identity theft in the 21st century, if not merely question the influence and impact that the United States might be having on its northern neighbor.

What do we actually know about The Canadian 700,000? This group has already been separated from its brethren (unauthorized purchases made with credit cards), but what does that leave us with? Since the answer to that question is unclear, one candidate would be other types of existing account fraud (e.g., bank accounts, social service accounts), which are also responsible for a portion of old you fraud in the United States—that is, the you who may have a credit card but was victimized through some other facet of your life.

This Canadian study also reported the following: "2.7% of the sample indicated that their personal data had been accessed by unauthorized people as part of a data breach or fraud operation in the last year. This represents *another* 700,000 Canadian adults who are at risk for identity fraud" (italics added).[52] Since Canada does not appear to have the equivalent of a U.S. social security number, what is the social substance of the personal data breached that puts this Other Canadian 700,000 at risk (distinguishable as being a different group from The Canadian 700,000)? If part of the personal data breached was credit card data, can these cases similarly be excluded? If so, and all of it is credit card data, then The Other Canadian 700,000 has just disappeared (*Poof!*). Based on just the information reported about these Canadian data, it is impossible to answer these kinds of questions, and painfully difficult to even ask them.

Canada has at least attempted to measure their problem, which reflects in some degree their commitment to understand it, but this is more than can be said for most other nations.[53] In part, the dearth of international data may stem from perceptions that identity theft really isn't a problem, or at least a large enough problem to warrant the cost of national research. The financial impact of identity theft may nevertheless be a primary concern for many members of the international community. The United Kingdom, for example, has been heavily invested in the fight against identity fraud for quite some time (and for about as long as the United States). Although one recent journalistic source noted that "fraud experts" believe the annual rate of victimization to be 0.17 percent of the population or 100,000 people,[54] this type of estimate is suspect for the same reasons as the original U.S. guesstimate. What is commonly available from the United Kingdom are cost estimates, however, which seems to reflect the bottom line of identity fraud for many societies across the globe, with the United States being no exception.

While cost estimates should be approached with even more caution than victimization estimates, it is important to consider all of the costs associated with identity theft, not just its financial ones. These costs are nevertheless shouldered differently by the victims of new you and old you, as well as shared (directly and indirectly) by the collective victims of identity fraud and the social co-owners of identities. Some of these finer points in the identity theft narrative will therefore be considered further in the last two chapters of Part II.

Just beneath the Surface

CLAIMS REGARDING THE acquisition of personal information are part of the overall narrative, but they are not as illogical as some of the others—at least on their surface. The effect that such claims might be having on actual behavior is another matter, which seems to justify taking a closer look at Act I and some of its popular reviews.

OPERATION IDENTITY

The dramatic action during Act I regards the kidnapping of mini you (Target #1), which is an embodiment of the interaction between identity and target as outlined in Part I. Although these elements could be viewed in a 5 x 4 table to consider their interactions in greater detail,[1] many types of information overlap across these categories. Many individual bytes of personal information also tend to exist simultaneously on a single target. A plastic credit card, for example, usually has a name, account number, existence information about the account (member since xxxx, expiration date), and a security code. Names in particular appear just about everywhere.

While it is usually not necessary to know everything about someone in order to wear their identity out in public, the need to know certain things is determined by where you intend to go thus donned. Wearing this cloak carries some element of danger at all times, but that too depends on where you are. The quality of its fabric is also a concern because the more you put it on, and the reasons for which you do so, will result in gradual wear and tear. Thus, society or its owner may eventually begin to see through to the true identity of the (wo)man underneath.

Crime prevention in practice focuses on a particular type of problem, such as a database breach, in order to examine the precise situational elements that contribute to its occurrence. Identity information literally exists everywhere, however, both physically and virtually. Although a full accounting of these social contexts is precluded by the nature of everything identity theft, the dynamics behind this act can be understood in an overall way. Personal information can generally be obtained along one of three main routes: (1) directly from you or your environment (e.g., residence, car, wallet, computer); (2) directly from an information guardian or its environment (e.g., store, office, database); or (3) during a transaction between parties.[2] This first category represents the environment radiating outward from your physical person: home base, the institutions and locations of your social life, and the world at large (represented by physical and virtual travel/communications).

With regard to the second category, the reputed status of Michele Brown's identity thief is a good example. According to at least one version of this story, Brown's information was stolen by her landlord's receptionist.[3] This category of the dishonest employee generally falls within the area of the guardian's domain, even though Michele Brown might have literally handed this information (in good faith) to her own thief. According to Brown's original testimony, however, the woman who stole her identity from her landlord's property management office was an acquaintance (not a receptionist). This scenario, however, also falls under the domain of the guardian.

The third realm is largely theoretical, representing an area somewhere in between guardians' and owners' domains of influence, thus representing an overall gray area of responsibility. This particular description might apply to an environment like cyberspace, and the lack of general law and order therein.[4] Personal information is not always acquired by criminal means, however, so the theft of this target might actually be a sale, or a basic situation of finders-keepers. These categories therefore represent the main avenues available to an offender in order to acquire Target #1, which can be further understood in terms of the types and forms of identity information that comprise it.[5] Distinctions can also be made regarding the means by which offenders obtain Target #1, particularly between high-tech and low-tech means as will now be discussed.

Friendly Fire

The role of technology is at the heart of a controversy surrounding the acquisition of personal information during this act. Although high-tech and low-tech methods may similarly be used to obtain a new identity, the question of which method is more prevalent has become extremely important in the realm of privacy, as personal records (particularly in the form of public records) have become increasingly available on the Internet. This topic is also tied into what people do with their identities while online, however, which is difficult to assess overall or in particular. One example of this is the economic issue of online shopping.

A few newspaper articles have cited different types of polls and research to suggest that some Americans are afraid of shopping online, or afraid of the Internet in general. Some of the most consistent research on this topic has been conducted by Pew Internet & Life. Since many of their reports focus on very specific topics, however, a complete picture of Internet usage cannot be gleaned as a whole or over time. As one example, it was reported that half of all U.S. adults did not have Internet access in 2000, and that 57 percent of those nonusers were not interested in ever obtaining access.[6] Just over half of those who were not online (54%) also believed that the Internet was dangerous. A similar 2001 report concluded that 87 percent of Americans were concerned about credit card theft online in addition to the role of the Internet in facilitating other types of criminal behavior.[7]

In relation to identity theft, the first study by the Federal Trade Commission (FTC) did ask respondents whether they had Internet access, but did not assess whether the Internet had any role in either the acquisition or misuse of the victims' personal information. While this gap was later addressed by Javelin Strategy & Research, a persistent problem has been the consistently high number of victims who do not know how their information was obtained. For example, Javelin reported that 44.5 percent of victims did not know and 53.4 percent did know how their information was obtained in 2003; in 2004, 43.3 percent did not know and 54.1 percent did.[8]

Victims who were aware of how their information had been obtained were then asked about the method used to obtain it. Table 8.1 shows two columns of results. Those to the far right are Javelin's, which were originally reported (as shown) to reflect 100 percent of the 54.1 percent of victims who knew how their information was obtained. In order to represent the distribution of this figure across all identity theft victims (i.e., as 100% of 100%), recalculations are presented in the middle column using available information for 2004.

Javelin used their figures to conclude that "[t]raditional means of accessing information, such as through lost or stolen wallets or purses and through burglarized paper mail, are still the most common ways thieves gained access to information," but this claim is not borne out by the figures in Table 8.1.[9] If all of the categories seeming to fit the description of "traditional means" were added together using the figures from the center column (43.23%), with the exception of those who did not answer the question (6.01%) and the last three rows that are expressly related to technology (4.92%), there would still be almost the exact same amount of victims who did not know how their information was obtained (43.3%).

While it would be difficult to speculate on how victims' information was acquired in almost half of the cases, it is conceivable that victims would be more likely to know when their personal information has been obtained by someone else while under their control—particularly if their information had been lost/stolen or taken by someone that they knew and trusted, also known as friendly fraud. This term also has a specific meaning within the credit industry, referring to cases where a consumer legitimately enters into a transaction with their own personal account and later denies doing so to the card-issuing company.[10]

Several unseeming categories in this table might also include technological (or nontraditional) means of accessing information. In particular, Javelin broke down the category "Accessed as part of a transaction" (12.9%) within

Table 8.1 Victims' Knowledge Regarding How Information Was Obtained

Method used	Recalculation of Javelin's findings for all victims (%)	Javelin's findings for victims who knew how information was obtained (%)
Method for obtaining information unknown or unavailable (total)	**45.9**	
Victims who did not know how their information was obtained	43.3	
Missing information	2.6	
Responses regarding the method used to obtain personal information (total)	**54.1**	**100** (of 54.1)
Don't know/Refused/No answer (after initially responding that they knew how their information had been obtained)*	6.01	11.1
Lost/stolen wallet, checkbook, or credit card	15.61	28.8
Accessed as part of a transaction	6.99	12.9
Friends/acquaintances/relatives with access to personal information	6.18	11.4
Corrupt employee who had access to the information	4.71	8.7
Stolen paper or mail/fraudulent change of address	4.33	8.0
Obtained in some other way	4.01	7.4
Taken from the garbage	1.40	2.6
Computer spyware	2.81	5.2
Computer viruses/hackers	1.19	2.2
E-mails sent by criminals posing as a legitimate business	0.92	1.7

*It is not entirely clear why someone who first admitted to knowing how their information was obtained would later say that they "don't know" the method through which it was obtained, but there is also no way of knowing how often this specific response was received in relation to refusals.

another part of their report as follows: "Online: 2.51% + Offline: 8.69% + Don't know type of transaction: 1.43% = 12.9%."[11] These figures were not calculated for Table 8.1 because 2.51 + 8.69 + 1.43 ≠ 12.9, but the inclusion of this detail would slightly reduce the overall category of traditional means and slightly increase the overall category of technological means. Similar reductions might also be witnessed if other categories were reported in this way; for example, "Corrupt employee" or "Friends/acquaintances."

In order to assess some of the additional things that this surveyor of all things identity theft had to say about these categories, five statements from the single quote that follows are considered separately:[12]

1. "Javelin believes that some criminal means of acquiring personal information are under- or over-reported while others are closer to actual incidence rates."

Translation: Positives, Negatives, False Positives, False Negatives

Based on what we know about victimization reporting in general, it is reasonable to expect under- and overreporting for a variety of reasons. While the issue of reporting was discussed earlier, the issue at hand here is not whether you were a victim but whether you knew how your personal information was obtained: yes or no. Those who say yes (positives) might be mistaken or lying (false positives = overreporting), and those who say no (negatives) might be incorrect or just not talking (false negatives = underreporting). The positives and negatives left standing therefore represent the truest incidence available, relative to fake yes and fake no. There may also be others, however, who refuse to commit (undecided), or refuse to answer at all (uncooperative).

2. "The reported rates of identity fraud from lost or stolen wallets and phishing (emails sent by criminals posing as legitimate businesses) may be closer to actual incidence rates because victims are more likely to have actually observed the identity thefts."

Translation: Victims who reported lost/stolen wallets and phishing are more likely to have observed the breach of their information, thus these reports should be closest to their actual incidence within society.

Lost wallets are not necessarily stolen, but if victims were a witness to this event then the wallet would probably not have gone missing. The likelihood of observing "the identity thefts," thus implying the victim was present at the breach, would therefore seem more likely in the case of theft rather than loss. There are many kinds of theft, however, some of which (like a robbery: Stick 'em up!) are more likely to involve victim-witnesses. Others, like burglary or larceny, are more likely than robbery to be discovered after the fact, but some may also be discovered as an act in progress. Witnesses in the "Yes,

I Saw It" category are therefore even further likely to resemble the incidence of these types of breaches within society.

With regard to phishing, defined as e-mails sent by criminals, there are two separate events requiring consideration: receiving fraudulent e-mails fishing for personal information (routine annoyance), and replying to those e-mails with the personal information requested (victimization). Victims are directly involved in both events, but they do not actually witness their personal information being stolen in the latter case, even though it might be their own fault. Such victims are not likely to suspect the potential for victimization, at least not strongly enough to prevent them from forking over the goods. This raises a more general question as to how victims, who might not observe the breach of their personal information, might be aware of it, as well as to how these victims know that the information involved in that particular breach was later misused in a particular way.

3. "Conversely, the reported rates of identity fraud from 'taken from garbage/mail,' and 'access from transaction' may be under-reported since many victims do not witness the thefts to these acts and either make educated guesses or are told by police or businesses how their information was taken."

Translation: Victims may not often witness breaches when they occur as the result of a garbage picking, mail theft, or a transaction, thus they may either: (a) not report (false negative), or (b) give anybody's best guess as an answer (if best guess wrong, false positive).

Victims may not be very likely to observe someone stealing their mail, or retrieving things from their garbage (whether at home or at the dump). These are both good candidates for underreported categories, considering that close to half of all victims do not know how their identity information was obtained. Since some people knew (or at least believed) that their information had been obtained in these ways, it stands to reason that some of the unaccounted cases might have resulted from these means. Some of them perhaps, but probably not all of them. Although victims may therefore be underreported in those particular categories, they are represented in some other way within the dataset, either as a false positive or false negative. This same logic also applies to the third category, access from transaction, except that the victims of offline transactions included within (according to Javelin's own testimony) might be more likely to witness the breach than their online or don't know counterparts.

4. "Finally, other responses, such as 'spyware' and 'computer viruses' and hackers' may be over-reported due to intensive media attention on those subjects."

Translation: Victims overreport techno-modern-global-related sources of a breach (implying false positives) because: (a) the media has browbeaten them into believing so without any evidence in their own case, or (b) the media is sensitizing criminals to new techno-modern-global means for committing breaches, thus resulting in increased offending and subsequent reporting (true positives).

The underlying question here is how media attention on any topic might lead to victim overreporting, and it is not an easy one to answer. In contrast to this claim, however, there are reasons to believe that access to personal information through techno-modern-global means might be underreported instead. Technological measures can be particularly difficult to detect, depending upon the environment and level of sophistication involved. Technology is also constantly evolving in humanity's race to emerge as the one best-armed, thus the chances for detection are greatest when opponents are evenly matched. In the case of *Everyman v. Bad Guys*, however, there might not be much chance of that at all.

> 5. "These findings demonstrate that government bodies, media, and financial institutions have an obligation to properly educate the public on the correct rates of means of access to identity fraud. The public must have accurate and updated information on fraud methods in order to adequately protect itself."

> Translation: The public must have accurate information in order to protect itself. [*Chorus:* Amen!] Governments, media, and financial institutions should properly educate the public. [*Chorus:* No Javelin, **everybody** should.]

Mission Accomplished

Returning for a moment to scenarios #3 and #4 involving the old and new John Schmidts, let's consider some of the ways in which his information might have been obtained. If his identity information was accessed from his computer, for example, this may have been physically stolen from his person (in the case of a laptop) or his home environment. If Mr. Schmidt was robbed of his computer (and thus his personal information) by traditional means, however, where does this act fall on the spectrum of technology? More importantly, should identity theft be classified by the objects involved in its commission or by the acts themselves?

There is another matter to be considered here as well: the quality, quantity, and location of activities taking place within the online environment. If Mr. Schmidt uses the Internet regularly, what is he doing while online? If he has an e-mail address, he may be a general target of phishing or some other form of scam, such as a pyramid scheme, which may have little if anything to do with identity theft except if it involves a credit card or other financial account. John may also be on Facebook or Twittering[13] with his friends, managing his personal or business affairs (e.g., monitoring his assets or paying his bills), or buying a new pair of shoes. The risks associated with all of these activities are different, but it should be kept in mind that the people and places he connects to via the Internet may either be around the corner from him or literally halfway around the world. Thus, the Internet can bring everyone in the world closer together in social ways that are not always global.

While Javelin's statistics on the issue of acquisition (the last column in Table 8.1) are generally presented with the disclaimer that they only represent victims who knew how their information was obtained, they were often misleadingly or mistakenly reported by other sources as totaling 100 percent of all victims. The Better Business Bureau presented Javelin's 2004 figures without this disclaimer, for example, thus suggesting that the findings represented 100 percent of all victims, not 100 percent of the 54.1 percent of victims who knew how their information was obtained in 2004.[14]

In a similar way, a report prepared for Congress intended to focus discussion on the IDT-Internet connection and what to do about it, summarizes the issue thusly:

> Many associate the rise in identity theft cases with the Internet, but surveys indicate that comparatively few victims cite the Internet as the source of their stolen PII [personally identifiable information]. . . . Still, the Internet may play a role, particularly through the practice known as "phishing."[15]

While Javelin's disclaimer appeared a few lines down, their findings were then reported in whole percentages and without any suggestion of how many victims were truly unaware of how their PII was obtained.

The issue of how personal information is obtained is also related to who obtains it, and Javelin's findings are even more problematic in this regard. Of the victims surveyed in 2003 and 2004, only 26.3 percent and 26.2 percent, respectively, knew the identity of their thief. Of those who did know, 35.1 percent and 32.0 percent (again, respectively) reported that it was a family member or relative.[16] Combined with other response categories suggesting that the victim knew the perpetrator in some way (e.g., friend, neighbor, in-home employee), these findings led Javelin to conclude:

> Of the 26% of cases where the victim is able to ascertain the identity of the criminal, the thief is more likely to be someone that the victim knows rather than a complete stranger.[17]

Once again, this aspect would be misreported within a number of sources. In an e-mail obtained by Hoofnagle under the Freedom of Information Act, Claudia Bourne Farrell from the FTC writes to one journalist about her misrepresentation of this finding:

> Since most surveyed—74 percent—could not identify the person who stole their identity, and half the 26 percent who could identify the thief either didn't personally know the thief or said it was someone other than a friend or relative, it would be misleading to suggest that the "Culprit is likely a friend or relative."[18]

In response, the journalist Robin Sidel wrote: "I spent some time on the phone with Javelin discussing the results, particularly because it outlined so many scenarios. I also was careful to review the wording with them so that it wasn't being misinterpreted."[19] This idea of the devil you know was similarly attributed to Ken Hunter, president of the Council of Better Business Bureaus, within another source: "Hunter said people's failure to realize that they are more at risk of identity theft from someone they know makes them even more likely to be victimized."[20] Overall, however, it would seem that the responsibility for transmitting statistics accurately must be shared between those who initially produce them and those who later report them.

The End for Now

MANY THINGS CAN actually be said about the U.S. experience of recovering from identity theft, particularly those involving the individual pains of victimization and the national response to date. While the United States does have an abundance of identity theft data relative to other countries, the quality of the information produced from or about those data thus far has left much to be desired. Many pieces of the U.S. story are also missing, especially those regarding the impact of criminalization and the effectiveness of other strategies, but a great deal of attention has been focused on the economic costs of identity theft because such concerns underlie much of the fuss about this issue as a whole. When it comes to you, however, the story of identity theft goes a little something like this—too little, too late, too bad.

TOO LITTLE

The initial response to the problem in the United States was to criminalize identity theft as an independent offense—a measure that was advocated by many groups of social actors. At the federal level, the 1998 Identity Theft Act was originally viewed as a new tool for employing "a more proactive approach to combating identity theft."[1] This was followed by the passage of the 2004 Identity Theft Penalty Enhancement Act, which was similarly intended to aid in the investigation and prosecution of identity theft cases.

While these are good goals, the Supreme Court recently ruled that federal prosecutors were misinterpreting the meaning of the 2004 law when using it to charge illegal immigrants who had knowing used "conjured" social security numbers that later turned out to be real.[2] According to Chief Justice John G. Roberts Jr.: "There's a basic problem here. You get an extra two years it if just so happens that the number you picked out of the air belonged to somebody else."[3] Although this decision would make "it more difficult for the agency to press criminal charges against immigrants with no other offenses but working illegally," it "will no longer be a weapon" in "the ordinary immigration case."[4] Thus, it is good to know that at least some headway is being made in the battle against identity theft laws.

There are currently no means for evaluating the effectiveness of new legislation, as many agencies do not record (or at least report) the number of cases that have been prosecuted under these statutes. According to the FBI, for example, there were "over 1,600 active investigations involving some aspect of identity theft" in 2005, but this agency "does not specifically track identity theft convictions and indictments, as identity theft crosses all program lines and is usually perpetrated to facilitate other crimes."[5]

One study examined more than 500 cases handled by the Secret Service between 2000 and 2006, but this research similarly focused on cases "with an identity theft component" and excluded cases of existing account fraud, which accounts for two-thirds of the problem.[6] Another recent study noted that the Executive Office of U.S. Attorneys had agreed to provide a list of all persons indicted, prosecuted, and convicted under the federal identity theft statute, but later reneged due to "legal issues."[7]

Many law enforcement agencies nevertheless focus their investigative efforts on the largest cases or those that involve networked criminal activities (i.e., the big fish), and the last round of federal identity theft legislation similarly focused on increased penalties for the most serious cases (i.e., aggravated identity theft). All of this occurred while some victims were being denied basic police assistance. Considering that the majority of identity theft victims must settle their disputes directly with financial institutions, however, the criminalization of identity theft appears to be largely symbolic as a whole.

Like the federal government, all states had legislation prior to 1996 that dealt with the offenses collectively underlying identity theft—with the exception perhaps of stealing information in certain forms, certain ways, or for certain purposes. The idea that none was sufficient to respond to the problem, or able to recognize individuals as victims, is a little more difficult to grasp beyond the adage of *nullum crimen, sine lege* (no crime without law), or the suggestion that individuals had no legal footing to stand on in order to recuperate from their losses. No substantive information is available regarding how any of these new "identity theft statutes" are actually being utilized, however, which is particularly surprising given the usual importance that these types of statistics have for illustrating the progress that is being made, or minimally justifying related budgetary expenses.

Anecdotes suggest that the states' focus has similarly been on the largest cases, and many seem to involve identity theft as a secondary, rather than a primary, charge. Within the newspaper sample, for example, there were a number of cases in which defendants were accused with a range of charges from forgery to larceny, not identity theft per se. As discussed, some states did not criminalize "identity theft" with that phrase. It was usually not clear within any report that defendants were being charged with new laws, however, just that these defendants' actions were symbolic of identity theft, independent of any specific charge. There were also several cases in which defendants pleaded guilty to charges other than identity theft. In one example, "[p]rosecutors said the case was the largest case of identity theft in the nation in terms of the number of victims . . . and the extent of their losses . . . [the defendant] pleaded guilty to . . . three counts of fraud, wire fraud and conspiracy."[8]

It is similarly difficult to assess prosecution even within a single state. For example, the first felony conviction in Virginia involved three counts of identity theft and three counts of computer fraud. There were five victims involved with these charges and at least $30,000 worth of damages, which resulted in a maximum sentence of 45 years, of which the defendant might only serve 5.[9] In order to obtain this conviction, however, identity theft had to be elevated from a Class 1 Misdemeanor because the losses in this particular case were greater than $200.

In relation to the actual out-of-pocket expenses incurred by individuals (see Table 9.1), it can be inferred from this case that a sizeable amount of identity theft victims across the nation may fall considerably short of finding any legal recourse. This is also true when considering estimates of the total loss involved in a given case. According to the 2003 FTC study, "16% of victims said that more than $5,000 was lost due to the misuse of their personal information. About 1-in-5 reported that less than $100 was involved."[10] The fact that many states similarly criminalized identity theft with a minimum dollar amount of loss is enough to justify at least some doubt regarding the effect that these laws were intended or can be expected to have.[11]

Additional evidence in support of this notion overall lies with the proposals that have not been passed. While cautions against the use of social security numbers as identifiers have been around for decades, their role in the commission of identity theft has always been acknowledged. Over a period of seven years, the Personal Information Privacy Act was repeatedly proposed at the federal level to prohibit social security numbers from being used as identification, as well as to prohibit their commercial distribution without an individual's consent. This bill was first introduced into the U.S. House and Senate in 1997 and then reintroduced in the House in 1999, 2001, and 2003. The Intelligence Reform and Terrorism Prevention Act of 2004 (Public Law No. 108–458) finally restricted states from displaying social security numbers on driver's licenses and other identification cards, but social security numbers are still used for a variety of industry purposes, thus preserving access for those with 'legitimate' interests.

Other proposals for legislation and reform have been more varied, but include consumer opt-out clauses for the disclosure of personal information,[12] allowing individuals to freeze their credit report, data security requirements, and the restriction of direct marketing tactics. Some federal legislation, particularly the Fair and Accurate Credit Transactions Act of 2003 (FACT Act), has nevertheless preempted states from passing stronger legislation to protect consumer interests.[13]

The problems of federalization extend to a number of related areas,[14] but the issue essentially boils down to a battle among the Defenders, the Producers, and the Ruling Class. In the privacy arena, Defenders attempt to protect individual rights, while industry lobbyists argue that restrictions on the flow of personal information would not only decrease consumer convenience, but actually increase the potential for fraud by limiting their ability to verify individual identity. The General Accounting Office nevertheless summarized this issue well in its first report on identity fraud: "Quite obviously . . . personal identifying information has a market value, and such information is widely used for many purposes within both the public and private sectors."[15] Resistance toward curtailing otherwise legitimate access to personal information, or providing individuals with more power over how their information is handled, has therefore been strong.

While it would be untrue to say that the Producers are the only group of social actors with an interest in the exchange of personal information, they have parlayed it into a multi-million-dollar industry. The GAO was ultimately unable to assess the effect that the Personal Information Privacy Act of 1997 might have on industries, but one official from Associated Credit Bureaus, Inc., reported that "pricing strategies are proprietary and members do not share revenue on specific product lines. However . . . aggregate revenues are in the 'tens of millions of dollars' annually."[16] The federal government is also one of their biggest clients due to restrictions set by the Privacy Act of 1974 (Public Law No. 93–579), and the ChoicePoint database in particular has "become an invaluable research tool for the FBI's analytical cadre in a number of ways."[17]

Proposed solutions for identity theft are largely a function of interest, like use of this term itself. Many of the specific bills that have been suggested focus on increased consumer protections or the empowerment of individuals to respond to their victimization, while others have focused on industry practices in the areas of marketing and the security of personal data. Grassroots organizations and some former victims have also taken a lead role in advocating for various legislative reforms, but the effects of federalization have watered down some of their successful campaigns at the state level.

A number of political leaders have similarly worked toward increasing awareness about the need for different types of legislative reforms, and private industry members have made lucrative strides in the area of individual prevention with the development of various fee-based services aimed at the apprehensive consumer. A great deal of attention has nevertheless been focused on the use of biometric and RFID (radio frequency identification)[18] technologies within a broad range of applications, from security locks to grocery shopping.

The federal government shares in this mainly private industry desire to improve the future of secured transactions—particularly through upholding the provisions of the Real ID Act of 2005, which will standardize state driver's licenses for the stated purpose of combating terrorism while supplying the added benefit of addressing the problem of identity theft. This law similarly provides for the use of biometric identifiers as part of the information that will be embedded in these new licenses, and there is much controversy surrounding this particular piece of legislation.

TOO LATE

This issue of what to do about identity theft will forever be tied to the area of physical identification, which includes proposals for the use of biometric identifiers (e.g., fingerprints, DNA, retina scans), smart cards, and RFID chips. Private industries and governments have been developing these types of technology for years, but they are accompanied by even greater privacy concerns. These types of issues have also surfaced many times since the birth of identity theft.

As an example from the newspaper sample, there was one particular controversy in Arizona that erupted after law enforcement officials began a pilot program to fingerprint drivers who had been stopped during routine traffic surveillance. There were many stated reasons for this particular program, one of which was to combat identity theft, but there seemed to be very strong opposition to (as well as very strong support for) this initiative and the man behind it.[19] The use of biometrics, in particular, is being considered under the provisions of the Real ID Act, with the intent of preventing terrorism by standardizing state driver's licenses and requiring states to link (or centralize) their motor vehicle databases together. Although not its stated purpose, this law has been denounced for creating a de facto national identity card,[20] an issue that the nation has been fighting over for about the past 100 years.

Debates are currently taking place that may affect the ultimate manifestation of this law in U.S. society, but this is not the first piece of legislation to impose standards resembling a national ID card. The Illegal Immigration Reform and Immigrant Responsibility Act of 1996 (Public Law 104–208), for example, prohibited federal acceptance of a driver's license, or comparable piece of identification, that did not display a social security number. Identification could also be accepted from a state as long as a social security number was required for its issuance, and this legislation was thus criticized for its attempt to use the social security number as a national identification number.

The Real ID Act was also not the federal government's first attempt to create a centralized national database of personal information. In 1997 (the year before the federal criminalization of identity theft), the federal government contracted with Image Data, LLC for an Identity Crime Prevention Pilot Program, which was designed to combat identity-based fraud. Controversy ensued in 1999 when it was discovered that the company had purchased drivers' photos from three states without the public's knowledge. Colorado had actually amended legislation to ensure the legality of the transaction in question (Colorado Rev. Statute § 42–1-206). Although this pilot program ended soon after, the federal government went on to create the Total Information Awareness Program (TIA), which was later renamed the Terrorism Information Awareness Program because its previous title "created in some minds the impression that TIA was a system to be used for developing dossiers on U.S. citizens."[21] While Congress ultimately stopped funding for this program in 2004, their action did not "restrict the National Foreign Intelligence Program from using processing, analysis and collaboration tools for counterterrorism foreign intelligence purposes."[22]

While this might seem to be the end of the matter as far as those not suspected of terrorism are concerned, the Multistate Anti-Terrorism Information Exchange (MATRIX) pilot project was created thereafter, "which leverages advanced computer/information management capabilities to more quickly access, share, and analyze *public* records" (italics in original).[23] "Confusion regarding the MATRIX project arose, however, in part because of misinformation disseminated in the early stages of organizing the project, as well as the project's failure to consider privacy from the inception of development."[24] If this project failed to respond to the same privacy concerns that sank the TIA and its predecessors, however, then what does that say about the people who designed it?

MATRIX is an information-sharing (as opposed to a data mining) project, but the federal government once again overlooked individual rights and repackaged a single agenda: the creation of a centralized information database. Related privacy concerns are nevertheless focused on the potential abuses of personal data collected in any form (public or private), rather than the manner in which such data is collected. Although clearly argumentative, the repeated actions of the federal government in this regard suggest that the issue of identity theft is being wielded to garner unwitting support for other agendas; the same might also be said for the issues of terrorism and illegal immigration.

In terms of the specific authentication procedures used during transactions, or any associated reform proposals, many cannot be directly assessed due to a lack of information. Some individuals have nevertheless tested the boundaries of standard credit card procedures with surprising success: a few dogs (and children) have been issued credit cards;[25] a credit card was issued from a torn up application;[26] and one man successfully began signing his credit card receipts in different ways: with hieroglyphs, as Mariah Carey, and once with "I stole this card."[27] The first time this fake Ms. Carey reported being questioned with regard to his signature involved the purchase of approximately $16,000 worth of merchandise from Circuit City. In this instance, he signed the receipt "Not Authorized" and the sales clerk called a manager. Both the clerk and the manager then asked him nicely to just sign his own name in order to complete the transaction.

Such stunts were intended to be funny, but they are also disturbing because they are true. These examples further highlight the human factor in authentication failure, which is why companies are mainly looking toward technology (particularly biometrics) for the future of identity verification. Aside from the potential success of such measures, which cannot currently be verified, their use can also be expected to grow in years to come as Generation Y matures: "Kids growing up now can't imagine that you needed a cord to use your telephone. Soon they're going to say, 'You mean you have to carry around a piece of plastic or a piece of paper to go buy something?'"[28]

As discussed, Javelin has suggested that personal information is most often obtained through traditional (i.e., offline) means, and subsequently recommended that individuals switch to online account monitoring for increased security. This particular claim, however, stands in opposition to the common belief that the Internet (or technology more generally) lies behind the contemporary phenomenon of identity theft. While the figures behind part of this claim were teased out earlier, this set of conclusions has perhaps had another impact.

The U.S. Senate declared March 2007 "Go Direct Month" as part of a national campaign, launched by the Department of the Treasury and Federal Reserve banks, which encourages citizens to use direct deposit because—among other reasons—it "helps protect against identity theft and fraud."[29] If not the immediate evidence behind this concern, Javelin's findings have minimally reinforced some long-standing perceptions on the part of the federal government that it "could save money, prevent crime, and help beneficiaries through the Electronic Funds Transfer program"—an initiative that was projected at the time to save the government $100 million and prevent $100 million in crime losses.[30]

Although this projection was published in 1999, the reference from which it came noted that the federal government recognized these benefits as early as 1996 (the year in which IDT was first criminalized). The Electronic Funds Transfer program also continues to operate and is currently reported to save 80 cents (89 cents down to 9 cents) on each check payment.[31] This move to virtual economics is somewhat consistent with the idea that identity theft is a serious problem that must be addressed through individual prevention, although the security of funds once transferred via direct deposit obviously remains a concern. While this particular method also happens to be aligned with the best interests of many social actors, it might actually go against the best interests of the public in terms of preventing identity theft, or their own well-being in general.

In many ways, it can be argued that the threat of identity theft is being used to herd the holdouts of U.S. society (the unfinanced, the unInternetted) into the future. The question of whether this threat was intentionally bolstered for this purpose can be left to conspiracy theorists, but it is not necessary to substantiate some type of Machiavellian plot in order to suggest that several groups of social actors have seized upon the opportunity that the topic of identity theft affords in this regard.

Resistance toward a paperless society, the Internet, and even human "chipping" (i.e., RFID implants) may slowly erode in the face of continued claims that technology has not only made modern life easier and more convenient, but safer from crime in all of its forms. The vision of a cashless society has also been pursued for more than 30 years, even though U.S. society has in fact been operating in this fashion for much longer than that.[32] Javelin's findings regarding the dangers associated with paper-based methods of account management, as well as the federal government's emphasis on virtual banking as a means to minimize fraud, nevertheless appear to be some of the final steps in making this dream a complete and total reality, maybe one just like *The Matrix* after it really is too late for us all.[33]

TOO BAD

The outcomes, or consequences, of victimization are considered in two ways within this final section: via the narrative directive that individuals must guard against identity theft, and with a focus on claims regarding the monetary costs of victimization for individuals and collectives.

Everyman for Himself

Although information regarding individual prevention is more common sense than a specific claim, a disproportionate amount of attention has been paid to the idea that individuals need to protect themselves from identity theft, relative to their ability to do so. This was less true when information about the problem was first being disseminated in the late 1990s, but the focus on this topic has remained consistently large over time while all attendant advice has remained unchanged for the most part. Much pessimism regarding the individual's ability to protect his or her identity also set in following ChoicePoint, but this reality was actually acknowledged from the very beginning:

> Can you completely prevent identity theft from occurring? Probably not, especially if someone is determined to commit the crime. . . . Despite your best efforts to manage the flow of your personal information or to keep it to yourself, skilled identity thieves may use a variety of methods—low- and hi-tech—to gain access to your data.
>
> —Federal Trade Commission (2000b)[34]

If individuals really can do very little to protect themselves, then why is the public repeatedly told to engage in this pointless exercise? Aside from educating individuals about the dangers of being careless with identities (in order to avoid making a bad problem worse), the consumer service industry in the United States has a particular interest in making sure that Americans jump through all available 'preventive' hoops. Three in particular deserve attention here: identity theft insurance, shredding, and credit report monitoring.

Although identity theft insurance scams seem to have begun approximately three years before this product was actually available to the public,[35] the question frequently being asked today is whether identity theft insurance or other types of services are merely new ways to rip off consumers. Identity theft insurance policies vary in coverage, but many seem to have a maximum benefit of between $15,000 and $25,000, which would only seem applicable to extensive cases of new you fraud. The Identity Theft Resource Center, for example, noted in 2003 that one victim reported $8,000 in losses, two reported $15,000, one reported $20,000, and one reported $30,000.[36] While these represent the extreme cases, there is no guarantee that all of their expenses would be covered under a given policy. These are nevertheless the cases for which insurance might be helpful, even though part of the stated impetus behind identity theft legislation was to assist victims in recovering from this "fast-growing financial offense."

The average annual cost of these policies varies, but combined with any associated deductibles, which might well exceed the minimum out-of-pocket costs experienced by victims (see Table 9.1), the ongoing costs involved might exceed even relatively substantial instances of victimization.[37] Identity theft insurance would further not apply to the majority of cases involving old you, specifically as federal law limits the responsibility of fraud victims to $50, and most companies now have a policy of $0 fraud liability in relation to existing accounts. According to a recent Javelin study, "100% of the top 25 U.S. card issuers offer zero liability for fraud losses" since this is the "number one most requested feature on a credit card account."[38] As such, this type of insurance does not seem able to provide many victims with much assurance that their associated costs will be covered at all, whether great or small. However, only time will tell whether the feeling of personal security that this service provides is actually effective, as opposed to symbolic.

Even specific services such as computer software and shredders will not prevent against all forms of identity theft, and some may not even be effective in their own purpose. The need to shred documents before their disposal was identified very early during the national emergence of identity theft. One of the first individual prevention guides, created by a few Defenders and published by Office Depot in 1999, even included sales coupons for shredding machines.[39] This market was later developed into the provision of shredding services, whereby individuals and companies could pay to have their sensitive documents destroyed by someone else, thus in effect breaking the chain of evidence where personal information is concerned.

The common practice of shredding documents into strips, rather than confetti, can also leave sensitive information exposed to prying eyes. Some documents can therefore be reconstructed after they are torn apart or damaged.[40] Many businesses, including shredding companies, are further in the practice of using or selling shredded documents as packaging material. Thus, some very sensitive personal information has literally been mailed out across the nation, which would certainly seem to defeat the purpose of shredding documents in the first place.[41] At best, individual prevention in the form of shredding documents is good common sense in practice, but these actions are arguably symbolic when compared to the larger realities of information handling practices in the United States. This assessment will also remain unaltered until some resolution can be found for the issue of how the personal information used to facilitate identity theft is actually obtained.

As mentioned earlier, credit monitoring services were available in the early 1990s, and one of Javelin's findings holds particular weight in relation to this area: "[v]ictims are more likely to discover identity fraud through self-detection than through other methods."[42] Javelin also found that the average time until detection and the average resulting loss were lower when accounts were monitored through some type of electronic means, which included ATMs and online management.

Taken together, this set of findings makes perfect sense. The delays normally associated with traditional paper account statements (i.e., a 30-day reporting cycle, mail delivery, etc.) means that fraudulent activity can occur repeatedly within that time frame before an individual has any chance to discover it. Further considering that the majority of identity theft is related to existing accounts, electronic resources now provide industrious people with the means to check their account status at any hour of the day. However, Javelin used this set of findings, in combination with their conclusion that personal information is most often obtained through traditional means, to suggest that online account management is safer than traditional paper-based monitoring:

> This report clearly demonstrates that consumers should cancel paper bills and statements wherever possible and instead pay bills and check statements online. Electronic monitoring reflects near real-time activity, can be accessed from almost anywhere, provides greater safety by sharply reducing time to detection, and potentially eliminates the paper records and mail that are possible avenues to many identity theft cases.[43]

The benefits of near-real-time monitoring have specifically been touted as a selling point for various electronic services. This sounds good to most people in the context of prevention because it implies that a thief can be caught red-handed, or the activity can otherwise be stopped. What happens in practice appears to be another matter. Detection in many cases still occurs after the fraudulent activity has taken place, and there currently seems to be little consumer benefit to discovering fraudulent activity while it is occurring, if indeed they can. Although a number of different claims have been made about what specific identity theft services can provide, the idea that any can completely prevent or protect against identity theft as it is happening is one of the most deceptive to date.

Monitoring existing accounts will not necessarily help to detect the creation of new accounts, which is why credit report monitoring has become so important. However, even the drawbacks of long-awaited federal legislation have been turned into a marketing ploy for identity theft services. As illustrated by another one of Javelin's conclusions: "The average detection time of 172 days indicates that more consumers are taking advantage of free legally mandated annual reports, rather than utilizing [i.e., paying for] credit monitoring services which would be expected to have shorter detection times."[44] This raises the question as to why U.S. consumers have not been granted unlimited free access to their own credit reports.

In 2006, Javelin concluded: "[new] accounts are almost impossible to detect, except through a credit report or credit monitoring service—a service which is, as yet, underutilized by consumers."[45] While it is true that new accounts are extremely difficult to detect, it is not necessarily true that monitoring services are more effective than individual credit report monitoring. In fact, the reverse may be true since individuals are seemingly in the best position to identify the fraudulent activities committed in their names. Individuals, however, are only "free" to check their credit report three times a year.[46]

One article from the *New York Times* recounted the story of a woman who, after paying $79.99 for a one-year subscription to a monitoring service from Equifax, found out that she had been a victim of identity theft through her car loan company.[47] She then signed up for two other credit monitoring services with Experian and TransUnion. At least one new credit application was filed under her name after she had paid for these additional services, and in spite of repeated notifications from all three agencies that there was no suspicious activity on her credit report. This victim, who at the time was in the process of suing several affiliates of these three major credit bureaus, was quoted as saying: "I still have credit monitoring because of the simple fact that it is the best tool available at this time. . . . It is not ideal, it is broken, and it is not as advertised."[48] Albeit an extreme example, this case raises a number of additional questions regarding the quality of identity theft services that consumers receive overall, not altogether irrespective of the frequency or real-timeliness with which they are provided.

The financial incentives behind identity theft are an issue for real concern. The national credit bureaus were particularly disgruntled with changes to the Fair Credit Reporting Act (enacted under the FACT Act of 2003), which mandated that each of them release one free credit report each year. While consumers were eligible to receive a free report under some circumstances prior to this amendment, credit reports were generally available for a fee. After this provision had gone into effect, however, the FTC filed a complaint against Consumerinfo.com, Inc. (a division of Experian) for requiring consumers to provide a valid credit card number to obtain their free report. This company did not properly disclose that the consumer was automatically enrolled in the company's credit monitoring service and charged a $79.95 fee if they did not cancel within 30 days. The ultimate settlement between these parties required the defendant "to pay redress to deceived consumers . . . [and] give up $950,000 in ill-gotten gains."[49]

Identity theft was then put to the public in the form of a "troubadour of the American masses"—a "baby-faced everyman caught in a Kafkaesque nightmare of credit score woes."[50] As is part of everyman's saga, however, this singing symbol of FreeCreditReport.com lost much of his popularity and credibility when the public discovered that he had lured them to a website where credit reports were not, in fact, free. (*Chorus:* Shame on you, too, *Fee-CreditReport.com*). If anything good resulted from this particular identity crisis, which certainly appeared to be the result of deliberate misrepresentation, perhaps it alerted some misguided parties to the fact that they can receive an honest-to-goodness free credit report from each of the three largest credit bureaus.[51]

Some companies have also chosen to offer free credit monitoring services to individuals whose information was compromised by a data breach. Aside from the issue of whether these services are actually effective, an individual's social security number will not expire when this free subscription ends, if in fact it was part of the breach to begin with. This type of gesture is therefore symbolic as well: The company responsible for the breach washes their hands of the matter with a year's worth of "protection," and then leaves its consumers hanging high and dry for the rest of their lives. This may nevertheless be the most advantageous and cost-efficient means for dealing with the aftermath of a breach, as opposed to cleaning up any of the routine practices that may have actually resulted in one.

As a related point, it was first suggested within the narrative that consumers close down all unused credit accounts as a preventative measure against identity theft. The exact opposite was then advocated since closing accounts can negatively affect a consumer's overall credit score, thus affecting their ability to obtain more credit in the future. In one instance, msn.com specifically admitted to changing its advice to consumers on this issue.[52] In this case then, individuals are specifically being advised to choose victimization along with consumerism.

Similar wishy-washiness has also been exhibited with regard to allowing consumers the right to freeze their credit report, because it would prove to be an "inconvenience" for both individuals and businesses. To be absolutely clear on this point however: identity theft victimization and the prevention of identity theft victimization are equally inconvenient, but particularly so for U.S. consumers. Taken together though, such examples illustrate a very strong profit motive on the part of many Producers, as well as their collective emphasis on expediency over security in the realm of individual prevention.

Javelin reported in 2006 that 12 million people subscribed to credit monitoring services.[53] Despite their previously stated opinion that these services are underutilized, the chorus might say at this point that these are already 12 million people too many. In addition to the fees involved, enrollment in some services requires individuals to provide companies with even more personal information, thus once again putting the consumer at increased risk. If it is true that eliminating paper statements and bills can reduce the risk for identity theft, arguably because this reduces the number of points at which information is handled, then perhaps this logic should also apply to information in every form. In reality, however, the onus of identity theft prevention falls on consumers, and thus many appear to find the immediate convenience of this type of service rather appealing because few other options are available.

A recent analysis by Consumer Reports concluded: "as currently designed, such services are often overrated, oversold, and overpriced."[54] Consumers therefore seem to have the most to lose in relation to identity theft prevention since such services may not only be ineffectual and costly, they can leave consumers with a false impression of what they can provide, which in turn might lead to a lapse in individual vigilance. As summarized by privacy consultant Robert Gellman: "Identity theft has essentially become a business—not just for bad guys but for good guys, too. . . . A lot of the people that are involved in profiting legally from identity theft are direct participants in the whole credit system that doesn't have protections in place to prevent identity theft in the first place."[55] As such, the disproportionality inherent to this particular set of claims might best be stated as caveat emptor (buyer beware), or everyman for himself.

The Quadrillions

The final set of claims fueling the U.S. crisis deals with the damages or costs of identity theft as they pertain to both individuals and collectives. In terms of the collective costs of identity theft, the earliest reports published by the GAO[56] included limited estimates based on the information provided by various public and private agencies, but this institution carefully concluded in 1998 that costs "appear to be growing." The first official figures reported by the FTC in 2003 were $47.6 billion in losses to businesses and $5 billion in losses to consumers.[57] Javelin estimated business losses to be $53.2 billion in 2003, $54.4 billion in 2004, and $56.6 billion in 2005.[58] Although Javelin later noted that the "total fraud amount dropped 12%, from $55.7 billion to $49.3 billion" in 2006,[59] the difference in figures reported for 2005 appears to be the result of a change in the method used to calculate cost estimates, which "leads to a lower estimate of the average fraud amount."[60]

Claims about the economic costs of identity theft are really just extensions of the idea that the problem is large and growing overall. While many identity theft claims have never been directly challenged, however, the proffered figures of financial losses to businesses have been targeted in more recent history. Specifically, the original figure of $47.6 billion reported by the FTC in 2003 has been deemed an incomprehensible and therefore "mythical" number. According to one assessment by law professor Fred Cate, if this "estimate were accurate, it would wipe out up to half the banking industry's $103 billion profits in 2005 . . . we'd have a *banking crisis* on our hands" (italics added).[61] Although there are problems with the methods used by the FTC to arrive at this estimate, Cate's comparison is not particularly helpful for illustrating this point as it only considers the banking industry and their profits.

The article in which Cate was quoted further noted that the $3.2 billion estimate for consumer losses over a six-month period, as reported by the National Crime Victimization Survey, may be "a more realistic figure." However, these authors do not acknowledge that the FTC originally estimated total consumer losses for a one-year period to be $5 billion. Although Javelin reported higher cost figures later on, these estimates have not been similarly criticized. As a note of interest, however, the Inspector General's Office of the Department of Health and Human Services estimated the cost of identity fraud—a term that actually appears to refer to fabricated as opposed to real identities in this context—at $30 billion a year nearly 20 years ago.[62]

While the subsequent suggestion that the FTC's $47.6 billion estimate be "exiled from news stories forever" is not altogether disagreeable,[63] there is no immediate solution for disentangling the elements that would ultimately contribute toward its fair evaluation. The FTC study, for example, asked victims to estimate "the approximate dollar value of what the person obtained," including the "value of credit, loans, cash, services, and anything else."[64] This type of information can be weighed against the total out-of-pocket expenses incurred by victims, but some consideration must also be given to the ways that financial institutions compensate for any resulting differences on their own balance sheets.

If such losses are considered a cost of doing business, then they are likely deflected back to society as a company's operational costs increase or their profits decrease. Victims' estimates are also likely to reflect their knowledge regarding an object's consumer value, which is much different than the actual production value of a given item/service, or the loss that might actually be absorbed by the Producers of this world. Cost is therefore another matter of perspective when it comes to identity theft because no one keeps very good records when it comes this type of accounting.

Individual costs were initially documented through the earliest research with victims, which focused on the most serious forms of this offense.[65] The extensive damages suffered by victims of true name fraud also helped to push the issues of criminalization and prevention into the limelight during the mid-1990s. The plight of individuals who have been victimized by new you continues to be a driving force behind efforts to assist the populace in responding to and recovering from the impact of this offense, as well as combating identity theft in general. This theme is reflected within all types of references, with the nation as a whole tending to focus on the most extreme consequences (or sensationalistic aspects) of identity theft victimization.

The pains of identity theft victimization are not equally distributed across all types of victims, however, individually or collectively. Given the diversity of what is represented by the label identity theft victim, discussing "averages" of any kind in relation to this group is extremely misleading. In essence, victims of new you are statistical outliers in relation to victims of old you with a credit card. While there are fewer victims of new you overall, the tangible and intangible consequences of this form of victimization are typically more severe. Almost every type of generalization regarding identity theft victims is therefore deceptive by nature.

The outcomes of identity theft have nevertheless been packaged to include financial and emotional devastation, as well as the more unclassifiable losses generally associated with an individual's access to the institutionalized means of social life (e.g., obtaining loans, employment, housing; being wrongly arrested or convicted of a crime). While the most devastating outcomes of identity theft are associated with new you, they are all too often used to depict the horrors of identity theft in general. As such, this is one of the few truths about identity theft that has publicly received a disproportionate amount of the wrong kind of attention.

As one example of this, Nationwide Mutual Insurance conducted its own survey in 2005 with a particular focus on the consequences of victimization, which as a group encompassed the best-known and best-established truths about identity theft at that time.[66] A spokesperson for the company commented on the results as follows: "recovering from identity theft can be difficult, costly and stressful, but what is most alarming is that despite the time, money and personal duress victims go through, resolution is not always achieved."[67] Hence, it would seem that their results confirm the need for identity theft insurance or some other type of recovery service, but the benefits of such measures would still only apply to a very small portion of identity theft cases overall. This is likely true according to their own results as well, perhaps lost somewhere in translation, unless Nationwide has stumbled upon an entirely new breed of IDT victim.

While the consequences of individual victimization are not often viewed in financial terms alone, Table 9.1 shows the distribution of out-of-pocket expenses across the three main categories of victims measured by the FTC's study. As shown, approximately 63 percent of all victims experienced no out-of-pocket losses, but the majority of this second column consists of victims who only experienced the misuse of an existing credit card. Specifically, the figures presented in the second column represent 50 percent of victims within the

Table 9.1 IDT Victim Out-of-Pocket Expenses

	Out-of-pocket loss: $0 (%)	Out-of-pocket loss: under $1,000 (%)	Out-of-pocket loss: over $1,000 (%)	Total (%)
New accounts or activities	18.54	10.01	5.93	**34.48**
Existing non–credit card account	9.12	4.87	.94	**14.93**
Existing credit card account	35.38	7.54	1.41	**44.33**
Total	**63.04**	**22.42**	**8.28**	**93.74**

Calculations for Table 9.1 were based on information reported by Synovate (2003): 43.

category of New Accounts, 58 percent of victims within the category of Existing Non-Credit Card, and 75 percent of victims within the category of Existing Credit Card. This outcome is nevertheless affected by a number of factors, particularly the length of time between the onset and discovery of misuse.

According to the FTC results, "[n]o out-of-pocket expenses were incurred by 67 percent of those who discovered the misuse less than 6 months after the misuse began"; however, "[d]iscovering the misuse was quickest for people who experienced misuse of existing non-credit card accounts . . . or who only experienced the misuse of existing credit cards."[68] Victims of new activities were also the most likely to discover the misuse six months or more after it began: 24 percent of the victims in the category of New Accounts compared with 3 percent of victims in the category of Existing Non-Credit Card and 8 percent of those in the category of Existing Credit Card.

When these findings are considered in light of the totals in the final column of Table 9.1, the largest category of victims (Existing Credit Card) experienced a relatively small percentage of the out-of-pocket losses experienced by all identity theft victims. The smallest category of victims (Existing Non-Credit Card) also shouldered a large percentage of the costs totaling less than $1,000, and this is due in part to the difficulties associated with resolving cases of bank fraud.[69] Victims of New Accounts, however, are the most likely to experience out-of-pocket expenses overall, particularly those totaling over $1,000.

A similar pattern of findings emerges in terms of the time spent by victims to resolve problems:

50% of those who experienced the misuse of an existing credit card were able to resolve problems within an hour, compared to 39% of victims who experienced the misuse of an existing non-credit card account, and 15% of those who experienced some form of new activity; 29% of the victims who experienced some form of new activity spent 40 hours or more resolving problems, compared to 8% of victims who experienced some form of existing non-credit card account misuse and 7% of the victims who only experienced the misuse of an existing credit card account.[70]

The intangible costs of identity theft victimization are more difficult to quantify: "Those who experienced more serious forms of Identity Theft—having new accounts opened in their names or having other forms of fraud committed using their personal information—are far more likely to report having one or more [of] the identified problems (64%) than those who only had existing credit card accounts misused (18%) or had other existing accounts misused (32%)."[71] And thus, victims of new you get the worst end of the deal in the end.

THE UNCALCULATED LIFE

The story of identity theft has ended for now, but the saga of identity theft lives on within global society. Reflecting upon the development of this issue over the past 15 years, it will likely do so well into the future. The basic problem remaining for everyone is nevertheless the one that defines it. Is identity theft (A) the kidnapping of mini you, (B) the abuse of mini you, or (C) the kidnapping and later abuse of mini you? This is how the problem of defining identity theft might be stated in dramatic terms, but everyman must answer some version of it for herself or himself. This wording captures the essence of individual ownership, however, which is the true spirit behind identity theft as an American phenomenon.

An identity is like a child in that it belongs to its owner for life, but that child also belongs to society. Millions of identities are being abused every year, so which parent can really be held more accountable? Whoever is at fault, something must finally be done about the problem of identity theft before it gets any further out of control. Selecting an answer to this multiple-choice question is therefore crucial, as it sets the limits of everything identity theft requiring a response. This has already been recognized by the international community, reflected in the following conclusion of the United Nations Core Group of Experts on Identity-Related Crime:

> It was not possible to count identity-crime cases without first defining what was being counted, while at the same time, governments were often reluctant to enact definitions and offence provisions without statistical evidence of the scope and seriousness of the problem.[72]
>
> *Translation:* Identity theft cannot be measured until it has been defined, but it cannot be defined until it has been measured.

If the U.S. experience can be any gauge, the international community might be staring down the barrel of a loaded gun when it comes to the issue of defining identity theft, but that option might be preferable to leaving that gun unattended altogether. The issue of whether the problem is better or worse for anyone is also rather meaningless in the context of The Billions, but perhaps the U.S. problem is big enough and bad enough for everyone right now. If that is the case, however, individuals and nations should be prepared to recognize identity theft if they see it on any soil. Let us consider the options together then.

A. Identity Theft Is the Kidnapping of an Identity

Identities are lost within societies all the time. Many of these identities are never found, but they are not being exploited (as far as we know). While we only have ourselves to blame for this neglect, the concept of identity theft cannot be understood or defined solely in relation to the disappearance of identities. The act of acquiring personal information may be criminal on its own (i.e., an infonapping), but the misuse of that personal information is the criminal heart of identity theft, no matter what it is called. The problem of lost identities is therefore a matter between individuals and various social collectives.

The problem of a kidnapped identity is a different matter—that is, one having been stolen with the intention of exchanging it for ransom. We do not know how many of these missing identities are lost as opposed to kidnapped, therein lying a threat of unknown proportion. We also do not know the quality or value of those identities on a grand scale. If serial numbers are involved—defined primarily as credit card numbers—then there might not be much of a threat at all. When viewed as the precursor to abuse, answer A would nevertheless seem to be more-true-than-not when it comes to capturing the essence of identity theft. Even so, it may not be the best answer available.

B. Identity Theft Is the Abuse of an Identity

Identities are misused in one of two ways: against owners (identity theft) and against handlers (identity fraud). The choice of answer B is therefore determined by a consideration of whether owners are victimized by identity fraud, or whether handlers are victimized by identity theft. Since identity theft really pertains to individuals rather than collectives, this answer would seem to be true at least in spirit. Is it the best answer? Perhaps not when considered in the larger context of social ownership (which establishes the worth of an identity), or in terms of the totality of social conditions that facilitate the kidnapping and abuse of identities.

C. Identity Theft Is the Kidnapping and Abuse of an Identity

Within this body of work, the term identity theft has implicitly been defined by the following equation: Identity Breach + Identity Fraud = Identity Theft. This is answer C, but there is really no other choice available when
faced with the challenge of understanding identity theft as a criminal act in
today's world. This may not be the best answer for everyone, but the math of
this equation does not lie. Answer C is thus the correct answer in a universal
sense as well, because this process is essentially the same no matter where you
are. Even if you insert and choose answer D (none of the above), you may still
want to know what the problem looks like in case it some day comes knocking
at your door some day uninvited.

Coming face to face with a problem usually prompts people to define it,
or impose some shape upon it for the purposes of description. Identity theft
is the shape of the U.S. problem, but there may be many others like it around
the world. Identity theft might also be a trickster in our midst, but it can likely
be found under every rock if one is so inclined to search. Once that problem
has a shape, however, it can be understood and then addressed. Thus begins
the process of research, which results in the collection of data, which informs
conceptual refinement and policy development, which spurs additional research and policy evaluation, and so on. Identity theft is not a special case in
this regard. It must be rediscovered by every person and every nation, just as
it was within the United States, and that process simply takes time.

In terms of what can be done about the problem of "identity theft," the
rational answer is clear: define and assess its occurrence within and between
different jurisdictions (i.e., personal, social, international, criminal) in order
to develop effective solutions. This work is already in progress on multiple
levels, so the only ones left with the choice of participating in this process are
individuals and individual nations. For anyone not yet decided, just remember that wherever you draw your line in the conceptual sand of identity theft,
there are still people in this world who might be willing to cross over it to get
to you.

The general question of what should be done about identity theft similarly boils down to how the problem is defined. Identity theft has already been
recognized universally as a criminal problem, and thus by extension of its
threat and resulting harm, as a personal, social, and global problem as well.
Who is responsible for the criminal problem of identity theft? Offenders can
certainly take a lot of the blame, but so can the social collectives who manage
the informational transactions of a society, particularly governments. Since
the latter is largely a social problem rather than a criminal one, the act of giving identity theft a name is really an exercise in problem definition.

If identity theft is not a problem by the standards of a country (or an individual), then no response is required. Identity fraud is globally recognized
as a problem at least, but the lion's share of identity abuse occurs within the

jurisdictional realm of credit, at least insofar as the figures from the United States, United Kingdom, and Canada outwardly suggest. Perhaps then the social problem is credit rather than identity theft, which requires a much different response than when the problem is primarily defined as a criminal act (credit card fraud). There is nevertheless much more to the problem of IDT than that. Identity theft is the big stuff and the small stuff, wherever your identity is accepted. In sum, the substance of identity theft is life, but the substance of life is not identity theft.

Are individuals the victims of identity fraud? Perhaps not in a strict legal sense, but this might be true in other ways that count, like when these individuals personally experience no-fault harm. As such, the litmus test of identity theft in the international arena will not necessarily be widespread adoption of the term itself, but when the idea behind it is reflected in the spirit if not the letter of international law: individuals (by virtue of being owners) are victims, too. This acknowledgment should not diminish the status of identity fraud victims, but rather strengthen a communal resolve to protect identities in all of their forms as they are churned through the day-to-day mechanics of social interaction. The social demand for identities, which thus fuels the social need for identity ownership, also creates the personal need for a good name, thus forming a timeless social cycle that has carried identity theft into the 21st century and the world beyond.

On the bright side of things, if the narrative is true, then the problem will get much worse very soon. When that happens, humanity will finally be bereft of all hope, and none of this should matter much anymore. In the meantime, some even bigger social disaster might come along (like an actual plague or war), which might make us forget about identity theft, even if only for just a moment in the United States.

While the problem of identity theft is serious the phenomenon of identity theft is suspect. As such, the only available course of action is to start solving the equations of identity theft, one at a time within the larger equation of life. The story of identity theft can therefore end however humanity wants it to, depending on how we define the variables. In the parting spirit of the narrative though, there are only two things you can do—don't be a victim and don't panic.

PART III

Life in Today's World

Don't Be a Victim

WHEN COMMUNICATING ABOUT how not to become a victim, preventative behavior is often discussed in terms of dos and don'ts (i.e., good behavior and bad behavior). Given the scope of identity theft in a global context, the list of things that everyone should or should not do in this regard might fill a separate volume, or several. As an alternative, this discussion prescribes rational thinking about identity theft in order to inform decision-making within the interactional dynamics of your own life, as well as that of everyman's.

The damage of identity theft has already been done, so the only recourse left for humanity is to act more responsibly toward this phenomenon from now on. This not only applies to how we behave (before, during, and after the fact of identity theft), but to how we discuss the issue as rational beings, whether in words, images, or numbers. While it may not seem practical to be concerned with everyone, everywhere, all the time—some of the bad guys are. This is also what the good guys must do in order to solve the equations of identity theft and life.

Despite the rather fantastical story of identity theft, there is no magic bean (or solution, or set of tips) that will stop IDT in all of its forms, except maybe this: Humanity can start acting like it's supposed to, just as if it were being watched all the time, but without the cameras or any of those little devils on our shoulders that tend to make very good arguments. Maybe we already know what we need to do about identity theft then, but not all of us want to do it, and that is an entirely different can of worms.

If every member of humanity got what he or she needed, then there might be fewer bad things in this world overall. Unfortunately, that is not how life works in the United States or anyplace else. It might also seem like there are more important problems in the world than identity theft, and there are, but its invasion of the mundane is perilous and cannot be overlooked any longer. To some, identity theft may only be a white-collar crime or a financial crime or a growing crime, or the latest marketing ploy. Identity theft is your life, however, and perhaps thou doth not protest enough when it comes to your own victimization. You might also be contributing to some of the circumstances surrounding it, even if unbeknownst to you.

Although the underlying issue of concern is criminal, identity theft prevention can be discussed in personal, social, and global terms. It can also be discussed situationally in relation to Acts I and II of the interactional drama, as well as Act III if the idea of prevention is extended to include desistance. These perspectives were considered throughout the narrative, which included many examples of how to effectively work against such purposes, but prevention is an ongoing reality for individuals as well. Thus, the hoi polloi of this world need to be armed with the right tool (i.e., the right information) in order to make informed decisions about identity theft in real time—as it occurs and however it appears—within their own lives. Assuming you intend to use this new tool in your own protection, you will also need a piece of paper and a pencil.

TALLYHO!

Different types, forms, quantities, and qualities of identity information are under the respective control of guardians at any given time in today's world, with different attendant responsibilities for preventing and responding to breaches if they should occur. Where can personal information be found within a society? It would be difficult to provide a comprehensive list of locations since few solid distinctions can presently be made between what constitutes an identity and what constitutes a suitable target for the purposes of identity theft. The social context of identity utilization is vitally important nonetheless.

Individual and collective guardians may fail to protect targets in a variety of ways and settings, depending on how different types and forms of identity information are used and stored, the number and reliability of people with access to identity information in different contexts, the methods through which identity information is intentionally discarded, and all related security features impacting these areas. Any useful evaluation of risk, however, can only be accomplished in specific terms.

Let's return to the example of auto theft for a moment, which has been a common problem in many societies for as long as cars have existed. During the intervening decades of personal car ownership, enough information has been collected to compare the incidence of auto theft across locations in at least general terms (i.e., as a ratio between the number of cars in operation and the number of cars that are stolen). However, the factors that drive the incidence of auto theft vary from place to place, even within a single nation. The problem in universal terms might therefore be stolen cars, but the ways in which cars can be stolen represent a number of distinct, smaller problems that are best examined and addressed in their particulars, just like identity theft.

As an inherently criminal act, the process of sizing up the risks for IDT is the same as it would be for any other crime, whether considered in terms of how an identity can be stolen or how it can be misused. Although traditional crimes such as auto theft can be discussed in more concrete and comparative terms due to their established presence within societies, identity theft is more problematic to assess overall because the act and the concept simultaneously traverse almost everything else criminal in this world. The first two John Schmidt scenarios outlined in Part I are therefore identity theft (at least by U.S. standards), but also auto theft (by universally criminal standards). If both scenarios were put on a scale, would it tip more toward identity theft or auto theft? It would depend of course on where you live (with the scales being at 0 percent identity theft for much of the world), but there might not be a clear winner in either scenario, even within the United States.

Since the assessment of risk is best performed in a localized fashion, you (as the owner of your identity) are about as local as it gets within a global discussion of identity theft prevention. Individuals do not have complete access to their identities in today's world, however, and such access (when provided) is never completely free. Further, owners can only prevent the theft of their identity insofar as their own actions or inactions lead to its kidnapping or abuse. In other words, owners everywhere only have the power to prevent the theft of the personal information that is within their realm of influence, which does not give them much power over the problem at all. Owners may also have the ability (rather than the desire) to monitor most of their lives 24 hours a day, but doing so in reality would not leave much time for living.

Whether you choose to actively examine your own life or not, someone else is probably doing it for you. That is another reality of today's world, the burden of which might be borne somewhat more evenly by everyman. While there is a standard litany of prevention tips available in the United States (see Box 10.1 for one example), not all may apply universally if the U.S. problem is truly different from its international counterparts. Even assuming that there were some pertinent universal lessons, such as guard your valuables or be wary of strangers, the complexities of identity theft are not easily or advisably reduced into tip-sized morsels or averages. Much of the advice available in the realm of personal identity ownership nevertheless falls under the rubric of crime prevention, which overall is a mixture of common sense and wise precaution relative to the dangers of different environments: at home, at work, online, out and about.

If your identity is truly valuable to you, then you might want to sit down and assess the security of the identity targets in your life. What information is there? What is paper, plastic, or digital? Who has access to what? How local is your life in relation to everything techno-modern-global? These questions will start you on your way to performing a personal risk assessment, and thus a customized plan for defense (and maybe some offense as well). Even if every target in your life were as secure as Fort Knox, however, you will never be able to eliminate your exposure to the risk of identity theft altogether, whether living primarily in the plain old world or the new shrinking one.

Box 10.1 Hark! The Call of American Prevention[1]

Helping Your Student to Deal with Identity Theft

A good start is to visit that Department of Justice Web site and to click on the Identity Theft tab.

There you will find an easy way for you to remember to take pro-active steps to prevent you – or your student – from becoming a victim of identity theft. Think about, and commit to memory, the word "SCAM," and treat it as an acronym. Then, attach these thoughts to each letter of the word:

For **S**: Be Stingy about giving personal info to others unless you trust them;
For **C**: Check on your personal information regularly;
For **A**: Ask periodically for a copy of your credit report; and
For **M**: Maintain careful records of your banking and financial accounts.

There is much more advice that is dispensed on the DOJ site, of course, and there are many more steps that College Parents of America suggests should be taken in order for you and your student to protect yourselves from identity theft.

Nevertheless, despite your best efforts and your student's best intentions, identity theft does sometimes occur and unfortunately, such occurrences are all too frequent in the college context.

That's why College Parents of America offers Identity Theft and Resolution Services as part of our Standard Membership offer.

To paraphrase Shakespeare: "To be or not to be, A member of College Parents of America? That is the question."

---

[1] http://www.collegeparents.org/blog/2010/09/23/helping-your-student-deal-identity-theft.

Rather than solely looking at an identity as a series of targets in need of protection, it might also be viewed as a commodity that must be cared for by every owner according to its intrinsic value. You are ultimately account-able for yourself and your identity, but you are also currently participating in identity management to some degree, even if only by guarding your wallet or locking your front door. The normal preventative techniques associated with identity theft do not extend far beyond that for the individual, however. Sim-ply put, be careful with your identity, wherever it is and whenever you use it.

Survival is a human instinct, and identities are necessary for social sur-vival. The protection of identity information may therefore be somewhat in-stinctual, insofar as it would go against the natural desire for self-preservation to put yourself in harm's way by allowing sensitive information (particularly a serial number) to fall into the hands of someone with ill intentions. The risk of harm might not always be apparent, however, hence why caution is always prudent when it comes to the transfer or exchange of personal information. This is especially true when the other party is anonymous, invisible, or oth-erwise a stranger to you, but it also applies to friends, relatives, neighbors, acquaintances, employers and co-workers, and all of the social collectives you do business with. Yes, that's right, everyone. No one can be trusted and thus everyone will remain unsafe in today's world, even if you persevere in securing the identity under your control.

If anyone has reached this point in the volume and is still thinking, "Not Me! I'm not a victim of identity theft" (as anywhere herein defined), then please contact someone immediately because the world needs to hear your story. If you are also thinking, "I'm not responsible for identity theft," then you might want to take a closer look at how you act toward your own identity and the identities of others, or how you might sometimes be "forced" to act within society. With whom do you share your information and why? How many times do you skip the fine print regarding how your personal information will be used for some purpose other than the one for which it is being surrendered? Monitoring your own identity is a thankless job that costs you time and potential money, but many individuals participate in the overall dysfunction that leads to identity theft, even if only under a form of coercion in some social contexts as required by vital exchanges.

Overall, the only surefire way to not be a victim is not to be labeled as one. This is a symbolic solution to the problem as well however, because it will not help anyone to endure the realities of identity theft victimization. Until anything can be done to stem the ongoing tide of IDT offenderization in today's world, refusing to be a victim may nevertheless be the best chance you have for prevention until tomorrow's world finally arrives.

Don't Panic

THE UNDERLYING NARRATIVE of this volume has maintained that identity theft is a moral panic via a preponderance of circumstance, but the tradition as a whole appears ill equipped to explain this phenomenon within evolving techno-modern-global societies. While Angela McRobbie and Sarah Thornton provided several constructive insights regarding why the concept of moral panics needs to be revised in order to incorporate the realities of "multimediated social worlds,"[1] the perspective cannot fully be retrofitted in this regard at the present time.

The proliferation of information within modern societies may either help or hinder the initiation and transmission of moral panics, not entirely irrespective of the manner in which such information is communicated. This might further be responsible for the impression that this is "the age of the moral panic,"[2] since a perceived increase in the frequency of moral panics over the past few decades may have more to do with our ability or desire to examine them, rather than their actual occurrence. However, this concept equally applies to the identity theft phenomenon as a whole, since technology and information not only worked together to create the problem, they were the same exact tools that allowed society to detect it more consistently while it was occurring, or at least afterward.

McRobbie and Thornton also discuss how "moral panics have become the way in which daily events are brought to the attention of the public."[3] This might be helpful for understanding several features of the identity theft phenomenon, such as the dramatic language used to describe it, or its common portrayal as a crisis in various forms (e.g., a national crisis, a financial crisis, an identity crisis). Yet while certain communication strategies do in fact make it appear as if "moral panics are constructed on a daily basis,"[4] this explanation alone does not seem to account for all of the distortion inherent to the identity theft narrative.

Proponents of the risk society have similarly argued that discrete moral panics "have now been replaced by a generalized moral stance, a permanent moral panic resting on a seamless web of social anxieties,"[5] but as Stanley Cohen noted, this idea is "less an exaggeration than a[n] oxymoron"[6] since a panic by its own definition is a temporary state. What these issues commonly reflect, however, is the influence that information and communication can have on levels of social anxiety, and the role that such anxiety might play in the occurrence or recurrence of moral panics. The identity theft phenomenon might therefore be a glimpse of what will happen if the moral panic of yesterday ever transforms itself into the unintended consequence of tomorrow.[7]

When thinking about identity theft in terms of being a moral panic at all, however, one question that arises is why? Why would otherwise rational people become unreasonably impassioned about some problematic aspect of social existence, particularly when they have some level of control over its occurrence? If the object of that passion represents a crisis to the beholder (or the opportunity for one), then this might be one mystery solved for the ages, and for the United States as well.

While the Federal Trade Commission and Javelin are both active in making claims about identity theft, the federal government is the primary definer of this problem—and the crisis—within the U.S. narrative. This label is not only appropriate due to their lead role in the criminalization and measurement of identity theft, it is one that they willfully adopted: "No accepted definition of identity theft existed until Congress passed the Federal Identity Theft and Assumption Deterrence Act of 1998."[8] Ironically, this statement is a claim in itself that cannot adequately be assessed.

Although there are some good reasons to question whether the U.S. government has tipped the scales in favor of its own interests in the case of identity theft, there can be no definitive answer to this type of inquiry without direct proof, especially when these types of tradeoffs are a normal part of doing business in the arena of governance. On the other hand, continued diligence will be necessary in order to detect and resolve any further "unintended injustices" on its part, but the same is also true for everybody else's part, whether good or bad.

Justice of any kind is always meted out in context, so moral justice (being the rebalancing of moral outrage during a panic) might be considered in terms of the four equations outlined in Part II, for both individual and collective actors:

The Road to Hell: Good Means + Bad Ends

The road to hell is paved with good intentions, but also with legitimate activities committed during the intentional pursuit of bad ends.

The Road to Prison: Bad Means + Bad Ends

The bad guys on this road might not always end up in prison, but they are well on their way to one. If every decision a person made could be classified solely in these terms, then he or she might truly be evil.

The Road to Nowhere: Bad Means + Good Ends

In the pursuit of good ends, Dirty Harry used a gun, the Great Imposter used identities, and the Inquisition used torture. Such strategies might be effective and expedient in the short term, but the use of bad means might be detected, even when the intention behind that misuse is not really bad or the outcomes are unexpectedly good.

The Road Less Traveled: Good Means + Good Ends

The actors consistently in this category are saints, or something of their ilk. If looked at in collective terms, however, this is the formula for a golden age of society.

Making judgments about good and bad is not always a subjective feat, even though such decisions are always made relative to the observer's perspective. While everyone's role in the U.S. crisis can be viewed in these terms, the real moral problem lies with reconciling all of the means and ends of identity theft when looked at through the eyes of everyman.

If considered in terms of the systems approach advocated in Part I, life consists of systems within systems, and equations within equations. Identity theft is systemic to most of them, but people are responsible for all of them. While no attempt has been made herein to construct the moral equation of identity theft in mathematical terms, its solution would be even more difficult to calculate: everyman (and every collective) must consider what he contributes to the problem relative to what it takes from him. Although many people might not be concerned with the ethical implications of the identity theft narrative, the eradication of identity theft hinges upon solving all of the equations (even the inconvenient ones) as individuals and nations, as well as a global society. This equation must also be considered during a moral panic when society's evaluation of, or reaction to, a threat might ultimately be classified as part of the problem, whether as a bad means or a bad end.

Identity theft will continue to evolve alongside civilization, but the act behind it will always be driven by the motivation to be invisible or otherwise unidentifiable within society for whatever reason. If humanity has not been able to stop that problem yet, chances are it will be with us for some time to come. In order to control it, however, identity theft must be approached with at least as much rationality as the criminal act itself. If the goal of anyone's search for identity theft is to understand and prevent its occurrence, then this same logic must also apply to that process and whatever information might be uncovered.

Even if no one ever chooses to set definitional limits upon the problem, it will be rather difficult to take a not-in-my-backyard attitude about identity theft within the international community. How does the safety of personal information stand within the networked context of life? How many people of this world are victimized by the U.S. problem and vice versa? These are the kinds of questions we need to start asking, because we are all doing "identity theft" to each other. Humanity must also consider whether it is prepared to offer identity theft victims any better brand of justice than the one they might be receiving at home. But perhaps if we start thinking about the problem of identity theft in universal terms now, we can avoid worrying about the problem of providing actual justice—or even global justice—for its victims in the future.

As a global community, we nevertheless have a responsibility to ensure that identity theft does not become a global crisis in any sense of the word. This not only requires active measures to prevent the spread of misinformation, it also implies that the problem cannot be controlled by any means or at any cost. In the final analysis, however, the primary means of our own destruction might be the only thing that can save us in the end. Like any tool, information can be wielded for good or bad. If used in the right way or for the right ends, information can be used to protect #1 (i.e., you), as well as everyone. If used in the wrong way or for the wrong ends, however, much evil might be committed in the name of "everyman's crime."

EVERYMAN'S WAR

Identity theft is a form of information warfare, both in relation to how it is perpetrated, and how information about it has been constructed and disseminated to the masses. The U.S. crisis is also at the heart of a larger information war, which unfortunately has been waged by most of humanity for as long as history cares to remember. After the arrival of The 9.9 Million, however, the U.S. crisis became an identity holocaust, replayed and relived in every detail of its horror (i.e., new you), each and every year, by you as a person and we as a society. Where then is the justice or humanity in allowing any of that to continue?

If the U.S. phenomenon of identity theft were put on trial by the International Criminal Court, one charge against it might be a crime against humanity. After all, identity theft victimization has the potential to rob everyman of his money, his job, his home, and his good name—leaving him virtually destitute and perhaps indebted, all while innocent. If this worst form of identity theft is not bad enough to warrant justice for its victims wherever they are, then what about their quantity: the compounding millions from the North American identity holocaust?

Identity theft currently represents a social death, not the end of life itself, unless the drives of human passion one day make it so. Life nevertheless provides occasional crises to remind us that we are all part of humankind, and the threat of identity theft is no different in that regard. The world is now on alert that the problem of identity theft is grave. If we are not careful about how we proceed as individuals or as nations, existence in the post-modern-techno-global world might soon be calculated in both inhuman and irrational terms, if and when identity is ever completely removed from that particular equation: ID = I am.[9] The world has also now been made aware that identity theft is a product of society, unintended or not, so some hope remains that solutions might one day be found in the best interests of everybody, literally meaning to the exclusion of no one: not you or even that other guy who sometimes pretends to be you.

Justice is about being made whole, or restoring a social imbalance without one person (or collective) profiting over another. How then can justice be provided to anyone in the case of identity theft? Who really profits the most and at whose expense? If the hypocrisies of identity theft cannot be acknowledged, then they will simply be reproduced within and by our social systems and mechanisms, thus creating further dysfunction. This approach will certainly work toward making one prediction of the narrative come true (identity theft will get worse), but that really does not seem to be what everybody wants.

When the object of human passion is something as vital as existence, representing the ultimate duality between life and death, actors might easily be corrupted into the adoption of bad means in order to achieve balance, however defined. This also seems to be true whether existence is viewed in real or symbolic terms relative to the perspective of actors, but the behavioral outcomes of such thinking are very real indeed. Identity theft is already changing the world one identity at a time, and seemingly in spite of everything we have already done about the problem. If the imbalance of identity theft must be addressed through some means going forward, however, why not let it be through a renaissance, rather than anomie or revolution or panic? The fate of mankind would literally seem to depend upon it, and the choice is all up to you, as well as us.

Notes

INTRODUCTION

1. United Nations Office on Drugs and Crime (2007). This particular source did not list the names of the six countries with relevant legislation, but the term identity theft was featured in both pieces of U.S. federal legislation: the Identity Theft and Assumption Deterrence Act of 1998 and the Identity Theft Penalty Enhancement Act of 2004. The United Nations also had 192 member states at the time of this writing (http://www.un.org/en/aboutun/index.shtml), but only 46 member states participated in this particular study. In terms of speaking globally about identity theft, it should also be noted that not all countries are members of the United Nations. Another article from that same year (van der Meulen [2007]) noted that eight European Union member states had "specific legislation on identity theft . . . [that] differs significantly." The Wikipedia entry for identity theft currently lists the following eight nations as having regional legal responses: Australia, Canada, France, Hong Kong, India, Sweden, the United Kingdom, and the United States. http://en.wikipedia.org/wiki/Identity_theft.

2. http://europa.eu/abc/panorama/index_en.htm.

3. Second Meeting of the Core Group of Experts on Identity-Related Crime (2008).

4. United Nations Office on Drugs and Crime (2007).

CHAPTER 1

1. The collective identity of a social entity, such as a company or a government, functions in the same way. Although the present discussion focuses on individual identity, these points can be extended to collective identities, as they too can be stolen and misused.

2. This military code of conduct is fairly standard and conforms to the Geneva Convention of 1949.

3. Choi (2007): *Two Snowflakes May Actually Be Alike.*

4. Cole (2001): *The Myth of Fingerprints.*

5. Kelly (2005). Written by Kevin Mullaney.

6. http://en.wikipedia.org/wiki/LifeLock.

CHAPTER 2

1. John Schmidt is best recognized by his middle names, Jacob Jingleheimer.

2. Although the primary target at this point is typically the information that comprises an identity, an offender with personal motives can target a specific identity.

3. For further information about the Chip and PIN system, see http://www.chipandpin.co.uk/.

4. Miller (2007).

5. McNally (2008a): 7.

6. http://www.privacyrights.org/ar/ChronDataBreaches.htm. The total number of breached records on February 27, 2011, was 514,701,406.

7. http://www.census.gov/main/www/popclock.html. The total U.S. population on February 27, 2011, was 310,897,015.

8. http://www.gao.gov/new.items/d07737.pdf.

9. *This Is Your Life* was a popular television series first aired during the 1950s in which guests were treated to a trip down memory lane within their own lives.

10. This concept of pain is from the classical work of English jurist and philosopher Jeremy Bentham.

CHAPTER 3

1. See McNally (2008b) for further discussion of scripting identity theft as a series of criminal acts.

2. Clue is a murder mystery game that has been around since 1949.

3. There is an entire tradition of systems research within criminology and other disciplines, but the term herein is used generally as a way to introduce the topic as a suggested area for future research.

4. The idea of mapping criminal networks is premised on work within the area of environmental criminology, even though the current discussion is not fully developed along those lines.

5. The evidence of transnational offending is largely anecdotal or piecemeal, based on the work of various agencies such as the FBI.

6. When talking about technology in a modern context, it is easy to focus on the flashy parts (like the Internet) to the exclusion of other things, such as telephones or pencils, which do fall under the category of technology and were at one point considered "modern" relative to the time of their invention. In today's terms, however, we have cell phones, the capability to talk face to face with others via Internet technology, word processing programs, and a host of other tools that mask the essence of the underlying social function involved—communication.

CHAPTER 4

1. Cohen (2002): xxxv.
2. Goode and Ben-Yehuda (1994): 12.
3. There is a very fine line of distinction between moral panics and moral crusades, but the latter generally involves activism regardless of public support. For further discussion of this topic, see Goode and Ben-Yehuda (1994).
4. Cohen (2002): 1.
5. Critcher (2003): 178.
6. Jewkes (1999): 31, discussing Kidd-Hewitt and Osborne (1995).
7. Hall, Critcher, et al. (1978).
8. Waddington (1986).
9. See, for example, Goode and Ben-Yehuda (1994): 135–136 for a treatment of Hall et al.'s work (1978) under an elite-engineered model of moral panics. For further discussion of this study in general, see Thompson (1998): 57–71 or Stabile (2001).
10. See, for example, the comparison in Critcher (2003): 14–16.
11. Jewkes (1999): 31.
12. Critcher (2003): 143.
13. Examples of systematic moral panics research include Baerveldt, Bunkers, et al. (1998); Victor (1998); Burns and Crawford (1999); Welch, Price, and Yankey (2002); Critcher (2003); Rothe and Muzzatti (2004).
14. Examples of less systematic moral panics research include Jenkins (1992, 1998); Chermak (2002); McCorkle and Miethe (2002); de Young (2004); Poynting, Noble, et al. (2004); Cole and Pontell (2006).
15. For a general overview of these criticisms, see Critcher (2003): 143–149 and Jewkes (1999). Cohen (2002) also responds to several criticisms in his introduction to the second and third editions of *Folk Devils*.
16. Hall et al. (1978): 16.
17. Nesbitt (2005) in the United Kingdom, and Cole and Pontell (2006) in the United States.
18. See McNally (2008a).
19. Cohen (2002): viii.
20. Not all topics of prior moral panics research fit neatly within these categories (e.g., terrorism) but there are some differences between the work that has been conducted in the United Kingdom and United States. For further discussion of this topic, see Thompson (1998) or the discussion of his work in Critcher (2003): 27–29.
21. For further discussion of this childhood theme, see chapter 11 in Critcher (2003).
22. McRobbie (1995).
23. One example consistent with the portrayal of threats that can occur during a moral panic comes from the Electricity Consumers Resource Council's (2002): 1 depiction of Enron's activities as being just the tip of the iceberg, "because they describe a real, ongoing problem with the electricity market." This can also be a common dramatic description of threats in general, however, so further research would be required to consider whether a moral panic might have been brewing around Enron.
24. Stabile (2001).
25. Cohen (2002): viii.
26. As discussed in Fattah (1993): 227.
27. Critcher (2003): 2.

28. There were a total of 39 questions in the original research, with many overlapping between models. See McNally (2008a) for a full description.

29. Critcher (2003): 150.

30. Critcher (2003): 2.

31. Cohen (2002): 134.

32. Goode and Ben-Yehuda (1994): 24.

33. Critcher (2003): 141.

34. Critcher (2003): 144.

35. The chorus is a classic group in Greek drama that provides running commentary on unfolding events for a variety of functions. The chorus, for example, might provide the audience with background information or act as a moral conscience for members of the cast. The chorus also often represented everyman, with the precise goal of translating how the events on stage pertained to those who were watching.

36. Cohen (2002): xxii.

37. The issue of morality was considered by Cohen, Critcher, and Goode and Ben-Yehuda, but it remains unresolved and undefined within the perspective.

38. The mathematical term *absolute value* refers to a number regardless of its sign (positive or negative).

39. There is an entire structure of ethical frameworks within the field of philosophy that cannot be fully outlined or explained in the present context. Relativism and absolutism are nevertheless two of the primary dueling concepts within that structure.

40. Downs (1972).

41. Baerveldt, Bunkers, et al. (1998): 42.

42. This theatrical heuristic happened to overlap between the two main schools of thought underlying the original research—rational choice and moral panics.

43. These five case studies were AIDS, ecstasy and raves, video nasties, child abuse in families, and pedophilia.

44. Nesbitt (2005).

45. Goode and Ben-Yehuda (1994): 38.

46. Goode and Ben-Yehuda (1994): 39.

47. Joint hearing before the Subcommittee on Oversight and Investigations (2002).

48. These were the most dominant subthemes of the narrative that could be distinguished among the clamor of identity theft, but there were many other important themes woven throughout its tapestry.

49. This lack of standardized methodology extends to the ways in which data are collected, as well as the ways in which they are displayed or used as evidence. Within Critcher's research, for example, media searches related to one case study focused on articles containing the word paedophile but apparently not paedophilia, which seems rather slanted in favor of finding a folk devil (one of the key characteristics of a panic). In relation to the issue of international comparisons, it is also unclear whether U.S. spellings (pedophile, pedophilia) would have produced different results. The articles retrieved via this search were also visually displayed by quarter, which does produce the very noticeable spikes in media attention that are consistent with the presence of a panic, but these data might have produced a very different picture had they been displayed by year or by month.

50. For a full discussion of the original research methodology, see McNally (2008a).

51. Newman and McNally (2005).

52. Critcher (2003): 141.

53. Critcher (2003): 152.

54. Lexis-Nexis and NewsBank have different issues with regard to the coverage of newspaper content, but neither is fully inclusive and both are subject to changes over time as a function of their agreement with various publishers. One specific limitation associated with using these databases is the inability to assess the physical characteristics of articles as they were published, particularly since photos and other types of graphics are not included. For a full discussion of the strengths and weaknesses of the original research design and these databases, see McNally (2008a).

55. There was one *Arizona Republic* article retrieved from the Privacy Rights Clearinghouse library (Leonard [1997]), which indicated that there was some type of identity theft coverage in this newspaper prior to 1999. A further Access World News search of the only Arizona newspaper with coverage prior to 1999 (*Arizona Daily Star* coverage beginning January 1, 1991) produced only four articles (one in 1996, two in 1997, and one in 1998). Since this pattern of scant coverage is witnessed in other newspapers as well, reporting in the *Arizona Republic* was likely similar.

CHAPTER 5

1. http://en.wikipedia.org/wiki/Trickster.

2. Schwanhausser (1995).

3. Bernstein (1999).

4. See, for example, the Federal Bureau of Investigation (n.d.); the National White Collar Crime Center (www.nw3c.org); or Rusch (2001), in which identity theft is described as "one of the most insidious forms of white-collar crime."

5. Quote attributed to Sergeant Jim Hyde of the Miami-Dade (Florida) Police Department, in Gayer (2003).

6. Copes and Vieraitis (2008): 37.

7. These are the basic principles of deterrence theory, as originally outlined by the English jurist and philosopher Jeremy Bentham.

8. Vasquez (2005).

9. Wagner (2005).

10. Goddard (2005).

11. Oxford English Dictionary Online: www.oed.com.

12. Federal Deposit Insurance Corporation (2004).

13. ID Analytics (2005b).

14. ID Analytics (2005a,b).

15. ID Analytics (2003).

16. Cook (2005): 3.

17. This particular definition also implies that identity fraud is only committed for financial gain. Compare this with an early statement made by the Federal Trade Commission (n.d.): "Identity theft and identity fraud are terms used to refer to all types of crime in which someone wrongfully obtains and uses another person's personal data in some way that involves fraud or deception, *typically for economic gain*" (italics added).

18. Javelin Strategy & Research (2006): 50–51.

19. Javelin Strategy & Research (2006): 51.

20. ID Analytics (2005a, 2006).

21. These descriptions of identity theft and identity fraud were found in an article on LifeLock (Galehouse 2005), and although the ideas were attributed to Todd Davis, they were not published as direct quotations and may only have been used as examples during the interview. As such, these excerpts may not truly be Davis's "definitions," but they represent another example of how identity theft can be misrepresented to the public—via either careless wording or careless reporting.

22. Fitch (1986).

23. " 'True Name' Credit Card Fraud . . ." (1988).

24. Billington (1989).

25. Neuffer (1991).

26. Merton (1957).

27. The U.S. Census estimate of the adult population as of July 1, 2002, was 215.47 million. Synovate (2003): 7.

28. Figure 5.1 also generally represents a decrease in the number of victims from left to right insofar as the two extremes (impersonation and assumption) are concerned. As shown in Table 5.1, however, there are fewer victims in the category of Existing Non-Credit Card Account Misuse than within the category of New Accounts and Other Fraud. While it was reported that "16% of victims who had their existing credit cards misused said that the person . . . also tried to 'take over' the account by doing such things as changing the billing address or adding themselves to the card as an authorized user" (Synovate [2003]: 14), this information does not suggest how many takeovers were successful in relation to existing credit card accounts or otherwise attempted in relation to other types of existing non–credit card accounts.

29. Synovate (2003): 5.

30. In reverse, the opportunities related to the commission of one type of fraud may lead to opportunities for the commission of other types of fraud. For further discussion of this issue, see Newman and McNally (2005) and McNally and Newman (2008).

31. *The Talented Mr. Ripley* has been called an "identity theft movie." Although the plot can be a useful example in several contexts, the title was borrowed here to represent the element of repeat victimization and the versatility of identity thieves as a group.

32. Brown (2000).

33. There are many movie examples of this (e.g., *Tootsie, Mrs. Doubtfire, Victor/Victoria*) in which the lead characters must impersonate someone of the opposite gender for different reasons. In two of these movies (*Tootsie* and *Victor/Victoria*), that reason was employment; in *Mrs. Doubtfire*, Robin Williams took the guise of a woman in order to be hired by his ex-wife as the nanny for his own children; thus his motivation was personal but the context was again employment.

34. These comparisons are based upon all references within the Theft and Fraud Samples. Comparisons between primary or secondary references were not performed because there were almost no primary references of any type within the Fraud Samples (33 primary references in total from four newspapers; 17 were primary articles). This nevertheless adds further credence to the conclusion that a greater amount of attention was given to the problem of identity theft by each of the newspapers.

35. There were no references to identity fraud within the Thief Sample due to the method in which it was selected.

36. For example, Caminer (1985) and Harper (1989).

37. See for example Perry (1995). This article is actually about stolen identities (i.e., identity theft), but the title refers to the "credit fraud epidemic."

38. See for example LaVally (1994). The title of this particular report is an interesting precursor to the way in which identity theft would later be described. Compare, for example, *Law Enforcement's View: The Growing Menace of Fraud in California* (LaVally), and *The Growing Menace of Identity Theft to New York Consumers* (Schumer 2002).

39. From the *New York Times*, 115 references were removed from the original search results and 13 were added. From the *Washington Post*, 125 were removed and 24 were added. These were the newspapers with the greatest amount of references, as well as the greatest amount of removed references overall.

40. These references only had alternate terms, with "theft of identity" common to both: Kisselgoff (1985) and Darling (1977). The 1985 article also referred to this idea figuratively, not literally in reference to a criminal act like the 1977 reference.

CHAPTER 6

1. For further reading about identity theft's ancient history, see Caslon Analytics (2003).

2. "What Can We Do About the Frauds?" (1864).

3. "Gets American Forger" (1926).

4. "Hold-Up Man Identified" (1951).

5. "Died" (1982). This is the earliest appearance of the term "identity thief" located to date. While there is at least some evidence to show that the concepts of stealing identities and assumed identities were associated with Ferdinand Demara ("The Great Imposter Returns!," 1961; Crichton 1960), the term identity theft does not appear to have any direct lineage to his legacy, except that it did first appear in 1964. His penchant for actions now fitting the description of *new you* was nevertheless well documented within the work of Robert Crichton.

6. Crichton (1960): 242.

7. Dirty Harry is a famous movie cop character played by Clint Eastwood, and this term is actually used within the field of ethics.

8. Crichton (1960): 58.

9. "The Great Imposter Returns" (1961).

10. A contemporary figure rivaling the Great Imposter is Frank Abagnale Jr., whose crimes, which were committed during the 1960s, were made famous in the 2002 movie *Catch Me if You Can*. Abagnale was primarily a check forger, however, and it is not clear from available accounts whether he ever stole real identities. In this way, Abagnale might best be called an identity fraudster rather than an identity thief, even though his reputation suggests otherwise. For more information on Frank Abagnale, visit http://www.abagnale.com/.

11. Oxford English Dictionary Online: http://www.oed.com/.

12. Billington (1989).

13. Effinger (1995).

14. Pierce (1991).

15. Maslin (1992).

16. Fitch (1986).
17. Sears (1993), PrivacyGuard (1993).
18. Richards (1998).
19. Travelers Insurance of Florida (2007).
20. Faron (1998).
21. Hartle and Hartle (2006).
22. The term *classic victim* generally represents the delayed discovery and repeated occurrence of identity theft victimization that specifically accompanies new you.
23. Brown (2000).
24. Newman and McNally (2005).
25. Washington (2006).
26. For example: "Life in the Legislature" (2000), Kopel (2003), and B. Johnson (2004).
27. IdentityTheft911 (2004), Schrager (2006).
28. Much of this author's analysis is also consistent with the presence of a moral panic insofar as some media reporting is concerned.
29. Kopel (2003).
30. The Identity Theft Clearinghouse was originally created as part of the Consumer Sentinel Network but appears to have been subsumed by it entirely, thus it is no longer known by this name: http://www.ftc.gov/sentinel/.
31. Federal Trade Commission (2001).
32. The accuracy of this particular figure and its origins will be considered during a later discussion.
33. Mayer and Schwartz (2000).
34. Federal Trade Commission (2000a): *Identity Crisis . . . What to Do If Your Identity Is Stolen.* This report was published only a few months after the FTC began collecting consumer complaint data on identity theft. This document was updated in 2005 with the subheading "Facts for Consumers." Taken together with the national awareness campaign launched in 2003 (Operation Identity Crisis), the continued linkage of this crisis frame to the federal government's stated goal of educating the public about the issue of identity theft is particularly disconcerting.
35. Ewen (1993): 247.
36. "An Identity Crisis" (1977).
37. See, for example, Wakin (2001): "The Nation: Identity Crisis; National I.D. Cards: One Size Fits All"; or Harper (2006): *Identity Crisis: How Identification Is Overused and Misunderstood.*
38. "What Can We Do About the Frauds?" (1864).
39. Effinger (1995).
40. Effinger (1995): xi.
41. Davis (1994).
42. Rother (1995).
43. "Are You a Target for Identity Theft?" (1997).
44. Laribee and Hogan (2001).
45. Clarke (2005).
46. U.S. General Accounting Office (1998).
47. U.S. General Accounting Office (2002a, c, d). There was also one other GAO report on identity fraud (2002b) that dealt specifically with its links to illegal immigration.

48. U.S. General Accounting Office (1998).

49. Rawe (1999).

50. Ball (2001).

51. Givens (2000b).

52. CBS News (1999).

53. New York Senate Majority Task Force on the Invasion of Privacy (2000), Kliewer (2000).

54. Federal Trade Commission (2001).

55. For further discussion of the types of identity theft information available during the early years, see Newman and McNally (2005).

56. EarthLink Identity Protection Center (2007), Equifax Learning Center (2007), Massachusetts Executive Office of Public Safety (2007).

57. White Canyon Software (n.d.).

58. Rivlin (2005).

59. Wilmouth, Grossman, and Hillebrand (2005).

60. Colorado Attorney General: http://www.ago.state.co.us/idtheft/IDTHEFT. cfm.

61. California Attorney General: http://caag.state.ca.us/idtheft/index.htm.

62. Virginia Attorney General: http://www.vaag.com/FAQs/FAQ_IDTheft. html.

63. New York Attorney General: http://www.oag.state.ny.us/consumer/tips/id_ theft_ victim.html.

64. New Mexico Attorney General: http://www.ago.state.nm.us/know/idtheft/ idtheft.htm.

65. For example: O'Connor (1996a), McLeod (1996).

66. For example: Faron (1996), Baca (1997).

67. Yavorsky (1997). Today, Keycorp continues to develop solutions for secure electronic transactions (www.keycorp.net).

68. Menefee (1998). Statement attributed to a spokesperson from the San Francisco Police Department.

69. One common departure on this theme is the claim that identity theft is an epidemic. Examples of the epidemic claim include Meece (1998), O'Harrow and Schwartz (1998), "Kleczka Leads . . ." (1998), "Fighting Identity Theft" (1998), Caniglia (1998), Associated Press Newswires (1999), Williams (1999), Hanson (1999), Dugas (1999), Rubin (1999), Pankratz (1999), Cliatt (1999), Vancheri (2000), Gardner (2000), Carlson (2000), Safire (2000), Bergal (2001), Mayer (2001), Sowers and Biggs (2002), Bauer (2003), Sullivan (2004), and Singer (2007).

70. Board of Governors of the Federal Reserve System (1997): 21.

71. Medine (1998).

72. Bernstein (1999).

73. Bush (2004a).

74. For example: Lease and Burke (2000), Michigan State Police (2007).

75. For example: *American Civil Liberties Union*, Steinhardt (2000); *Privacy Rights Clearinghouse*, Givens (2000a).

76. For example: Schumer (2002), Feinstein (2005).

77. Wiles (2001).

78. Yip (2001).

79. LaVally (1994).

80. McLeod (1997).

81. Foley (2002).
82. O'Brien (2004).
83. Quote by Chuck Whitlock, investigative reporter and professional scam buster, in Oldenburg (1997).
84. Copes and Vieraitis (2008).
85. 86/2106 = 4.08 percent.
86. *Arizona Republic* (13/369 = 3.52%), *Boston Globe* (12/262 = 4.58%), *USA Today* (9/215 = 4.18%), *New York Times* (28/452 = 6.19%), *Washington Post* (22/648 = 3.39%), *Rocky Mountain News* (2/160 = 1.25%).
87. Each sample was coded for the occurrence of the term identity thief or one of its variants (e.g., thief of identity). The term identity thief also appeared within two references from the Fraud Sample, which were not included here. Given that this sample did not include the term identity theft, the presence of the term identity thief was rather anomalous (2 out of 181 references). It therefore seemed that their inclusion would underestimate the true proportion of references in which this term appeared. However, this is further evidence that the identity thief had a status separate from that of identity theft.
88. *Arizona Republic* (41/352 = 11.64%), *Boston Globe* (39/216 = 18.05%), *USA Today* (60/207 = 28.98%), *New York Times* (72/422 = 17.06%), *Washington Post* (85/580 = 14.65%), *Rocky Mountain News* (8/148 = 5.40%).
89. Goode and Ben-Yehuda (1994): 28.
90. For example: Sullivan (2004), State of California (2005).
91. For example: Koenenn (1997), O'Harrow and Schwarz (1998), Yip (1999), Brown (2000), Federal Trade Commission (2000b), Nelson (2000), Stanley (2001).
92. For example: Identity Theft Prevention Special Interest Group (2005), Swartz (2005a).
93. Jarman (2005).
94. Bray (2005a).
95. Cohen (2002): 1.
96. O'Harrow (2003).
97. Silva and Pratt (2004): 1.
98. Cohen (2002): 27.
99. Immigration (2/1,839 = 0.10%), terrorism (15/1,839 = 0.81%), drugs (12/1,839 = 0.65%).
100. Immigration (14/1,839 = 0.76%), terrorism (26/1,839 = 1.41%), drugs (16/1,839 = 0.87%).
101. This tactic has successfully been used before. Pol Pot, for example, employed it in Cambodia during the 1970s.
102. Crenshaw (2000).
103. Moore (2001).
104. Summers (1999).
105. http://www.javelinstrategy.com/true_false_08_22_07.html.
106. Synovate (2003).
107. Anderson (2005).
108. Beales (2002).
109. Beales (2002).
110. Anderson (2005): 23.
111. Javelin Strategy & Research (2006): 3.

112. This issue becomes more difficult to assess for other vulnerable groups. Students, for example, have fallen into this at-risk category because many schools were in the habit of using social security numbers as identification numbers. However, the same can be said about all drivers from states that used to print social security numbers on their licenses.

113. Singletary (2003).

114. There were only eight articles with a primary focus about children, and seven regarding the military across all six newspapers; each paper also had seven articles with a secondary focus on these topics.

115. Altheide (2002).

116. Critcher (2003): 140.

CHAPTER 7

1. Lee (2003).

2. Mayer (2003).

3. A few studies had been conducted before the FTC released its results in the summer of 2003, but their study was the largest and the best at that time. For further discussion regarding the limitations of previous research, see Appendix 1 in Newman and McNally (2005). There was also a second study conducted on behalf of the FTC in 2006, but those results are not considered here (Synovate 2007).

4. U.S. Postal Service (2003).

5. Jerry Orbach died in 2004 but was probably best known for his role as a detective on the TV show *Law & Order*, which premiered in 1990 and is now one of the longest running series in television history (http://www.nbc.com/Law_&_Order/about/).

6. U.S. Postal Inspection Service (2004).

7. http://www.usps.com/postalinspectors/dvdorder.htm. While this operation appears to have been abandoned and the video is now difficult to locate, one viewer reported that it aired on a cable access channel in Colorado as recently as 2006: http://imdb.com/title/tt0385770/.

8. There was a U.S. television show *The 4400*, in which a group of alien abductees (4,400 in total) had been returned en masse to society from outer space. This plot is reminiscent of discovering the 9.91 million victims of identity theft in the United States.

9. Javelin Research & Strategy (2005, 2006, 2007a, 2010).

10. This is the catchphrase of *The Shadow*, a fictional "crime-fighting vigilante with psychic powers." http://en.wikipedia.org/wiki/The_Shadow.

11. Blurry photographs refer to measures designed to take a snapshot of the dark figure (such as the NCVS), which never create an entirely clear picture of crime. Discredited eyewitnesses refer to the bystanders of (or participants in) such acts, who for whatever reason (many times criminal) do not call the police for help.

12. NCVS: http://bjs.ojp.usdoj.gov/content/glance/house2.cfm; UCR: http://www2.fbi.gov/ucr/cius2006/offenses/property_crime/index.html.

13. Gartner, Inc. (2003, 2007).

14. Kraft (2007).

15. Javelin Strategy & Research (2007a): 18.

16. Klaus (2006).

17. Baum (2006). A more recent example of media confusion relates to these first identity theft results from the NCVS. Estimates previously provided by the FTC in 2003 indicated that approximately 9.91 million adults had been victimized during the one-year period prior to their survey. Results from the NCVS later revealed that 3.6 million U.S. households had discovered that at least one member had been a victim of identity theft during a six-month period in 2004. These figures were inappropriately compared within some media sources to suggest that victimization had either declined or been overestimated by the FTC. Aside from the difference in reference periods (one year versus six months), the FTC's study measured individual victimization while the NCVS measured household victimization. This mistake seems to have originated from an Associated Press newswire (Jelinek 2006), and even though it was caught rather quickly and corrected within most sources, uncorrected examples could still be found on the Internet in 2008, for example, Bosworth (2006).

18. Baum (2006): 6.

19. A full year's figure for 2004 has never been published to my knowledge. A second report released in November 2007 noted that 6.4 million households (or 5.5% of all U.S. households) experienced some form of identity theft victimization in 2005 (Baum 2007). According to a third report, at least one member of 7.9 million households (6.6% of all U.S. households) had discovered their victimization in 2007, representing a "significant" increase from 5.5 percent in 2005 (Langton and Baum 2007).

20. Synovate (2003): 50.

21. Results from the FTC and Javelin surveys are not directly comparable. Differences between their estimates largely result from Javelin's extension and recalculation of the FTC's original data, which measured victimization during a five-year period ending in March/April 2003. Javelin also made changes to the study's methodology during subsequent surveys.

22. These are the figures reported by Javelin, but the totals for 2003 and 2004 do not equal 100 percent, which is probably due to rounding.

23. An unknown percentage of these victims also contacted another type of agency (e.g., the FTC, credit card company, bank, credit bureau).

24. Aside from the missing results for 2005, there are missing percentages for 2003 (9.1%) and 2004 (2.9%) in which information regarding whether a police report had been taken was unknown; thus, these columns do not equal 100 percent.

25. When these figures are added to those who "Contacted an agency other than the police," the resulting figures are: 77.36 percent (reported by Javelin in Table 7.3 as 77.4%) and 66.88 percent in 2004 (reported by Javelin in Table 7.3 as 66.9%). These differences are also the result of the recalculation.

26. U.S. Bureau of Justice Statistics (2005, 2006).

27. In the NCVS reports, the category "Completed Theft" is further divided into four subcategories: Less than $50, $50–$249, $250 or more, and Amount Not Available.

28. Javelin Strategy & Research (2005). While it is practically meaningless to discuss the mean or average out-of-pocket losses suffered by identity theft victims, the common perception—based on statistics such as these—is that they are high.

29. Hart and Rennison (2003).

30. This is a variation of the title from a famous Agatha Christie novel.

31. Hoofnagle (2007b).

32. Javelin Strategy & Research (2006: 50–51).

33. Hoofnagle (2007b).

34. Van Dyke (2007).

35. Can the IDT victims from the Javelin studies be added together? While the exact procedures used by Javelin are unclear, research of this nature might be expected to screen out prior respondents. Javelin (2005): 5 once noted that there were "9.3 million *new* victims of identity fraud" (italics added), which seems to add credence to this assumption. Either way, there is no available information to suggest that identity theft victims have been recycled in any way over past surveys, and thus the results appear to be additive.

36. The Consumer Sentinel Network continues to act as a centralized repository for identity theft complaint data in the United States, which is utilized by various law enforcement agencies to investigate cases and identify national trends across jurisdictional boundaries.

37. For further discussion of the issues related to the reporting and recording of identity theft data, and the information collected by the FTC's Identity Theft Clearinghouse/Consumer Sentinel, see Newman and McNally (2005).

38. Monahan (2007).

39. Synovate (2003): 50.

40. Javelin (2005): 49.

41. Kim (2007).

42. Information regarding contributors to the Consumer Sentinel Network, which includes the former Identity Theft Clearinghouse, can be found in the appendix of later annual reports from the Federal Trade Commission (2006, 2007a), as well as their website: www.consumer.gov/sentinel/.

43. Hoofnagle (2007a).

44. Federal Trade Commission (2011).

45. Full Javelin reports can only be purchased, ranging in cost up to $2,500.

46. Javelin Strategy & Research (2007b).

47. Javelin Strategy & Research (2007b). Posting attributed to Harry J. Houck Jr.

48. Hoofnagle (2007b).

49. Sproule and Archer (n.d.).

50. Javelin (2010).

51. There are many challenges involved with making international comparisons under the best of terms, but the Canadian survey was conducted with an Internet panel, which is hardly traditional. This sends up at least one red flag in terms of whether the sample is representative of the Canadian population as a whole, but it is also very different from the methodology used in the U.S. survey. It is interesting that the Canadian rate is higher under these circumstances, and it begs the question of how this techno-modern-global methodology might have impacted the findings.

52. Sproule and Archer (n.d.).

53. Aside from the rigors of international research in general, finding identity theft in the world is not an easy task. As noted by van der Meulen (2007): "[w]ithin the European Union, officials make global statements usually without mentioning concrete figures." If national estimates do exist, they may therefore be well-kept secrets for different reasons.

54. Weston (n.d.).

CHAPTER 8

1. Name, rank, serial #, physical existence and lived existence × paper, plastic, digital, and virtual.

2. McNally (2008b).

3. http://feinstein.senate.gov/legislation/idtheft.html. This particular version of the story identifies Michele Brown's identity thief as the receptionist in the property management office where she lived.

4. As conceptualized in McNally (2008b), the category of transaction included physical and virtual transfers of information. When reconsidering this issue in light of jurisdictions, person-to-person transactions seemed to fall more within the second area of guardianship, since such information is transferred in good faith by at least one party, if not both initially. This third area of activity nevertheless remains a catchall for any breach in which sole responsibility cannot be attributed because it lies in the borderland of a transaction.

5. For further discussion about scripting identity theft by Act, see McNally (2008b).

6. Lenhart (2000).

7. Fox (2001).

8. Javelin (2005): 23. Although no specific explanation is given, these figures do not total 100 percent for either year and this is likely due to missing responses: 97.9 percent in 2003 and 97.4 percent in 2004. Synovate (2003: 30) only reported that 51 percent of identity theft victims over a five-year period knew how their information had been obtained. For the same reason, however, it cannot be assumed that a full 49 percent of victims did not know.

9. Javelin (2005): 74.

10. Kahn and Roberds (2005): 22.

11. Javelin (2005): 25.

12. Javelin (2005): 25–26.

13. Facebook and Twitter, although different, both represent online communities or networks.

14. Better Business Bureau (2005).

15. Smith (2005): 1.

16. Javelin (2005): 20.

17. Javelin (2005): 20.

18. Hoofnagle (2007a).

19. Hoofnagle (2007a).

20. Singletary (2005).

CHAPTER 9

1. Finkelstein (1999).

2. http://law.rightpundits.com/?p=82.

3. Liptak and Preston (2009a).

4. Attributed to Stephen H. Legomsky, professor of immigration law at Washington University in Liptak and Preston (2009b).

5. Swecker (2005): 1.

6. Gordon, Rebovich, et al. (2007).

7. Copes and Vieraitis (2008).

8. Preston (2004).

9. Commonwealth of Virginia, Office of the Attorney General (2006).

10. Synovate (2003): 41.

11. For additional discussion regarding the strengths and weaknesses of different identity theft legislation, see Perl (2003) regarding the failure of state laws to address criminal record identity theft; Pastrikos (2004) for an examination of federal and various state statutes; and Saunders and Zucker (1999) for an assessment of the 1998 Identity Theft and Assumption Deterrence Act.

12. Opt-out legislation is symbolic on its own; business will go on as usual and it is up to you (the individual/consumer) to read the fine print. If such laws were truly intended to help individuals, then they probably should have been given the choice to opt in rather than opt out. As it stands, many collectives are unhappy with having to give individuals any choice at all.

13. The FACT Act solidified the provisions of a 1996 amendment to the Fair Credit Reporting Act of 1970. While the FACT Act now provides consumers with a free annual copy of their credit report from each of the three main national credit bureaus, it also permanently blocks states from passing more stringent privacy rules than the federal government (Newman and McNally [2005]: 81). One section also directs the secretary of the Treasury "to conduct a study of the use of biometrics and other similar technologies to reduce the incidence and costs of identity theft by providing convincing evidence of who actually performed a given financial transaction" (Gordon, Willox, et al. [2004]: 27).

14. For example, see Curtis (1996) on the federalization of crime, and the U.S. House of Representatives Committee on Government Reform (2006) for an assessment of congressional preemption more generally. See also Cassady (2004) for further discussion on a range of issues from consumer privacy to global warming, and Mierzwinski (2004) for specific consideration of federalization in the area of consumer protection.

15. U.S. General Accounting Office (1998): 57.

16. U.S. General Accounting Office (1998): 55.

17. Swecker (2005).

18. RFID (radio frequency identification) is similar to the technology used in smart cards, which contain a machine-readable chip that stores information. RFID technology is currently used in a number of products and services, such as passports and E-Z Pass, but the Federal Drug Administration has approved the implant of RFID chips into humans for a range of health-care applications (http://www.epic.org/privacy/rfid/verichip.html).

19. "Sheriff Joe" Arpaio has often been at the center of controversy in Arizona. See http://en.wikipedia.org/wiki/Joe_Arpaio for a summary.

20. See, for example, Electronic Privacy Information Center (2007).

21. U.S. Defense Advanced Research Projects Agency (2003): 1. The "war on terror" has apparently been misnamed as well, as the House Armed Services Committee banished this term from the 2008 defense budget (Maze, 2007). While President Bush (2004b) previously suggested it be called "the struggle against ideological extremists who do not believe in free societies who happen to use terror as a weapon to try to shake the conscience of the free world," no replacement term appears to have been selected.

22. U.S. House of Representatives (2003): 327.

23. Krouse (2004): i.

24. U.S. Department of Homeland Security (2006): 2.

25. Hoofnagle (2005).

26. Cockeyed.com (2006).

27. Zug.com (n.d.).

28. Tim Robinson, president of BioPay LLC, quoted in McCarthy (2005).

29. U.S. Senate (2007).

30. Summers (1999).

31. http://fms.treas.gov/eft/index.html.

32. See, for example, Hendrickson (1972).

33. In the movie *The Matrix*, people live within a world of virtual reality.

34. Federal Trade Commission (2000b): 1, 7.

35. Faron (1998).

36. Identity Theft Resource Center (2003): 25.

37. Ryst (2006) provides further information about these types of insurance policies and their subscription rates. American International Group, for example, reported insuring 7 million people compared with approximately 5 million people in the previous year.

38. http://www.javelinstrategy.com/true_false_08_22_07.html.

39. Frank and Givens (1999).

40. Aside from simple measures such as Scotch Tape, see Cockeyed.com (2006), there are in fact very sophisticated forensic procedures that can be used to reconstruct documents. See, for example, Justino, Oliveira, and Freitas (2006).

41. Examples of this can be found in Givens (2004) and WFSB (2006), the latter of which involved shredded police reports from Colorado. One Enron employee had also discovered evidence of the company's illicit activities in a pile of paper shreddings that she had taken home to use as packing material (Lavandera and Barrett, 2002).

42. Javelin (2005): 38.

43. Javelin (2005): 7.

44. Javelin (2006): 3.

45. Javelin (2006): 15.

46. Individuals can stagger their review of these three credit reports over the course of a year in order to increase the effectiveness of such monitoring activities.

47. Dash (2006).

48. Dash (2006).

49. FTC (2005b). This ruling did not seem to deter others, like FreeCreditReport.com from luring the public to their services with a similar promise.

50. Popkin (2008).

51. AnnualCreditReport.com is the place to go for free credit reports in the United States.

52. Weston (n.d.).

53. Dash (2006).

54. Consumer Reports (2007).

55. Quoted in Dash (2006).

56. U.S. General Accounting Office (1998, 2002c).

57. Synovate (2003).

58. Javelin Strategy & Research (2006).

59. Javelin Strategy & Research (2007b).

60. Javelin Strategy & Research (2007a): 16.

61. Quoted in Foust and Ryst (2006).

62. Anderson (1988).

63. Shafer (2006).

64. Synovate (2003): 82.

65. For example: California Public Interest Research Group (1996, 1997); Benner, Mierzwinski, and Givens (2000).

66. The intangible costs suffered by victims of new you are well documented by other research. See, for example, Benner, Mierzwinski, and Givens (2000); and Identity Theft Resource Center (2003, 2005).

67. "Recovering from ID Theft Can Be Difficult . . ." (2005).

68. Synovate (2003): 20, 43.

69. Givens (2006).

70. Synovate (2003): 93.

71. Synovate (2003): 47.

72. http://www.unodc.org/documents/organized-crime/Final_Report_ID_C.pdf.

CHAPTER 11

1. McRobbie and Thornton (1995).

2. Thompson (1998): 1.

3. McRobbie and Thornton (1995): 560.

4. McRobbie and Thornton (1995): 560.

5. Cohen (2002): xxix.

6. Cohen (2002): xxx.

7. The original research concluded that moral panics and the risk society were separate concepts, but all of the distinctions between them cannot be explicated here. There are also several similarities between them, however, which suggest that one might replace the other within some futures. See McNally (2008a) for further discussion.

8. National Institute of Justice (2007): 2.

9. In René Descartes's analysis of existence, *Cogito ergo sum* (I think therefore I am).

References

Aamidor, Abe. 2002. "Identity Crisis: Thief's Use of Your Social Security Number Can Create Financial Havoc." *Indianapolis Star*, April 7, p. J02.

Allen, H. Torrence, and Boyoon Choi. 2005. *Identity Crisis: New Yorkers' Personal Information Needs Protection*. A Staff Report to the Council of the City of New York. Available at http://www.nyc.gov/html/records/pdf/govpub/1874idtheft.pdf

Alter, Jonathan. 2002. "America's Real Identity Crisis." *Newsweek*, December 9, p. 51.

Altheide, David L. 2002. *Creating Fear: News and the Construction of Crisis*. Hawthorne, NY: Aldine de Gruyter.

Alvarez, Ashanti M. 2005. *Preventing an Identity Crisis: Rutgers Officials Protect Students, Strengthen Data Security*. Rutgers Focus. May 9. Available at http://ur.rutgers.edu/focus/article/Preventing%20an%20identity%20crisis/1579/

"An Identity Crisis." 1977. *Washington Post*, April 27, p. A16.

Anderson, Jack. 1988. "Bogus Birth Certificates." *San Francisco Chronicle*, April 5, p. A19.

Anderson, Keith B. 2005. *Identity Theft: Does the Risk Vary with Demographics?* Washington, D.C.: Bureau of Economics, Federal Trade Commission.

"Are You a Target for Identity Theft?" 1997. *Consumer Reports*: 10–16, September.

Armour, Stephanie. 2003. "Employment Records Prove Ripe Source for Identity Theft." *USA Today*, January 23, p. 1B.

Associated Press. 1998. "Identity Theft Bill Caught in Congressional Logjam." October 14.

Associated Press Newswires. 1999. "High-Tech Criminals Take to Stealing Identities." August 15.

"Avoid Online ID theft." 2005. *Washington Post*, July 24, p. M03.

Baca, Aaron. 1997. "Check Fraud Easy to Do, Hard to Stop." *Albuquerque Journal*, August 11, p. 1.

Baerveldt, Chris, Hans Bunkers, Micha DeWinter, and Jan Kooistra. 1998. "Assessing a Moral Panic Relating to Crime and Drugs Policy in the Netherlands: Towards a Testable Theory." *Crime, Law and Social Change* 29(1): 31–47.

Balint, Kathryn. 2003. "Identity Crisis; Technology and the Web Make Fake IDs Easier to Produce and Harder to Spot." *San Diego Union-Tribune*, February 17, p. E1.

Ball, Andrea. 2001. "Interagency Task Force Battling Identity Theft." *Austin American-Statesman*, September 24, p. B1.

Bauer, Kurt R. 2003. "Arizona Banker Says We Can Meet the Challenges; Corralling Identity Thieves." *Arizona Republic*, August 3, p. D3.

Baum, Katrina. 2006. *Identity Theft, 2004*. Washington, D.C.: U.S. Bureau of Justice Statistics.

Baum, Katrina. 2007. *Identity Theft, 2005*. Washington, D.C.: U.S. Bureau of Justice Statistics.

Beales, Howard. 2002. *Prepared Statement of the Federal Trade Commission on "Identity Theft: The Impact on Seniors" Before the Senate Special Committee on Aging*. July 18. Available at http://www.ftc.gov/os/2002/07/020718identitytheft.htm

Beck, Ulrich. 1992. *Risk Society: Towards a New Modernity*. London: Sage Publications Ltd.

Beckage, Joseph. 2005. "Don't Make it Easy for ID Thieves." *Arizona Republic*, June 5, p. V4.

Becker, Howard S. 1963. *Outsiders: Studies in the Sociology of Deviance*. New York: Free Press.

Benner, Janine, Edmund Mierzwinski, and Beth Givens. 2000. *Nowhere to Turn: Victims Speak Out on Identity Theft*. California Public Interest Research Group and the Privacy Rights Clearinghouse. Available at http://www.calpirg.org/consumer/privacy/idtheft2000/idtheft2000.pdf

Bergal, Jenni. 2001. "Identity Theft Becoming an Epidemic, Investigators Say." *Charleston Gazette*, August 7, p. 5D.

Bernstein, Jodie. 1999. *Prepared Statement of the Federal Trade Commission on "Financial Identity Theft" Before the Subcommittee on Telecommunications, Trade and Consumer Protection and the Subcommittee on Finance and Hazardous Materials of the Committee on Commerce, United States House of Representatives*. April 22. Available at http://www.ftc.gov/os/1999/04/identitythefttestimony.htm

Bernstel, Janet Bigham. 2001. "Identity Crisis." *Bank Marketing* 33(7): 16.

Better Business Bureau. 2005. *New Research Shows that Identity Theft Is More Prevalent Offline with Paper than Online*. Available at http://www.bbb.org/alerts/article.asp?ID=565

Billington, Mike. 1989. "Identity Theft Besmirches Victims' Records." *Sun-Sentinel*, July 6, p. 1B.

Block, Sandra. 2000. "Don't Fall Prey to Identity Thieves." *USA Today*, September 12, p. 3B.

Block, Sandra. 2002. "Act Now to Prevent Identity Thief from Stalking the True You." *USA Today*, November 26, p. 3B.

Block, Sandra. 2003a. "How to Protect your Credit Card from Headaches of ID Theft." *USA Today*, January 28, p. 3B.

Block, Sandra. 2003b "Banks Could Be Forced to Alert Customers of Cybertheft." *USA Today*, August 13, p. 3B.

Board of Governors of the Federal Reserve System. 1997. *Report to the Congress Concerning the Availability of Consumer Identifying Information and Financial Fraud.* Available at http://www.federalreserve.gov/boarddocs/rptcongress/privacy.pdf

Bosworth, Martin H. 2006. *Identity Theft Study Leaves Questions Unanswered.* April 4. Available at http://www.consumeraffairs.com/news04/2006/04/id_theft_stats02.html

Boulard, Garry. 1999. "Identity Crisis in the Information Age." *State Legislatures Magazine.* March. Available at http://www.ncsl.org/programs/pubs/399ID.HTM#UP

Bray, Hiawatha. 2005a. "Let's Focus on the Theft, not the Identity." *Boston Globe*, March 21, p. C3.

Bray, Hiawatha. 2005b. "iPod Can be Music to a Data Thief's Ear." *Boston Globe*, June 6, p. C2.

Brown, Michelle. 2000. *Verbal Testimony by Michelle Brown Before the U.S. Senate Committee Hearing on the Judiciary Subcommittee on Technology, Terrorism and Government Information—"Identity theft: How to Protect and Restore Your Good Name," July 12, 2000.* Available at http://www.privacyrights.org/cases/victim9.htm

Burns, Ronald, and Charles Crawford. 1999. "School Shootings, the Media, and Public Fear: Ingredients for a Moral Panic." *Crime, Law & Social Change* 32(2): 147–168.

Bush, George W. 2004a. *President Bush Signs Identity Theft Penalty Enhancement Act. Remarks by the President at Signing of Identity Theft Penalty Enhancement Act.* July 15. Available at http://www.whitehouse.gov/news/releases/2004/07/20040715–3.html

Bush, George W. 2004b. *President's Remarks to the Unity Journalists of Color Convention.* August 6. Available at http://www.whitehouse.gov/news/releases/2004/08/20040806–1.html

Bush, George W. 2006. *Executive Order: Strengthening Federal Efforts to Protect Against Identity Theft.* May 10. Available at: http://www.whitehouse.gov/news/releases/2006/05/20060510–3.html

California Public Interest Research Group. 1996. *Theft of identity: The consumer x-files.* Los Angeles, CA.

California Public Interest Research Group. 1997. *Identity theft II: Return to the consumer x-files.* Sacramento, CA.

Cambanis, Thanassis. 2002. "Alleged ID Thief Arrested in NYC Scam Had Targeted 12 Boston Lawyers." *Boston Globe*, August 20, p. B1.

Caminer, Brian F. 1985. "Credit Card Fraud: The Neglected Crime." *Journal of Criminal Law & Criminology* 76(3): 746–763.

Caniglia, John. 1998. "Police Say ID Thefts on Rise; Internet, Easy Credit Create an 'Epidemic.'" *The Plain Dealer*, December 28, p. 1B.

Carlson, Tina. 2000. "Identity Theft Increasingly Results from Inside Job." *Credit Union Journal* 4(46): 12.

Caslon Analytics. 2003. *Caslon Analytics Profile: Identity Theft, Identity Fraud.* Available at http://www.caslon.com.au/idcrimeguide.htm

Cassady, Alison. 2004. *Tying the Hands of States: The Impact of Federal Preemption on State Problem-Solvers.* National Association of State PIRGs. Available at http://www.

calpirg.org/uploads/w0/4o/w04oTh5Hqu5Gi7J6c84Fmg/TyingtheHandsof States.pdf

Catalano, Shannan M. 2004. *Criminal Victimization, 2003*. Washington, D.C.: U.S. Department of Justice, Office of Justice Programs, U.S. Bureau of Justice Statistics.

Catalano, Shannan M. 2006. *Criminal Victimization, 2005*. Washington, D.C.: U.S. Department of Justice, Office of Justice Programs, U.S. Bureau of Justice Statistics.

CBS News. 1999. *Credit Is Hard to Restore*. Available at http://www.cbsnews.com/ stories/1999/10/05/eveningnews/main65044.shtml

Chermak, Steven M. 2002. *Searching for a Demon: Media Construction of the Militia Movement*. Boston, MA: Northeastern University Press.

Choi, Charles Q. 2007. *Two Snowflakes May Actually be Alike: Smaller Crystals Sometimes Fall Before They Have a Chance to Fully Develop.* January 22. Available at http://www.msnbc.msn.com/id/16759121/ns/technology_and_ science-science/

Clarke, Richard A. 2005. "You've Been Sold." *New York Times*, April 24, p. 39.

Cliatt, Cass. 1999. The Big Business of Fake IDs; Elgin Authorities Cracking Down on Plants Churning out Documents. *Chicago Daily Herald*, November 3, p. F2.

Cockeyed.com. 2006. *The Torn Up Credit Card Application*. Available at http://www .cockeyed.com/citizen/creditcard/application.shtml

Cohen, Stanley. 2002. *Folk Devils and Moral Panics: The Creation of the Mods and Rockers*. 3rd ed. London: Routledge.

Cole, Simon. 2001. "The Myth of Fingerprints." *New York Times*, May 13. Available at http://truthinjustice.org/fingerprint-myth.htm

Cole, Simon A., and Henry N. Pontell. 2006. "'Don't Be a Low Hanging Fruit': Identity Theft as a Moral Panic." In *Surveillance and Security: Technological Politics and Power in Everyday Life*, ed. T. Monahan, 125–147. New York: Routledge.

Commonwealth of Virginia, Office of the Attorney General. 2006. *McDonnell Announces Felony Conviction in First Identity Theft Case*. August 2. Available at http://www.oag.state.va.us/PRESS_RELEASES/NewsArchive/080206_Felony_ Conviction_First_Identity_Theft_Case.html

Connelly, D. Barry. 1999. *Testimony of Barry D. Connelly, President of Associated Credit Bureaus. Identity Theft: Is There Another You? Joint Hearing Before the Subcommittee on Telecommunications, Trade, and Consumer Protection and the Subcommittee on Finance and Hazardous Materials of the Committee on Commerce, House of Representatives.* April 22.

Consumer Reports. 2007. *Costly Credit-Monitoring Services Offer Limited Fraud Protection: You Can Guard Against Identity Theft Better by Taking Other Steps.* Available at http://www.consumerreports.org/

Cook, Mike. 2005. "The Lowdown on Fraud Rings." *Collections & Credit Risk* 10(6): 1–4.

Copes, Heith, and Lynne Vieraitis. 2008. "The Risks, Rewards and Strategies of Stealing Identities." In *Perspectives on Identity Theft*, ed. Megan M. McNally and Graeme R. Newman, 87–110. Crime Prevention Studies, 23. Monsey, NY: Criminal Justice Press.

Cornish, Derek. 1994a. "Crimes as scripts." In *Proceedings of the International Seminar on Environmental Criminology and Crime Analysis, University of Miami, Coral Gables, FL, 1993*, ed. D. Zahm and P. Cromwell, 30–45. Tallahassee, FL:

Florida Statistical Analysis Center, Florida Criminal Justice Executive Institute, Florida Department of Law Enforcement.

Cornish, Derek. 1994b. "The Procedural Analysis of Offending and Its Relevance for Situational Prevention." In *Crime Prevention Studies*, ed. R.V. Clarke, 151–196. Vol. 3. Monsey, NY: Criminal Justice Press.

Correa, Tracy. 2000. "Identity Crisis—With a Few Pieces of Personal Data, Identity Thieves Can Wreck Victims' Financial Standing." *Fresno Bee*, July 9, p. D03.

Crawford, Amanda J. 2005. "2 Just Tip of Identity Theft Iceberg: Arizona Is Leading the Nation in the Increasingly Common Crime." *Arizona Republic*, February 6, p. B1.

Crenshaw, Albert B. 1996. "Identity Crisis: The Theft That's Tough to Thwart." *Washington Post*, August 25, p. H01.

Crenshaw, Albert B. 2000. "Stressing the 'Security' in SSNs; New Government Measures Needed to Curb Identity Theft." *Washington Post*, October 29, p. H02.

Crichton, Robert. 1960. *The Great Imposter: The Amazing Careers of the Most Spectacular Imposter of Modern Times*. New York: Permabooks.

Crichton, Robert. 1961. *The Rascal and the Road*. New York: Random House.

Critcher, Chas. 2003. *Moral Panics and the Media*. Buckingham, UK: Open University Press.

Curtis, Dennis E. 1996. "The Effect of Federalization on the Defense Function." *Annals of the American Academy of Political and Social Science* 543(1): 85–96.

Daniel, Mac. 2005. "State Details Plan for Safer, High-Tech Licensing." *Boston Globe*, October 19, p. B5.

Darling, Lynn. 1977. "Imposter Snarled in Weird Kidnap Plot." *Washington Post*, May 22, p. A1.

Dash, Eric. 2006. "Stolen Lives: Protectors, Too, Gather Profits from ID Theft." *New York Times*, December 12, p. 1.

Davis, Kevin. 1994. "Imposters Leave Victims of Theft in Identity Crisis." *Sun-Sentinel*, November 6, p. 1B.

de Young, Mary. 2004. *The Day Care Ritual Abuse Moral Panic*. Jefferson, NC: McFarland & Company.

Dean, Joshua. 2000. "The Internet Identity Crisis." *Government Executive*, December 1. Available at http://www.govexec.com/features/1200/1200persontech.htm

Del Grosso, Robert J. 2001. "How to Avoid an Identity Crisis." *Security Management*, December. Available at http://www.securitymanagement.com/library/001150.html

"Died." 1982. *Newsweek*, June 21, p. 75.

Dinerstein, Marti. 2002. "America's Identity Crisis: Document Fraud is Pervasive and Pernicious." *Backgrounder*: 1–12, April.

Downs, A. 1972. "Up and Down with Ecology: The 'Issue-Attention' Cycle." *The Public Interest* 28: 38–50.

Dugas, Christine. 1999. "Protect your Social Security Number; Don't Be a Victim of Identity Theft." *USA Today*, July 2, p. 6B.

EarthLink Identity Protection Center. 2007. *Identity Theft Basics*. Available at http://www.equifax.com/sitePages/EarthLink/protectionCenter/

Effinger, Bill. 1995. *Making Crime Pay: How Identity Thieves Cash in on Your Credit; What You Can Do to Stop It*. La Jolla, CA: New Hope Press.

Electricity Consumers Resource Council. 2002. "Enron Tip of Iceberg, ELCON Tells FERC." *ELCON Report*, Number 2. Washington, D.C.

Electronic Privacy Information Center. 2007. *National ID Cards and Real ID Act.* Available at http://www.epic.org/privacy/id_cards/

Ellement, John. 2003. "Second Batch of Paul Caseys Say They Are Victims of ID Theft; Dorchester Man Arrested in Case." *Boston Globe*, November 27, p. B3.

Encarnacao, Jack. 2004. "Firms Hit Hard by Identity Theft." *Boston Globe*, July 14, p. C3.

Equifax Learning Center. 2007. *Identity Theft—Facts and Statistics.* Accessed at https://www.econsumer.equifax.com/consumer/sitepage.ehtml?forward=elearning_idtheft4

Ewen, Robert B. 1993. *An Introduction to Theories of Personality,* 4th ed. Hillsdale, NJ: Lawrence Erlbaum Associates.

Faron, Fay. 1996. "Identity Theft Can Be the Costliest of All." *Dallas Morning News*, November 15, p. 8C.

Faron, Fay. 1998. "Scam Artists Know Elderly Will Be Polite." *Dallas Morning News*, April 17, p. 6C.

Fattah, E. A. 1993. "The Rational Choice/Opportunity Perspectives as a Vehicle for Integrating Criminological and Victimological Theories." In *Routine Activity and Rational Choice*, ed. Ronald V. Clarke and Marcus Felson, 225–258. Advances in Criminological Theory, Vol. 5. New Brunswick, NJ: Transaction Books.

Federal Bureau of Investigation. n.d. *White-Collar Crime.* Available at http://www.fbi.gov/whitecollarcrime.htm

Federal Bureau of Investigation. 2006. *Crime in the United States by Volume and Rate per 100,000 Inhabitants.* Available at http://www.fbi.gov/ucr/05cius/data/table_01.html

Federal Bureau of Investigation. 2007. *Something Vishy: Be Aware of a New Online Scam.* Available at http://www.fbi.gov/page2/feb07/vishing022307.htm

Federal Deposit Insurance Corporation. 2004. *Putting an End to Account-Hijacking Identity Theft.* Available at http://www.fdic.gov/consumers/consumer/idtheftstudy/

Federal Trade Commission. n.d. *Identity Theft and Identity Fraud.* Available at http://www.usdoj.gov/criminal/fraud/idtheft.html

Federal Trade Commission. 2000a. *Identity Crisis . . . What To Do If Your Identity Is Stolen.* FTC Consumer Alert. The 2005 update of this document is available at http://www.ftc.gov/bcp/conline/pubs/credit/idcrisis.htm

Federal Trade Commission. 2000b. *ID Theft: When Bad Things Happen to Your Good Name.* Washington, D.C.

Federal Trade Commission. 2001. *Identity Theft Victim Complaint Data: Figures and Trends on Identity Theft, January 2000 through December 2000.* Washington, D.C.

Federal Trade Commission. 2003a. *National and State Trends in Fraud and Identity Theft, January–December 2002.* Washington, D.C.

Federal Trade Commission. 2003b. *Report: Federal Trade Commission Overview of the Identity Theft Program, October 1998–September 2003.* Available at http://www.ftc.gov/os/2003/09/timelinereport.pdf

Federal Trade Commission. 2004. *National and State Trends in Fraud and Identity Theft, January–December 2003.* Washington, D.C.

Federal Trade Commission. 2005a. *National and State Trends in Fraud and Identity Theft, January–December 2004.* Washington, D.C.

Federal Trade Commission. 2005b, *Marketer of "Free Credit Reports" Settles FTC Charges*. August 16. Available at http://www.ftc.gov/opa/2005/08/consumerinfo.htm

Federal Trade Commission. 2006. *Consumer Fraud and Identity Theft Complaint Data, January–December 2005*. Washington, D.C.

Federal Trade Commission. 2007a. *Consumer Fraud and Identity Theft Complaint Data, January–December 2006*. Washington, D.C.

Federal Trade Commission. 2007b. *FTC to Host Identity Authentication Workshop: Agency Seeks Development of Tools to Thwart Identity Theft*. February 21. Available at http://www.ftc.gov/opa/2007/02/authentication.shtm

Federal Trade Commission. 2011. *FTC Releases List of Top Consumer Complaints in 2010; Identity Theft Tops the List Again*. March 8. Available at: http://www.ftc.gov/opa/2011/03/topcomplaints.shtm

Feinstein, Dianne. 2005. *Testimony of Senator Feinstein at Commerce Committee Hearing on Identity Theft*. June 16. Available at http://feinstein.senate.gov/05releases/r-commerce-hrg0616.htm

Fields, Gary. 2000. "Victims of Identity Theft Often Unaware They've Been Stung." *USA Today*, March 15, p. 6A.

"Fighting Identity Theft—New Law Could Help Stem Epidemic of Imposters Assuming IDs, Wreaking Economic Havoc." 1998. *Austin American-Statesman*, November 22, p. E2.

Finkelstein, Barry J. 1999. *Memorandum for Assistant Regional Council (Criminal Tax)*. January 22. Available at http://www.unclefed.com/ForTaxProfs/irs-wd/1999/9911041.pdf

Fitch, Thomas P. 1986. "To Catch a Thief." *United States Banker*: 92, November.

Foley, Linda. 2002. "Dear Ann." *Washington Post*, January 11, p. C10.

Foust, Dean, and Sonja Ryst. 2006. "ID Theft: More Hype Than Harm." *Business Week*, July 3. Available at http://www.businessweek.com/magazine/content/06_27/b3991041.htm?chan=tc&chan=technology_technology+index+page_more+of+today's+top+stories

Fox, Susannah. 2001. *Fear of Online Crime: Americans Support FBI Interception of Criminal Suspects' Email and New Laws to Protect Online Privacy*. Washington, D.C.: Pew Internet & American Life Project.

Frank, Mari, and Beth Givens. 1999. *Privacy Piracy! A Guide to Protecting Yourself from Identity Theft*. Office Depot.

Freeman, Mike. 2007. *Mike Freeman's 2007 Initiatives for the Hennepin County Attorney's Office*. Available at http://www.votemikefreeman.com/Initiatives

Fryburg, Marc. 2000. "Identity Thieves Divert Mail." *USA Today*, September 11, p. 23A.

Fulton, Delawese. 2005. "ID Theft: The New Identity Crisis." *Macon Telegraph*, August 9, p. B.

Galehouse, Maggie. 2005. "Firm Targets ID Thieves—New Company Claims It Can Prevent Theft." *Arizona Republic*, November 7, p. 1.

Gardner, Michael. 2000. "Privacy Is Red-Hot Issue in the State; Lawmakers Clash Over Protections." *San Diego Union-Tribune*, May 2, p. A-1.

Gartner, Inc. 2007. *Gartner Says Number of Identity Theft Victims Has Increased More than 50 Percent Since 2003*. March 6. Available at http://www.gartner.com/it/page.jsp?id=501912

Gartner, Inc. 2003. *Gartner Says Identity Theft Is Up Nearly 80 Percent: 7 Million U.S. Adults Were Identity Theft Victims in the Past 12 Months.* July 21. Available at http://www.gartner.com/5_about/press_releases/pr21july2003a.jsp

Gayer, J. 2003. *Policing Privacy: Law Enforcement's Response to Identity Theft.* CA: CALPIRG Education Fund. Available at http://www.calpirg.org/reports/policingprivacy2003.pdf

"Gets American Forger: Detective Seizes in Paris Imposter Who Swindled Several Capitals." 1926. *New York Times*, October 2, p. 4.

Givens, Beth. 2000a. *Identity Theft: How It Happens, Its Impact on Victims, and Legislative Solutions.* Written Testimony for U.S. Senate Judiciary Subcommittee on Technology, Terrorism, and Government Information. July 12, 2000. Available at http://www.privacyrights.org/ar/id_theft.htm

Givens, Beth. 2000b. *Identity Theft: The Growing Problem of Wrongful Criminal Convictions.* Presented at the SEARCH National Conference on Privacy, Technology and Criminal Justice Information, Washington D.C. Available at http://www.privacyrights.org/ar/wcr.htm

Givens, Beth. 2004. *The Saga of Shredding in the U.S.: A Privacy Advocate's Perspective.* Available at http://www.privacyrights.org/ar/NAID.htm

Givens, Beth. 2006. Interview with Beth Givens; San Diego, CA. April 1.

Goddard, Terry. 2005. "Crying Wolf About Meth Abuse?" *New York Times*, August 11, p. 2.

Goode, Erich, and Nachman Ben-Yehuda. 1994. *Moral Panics: The Social Construction of Deviance.* Cambridge, MA: Blackwell Publishers Ltd.

Gordon, Gary R., Norman A. Willox Jr., et al. 2004. "Identity Fraud: A Critical National and Global Threat." *Journal of Economic Crime Management* 2(1): 1–48.

Gordon, Gary R., Donald J. Rebovich, et al. *Identity Fraud Trends and Patterns: Building a Data-Based Foundation for Proactive Enforcement.* Center for Identity Management and Information Protection.

Gusfield, Joseph R. 1963. *Symbolic Crusade: Status Politics and the American Temperance Movement.* Urbana: University of Illinois Press.

Hall, Stuart, Chas Critcher, et al. 1978. *Policing the Crisis: Mugging, the State, and Law and Order.* New York: Holmes & Meier Publishers.

Hansell, Saul. 1996. "Identity Crisis: When a Criminal's Got Your Number." *New York Times*, June 16, p. 1.

Hanson, Cynthia. 1999. "The Identity Snatchers." *Ladies Home Journal* 116(6): 84.

Harney, Kenneth R. 2003. "Helping Consumers Check Up On Credit." *Washington Post*, November 29, p. F01.

Harper, Dennis. 1989. "High-Flying Fraud (Credit Cards)." *Security Management* 33(2): 62–65.

Harper, Jim. 2006. *Identity Crisis: How Identification Is Overused and Misunderstood.* Washington, D.C.: Cato Institute.

Hart, Timothy C., and Callie Rennison. 2003. *Reporting Crime to the Police, 1992–2000.* Washington, D.C.: U.S. Department of Justice, Office of Justice Programs, Bureau of Justice Statistics.

Hartle, Bob, and JoAnn Hartle. 2006. *Identity Theft: Problems and Solutions.* Arizona: ID Theft Services. Available at www.idfraud.org

Hendrickson, Robert A. 1972. *The Cashless Society.* New York, NY: Dodd, Mead & Company.

Hier, Sean P. 2002. "Raves, Risks and the Ecstacy Panic: A Case Study in the Subversive Nature of Moral Regulation." *Canadian Journal of Sociology* 27(1): 33–57.

"Hold-Up Man Identified: Prints Show 'John Alexander' to be Armand Latraverse." 1951. *New York Times*, June 24, p. 36.

Hoofnagle, Chris. 2005. *Written Testimony of the Electronic Privacy Information Center to the New York Senate Standing Committee on Consumer Protection and the Assembly Standing Committee on Consumer Affairs and Protection. Public Hearing on Security Freeze.* November 21. Available at http://www.epic.org/privacy/idtheft/nystate11.21.05.html

Hoofnagle, Chris. 2007a. *Response to Request Under the Freedom of Information Act, Re: Javelin Strategy & Research.* Available at http://chrishoofnagle.com/blog/wp-content/uploads/2007/02/ftc_email_on_javelin.pdf

Hoofnagle, Chris. 2007b. *Javelin's Bogus Analysis of Identity Theft.* February 2. Available at: http://www.chrishoofnagle.com/blog/?p=680

Huntley, Sarah. 2002. "A Major Identity Crisis; Info Stolen from Motor Vehicles Offices Has Residents Worried." *Rocky Mountain News*, August 20, p. 5A.

ID Analytics, Inc. 2003. *ID Analytics Announces Findings from Largest-Ever Research into Identity Fraud with Cooperation of Business Leaders Across Multiple Industries.* September 23. Available at http://www.idanalytics.com/news_and_events/20030923.html

ID Analytics, Inc. 2005a. *ID Analytics' First-Ever National Data Breach Analysis Shows the Rate of Misuse of Breached Identities May Be Lower than Anticipated.* December 8. Available at http://www.idanalytics.com/news_and_events/20051208.htm

ID Analytics, Inc. 2005b. *ID Analytics Announces New Data Analysis Findings; Synthetic Identity Fraud Poses New Challenges.* February 9. Available at http://www.idanalytics.com/news_and_events/2005209.html

ID Analytics, Inc. 2006. *ID Analytics Analysis of 70 Data Breaches in 2005 Shows the Largest Volume Occurred in Education Sector.* February 9. Available at http://www.idanalytics.com/news_and_events/20060209.htm

"Identity Crisis; An Epidemic of High-Profile Laptop Heists Shows How Vulnerable Americans' Personal Information Is." 2006. *Washington Post*, August 6, p. B06.

"Identity Crisis: Fraud Victims Have Hard Time Getting Back Their Good Name." 1999. *Florida Times-Union*, March 7, p. G-1.

Identity Theft Prevention Special Interest Group. 2005. *Identity Theft Primer.* Liberty Alliance. Available at www.projectliberty.org

Identity Theft Resource Center. 2003. *Identity Theft: The Aftermath 2003.* Available at http://www.idtheftcenter.org/artman2/uploads/1/The_Aftermath_2003.pdf

Identity Theft Resource Center. 2005. *Identity Theft: The Aftermath 2004.* Available at http://www.idtheftcenter.org/artman2/uploads/1/The_Aftermath_2004_1.pdf

IdentityTheft911. 2004. *Colorado Identity Theft Bill Killed Over Budget Concerns.* April 4. Available at www.identitytheft911.com/education/articles/art20040409colo.htm

IdentityTheft911. 2006. "Identity Crisis in the Workplace." *IdentityTheft911 Newsletter* 3(7): 2–3.

Jain, Anil. 2006. *Biometric Science Seeks to Avert Identity Crisis.* February 20. Available at www.physorg.com/news11019.html

Jarman, Max. 2005. "Damages From ID Theft Hitting Hard in Phoenix." *Arizona Republic*, July 30, p. D1.

Javelin Strategy & Research. 2005. *2005 Identity Fraud Survey Report.* Pleasanton, CA.

Javelin Strategy & Research. 2006. *2006 Identity Fraud Survey Report.* Pleasanton, CA.

Javelin Strategy & Research. 2007a. *2007 Identity Fraud Survey Report, Consumer Version: How Consumers Can Protect Themselves.* Pleasanton, CA.

Javelin Strategy & Research. 2007b. *U.S. Identity Theft Losses Fall: Study.* Available at http://www.javelinstrategy.com/2007/02/01/us-identity-theft-losses-fall-study/

Javelin Strategy & Research. 2010. *2010 Identity Fraud Survey Report: Identity Fraud Continues to Rise—New Accounts Fraud Drives Increase; Consumer Costs at an All-Time Low.* Pleasanton, CA.

Jelinek, Pauline. 2006. *Justice Report Finds Fewer Victims of Identity Theft than did Earlier Government Study.* Associated Press, April 3.

Jenkins, Philip. 1992. *Intimate Enemies: Moral Panics in Contemporary Great Britain.* New York: Aldine de Gruyter.

Jenkins, Philip. 1998. *Moral Panic: Changing Concepts of the Child Molester in Modern America.* New Haven, CT: Yale University Press.

Jerome, Marty. 2000. "Web Rip-Off: Who Ya Gonna Call?" *Boston Globe*, June 25, p. C7.

Jewkes, Yvonne. 1999. *Moral Panics in a Risk Society: A Critical Evaluation.* Studies in Crime, Order and Policing Occasional Paper No. 15. Leicester, U.K.: Scarman Centre for the Study of Public Order, University of Leicester.

Johnson, Bill. 2004. "A Shower of Hope Among Drought of Useful Bills." *Rocky Mountain News*, January 28, p. 7A.

Johnson, Holly. 2004. "Criminals Taking Scottsdale Residents' Names, Cashing In/ID Thieves Love Arizona—Police Step Up Efforts to Fight Identity Theft." *Arizona Republic*, November 8, p. 1.

Joint hearing before the Subcommittee on Oversight and Investigations of the Committee on Financial Services and the Subcommittee on Social Security of the Committee on Ways and Means of the U.S. House of Representatives. 2002. *Preventing Identity Theft by Terrorists and Criminals.* 107th Congress, first session, November 8, 2001. Washington, D.C.: Government Printing Office.

Jones, Charisse. 2002. "His Life Was Stolen, Then His Name." *USA Today*, November 15, p. 3A.

Justino, Edson, Luiz S. Oliveira and Cinthia Freitas. 2006. "Reconstructing Shredded Documents Through Feature Matching." *Forensic Science International* 160(2–3): 140–147.

Kahn, Charles M., and William Roberds. 2005. *Credit and Identity Theft.* Federal Reserve Bank of Atlanta, Working Paper Series. Working Paper 2005–19. Available at http://www.frbatlanta.org/filelegacydocs/wp0519.pdf

Kelly, John. 2005. "A Hint He Can't Refuse." *Washington Post*, June 24, p. C08.

Kidd-Hewitt, D., and Osborne, R. 1995. *Crime and the Media: The Post-Modern Spectacle.* London: Pluto.

Kim, Rachel. 2007. *FBI Report Shows Internet Fraud Is Down.* March 19. Available at http://www.javelinstrategy.com/2007/03/19/fbi-report-shows-internet-fraud-is-down/#more-661

Kisselgoff, Anna. 1985. "Dance; How Realism in Mime and Romantic Ballet Began." *New York Times*, May 5, p. 6.

Klaus, Patsy. 2006. *Crime and the Nation's Households, 2004.* U.S. Department of Justice, Office of Justice Programs, Bureau of Justice Statistics.

"Kleczka Leads Congressional Battle Against ID Theft." 1998. *Wisconsin State Journal*, September 13, p. 1B.

Klein, Gil. 1998. "Name Theft a Real Identity Crisis for the Victim; About 500,000 Yearly Undergo Long, Costly Ordeal of Trying to Regain Reputations." *Pittsburgh Post-Gazette*, July 19, p. A-8.

Kliewer, Laura. 2000. "With Identity Theft on the Rise, Lawmakers Explore New Ways to Protect Consumers." *Firstline Midwest* 7(11): 1–4.

Koenenn, Connie. 1997. "The New Identity Crisis: Can You Stop a Thief From Stealing Your Good Name?" *Palm Beach Post*, December 3, p. 1D.

Kollars, Deb. 2005. "Identity Crisis: Theft of Private Data Grows." *Sacramento Bee*, June 12, p. A1.

Kopel, Dave. 2003. "Sloppy Advocacy Journalism ID'd; Thinly Veiled Support for Identity-Theft Legislation Takes Form of Story at Post." *Rocky Mountain News*, December 6, p. 14C.

Kraft, Harold. 2007. "Identity Scoring: New Defenses Against Data Breaches." *E-Commerce Times*. February 15. Available at http://www.ecommercetimes.com/story/55770.html

Krouse, William J. 2004. *The Multi-State Anti-Terrorism Information Exchange (MATRIX) Pilot Project.* CRS Report for Congress. Available at http://www.fas.org/irp/crs/RL32536.pdf

Langton, Lynn, and Katrina Baum. 2007. *Identity Theft Reported by Households, 2007—Statistical Tables.* Available at http://bjs.ojp.usdoj.gov/content/pub/pdf/itrh07st.pdf

Laribee, Stephen F., and Stephen D. Hogan. 2001. "Identity Theft: Will You Be the Next Victim?" *National Public Accountant* 46(4): 8, 10–11.

LaVally, Rebecca. 1994. *Law Enforcement's View: The Growing Menace of Fraud in California.* Sacramento, CA: California Senate Office of Research.

Lavandera, Ed, and Ted Barrett. 2002. *Enron Posts Guards to Stop Shredding.* CNN.com Law Center. January 23. Available at http://archives.cnn.com/2002/LAW/01/23/enron/index.html

Lease, Matthew L., and Tod W. Burke. 2000. "Identity Theft: A Fast-Growing Crime." *FBI Law Enforcement Bulletin* 69(8): 8–13.

Lee, Jennifer. 2003. "Identity Theft Victimizes Millions, Costs Billions." *New York Times*, September 4, p. 20.

Lenhart, Amanda. 2000. *Who's Not Online: 57% of Those Without Internet Access Say They Do Not Plan to Log On.* Washington, D.C.: Pew Internet & American Life Project.

Leonard, Christina. 1997. "Thieves Today Take Identities: Fast-Growing Fraud Outstripping Law." *Arizona Republic*, August 25, p. B1, B3.

"Life in the Legislature: Theft-of-Identity Bill Advances." 2000. *Rocky Mountain News*, April 18, p. 12A.

Liptak, Adam, and Julia Preston. 2009a. "Supreme Court Hears Challenge to Identity-Theft Law in Immigration Cases." *New York Times*, February 25. Available at http://www.nytimes.com/2009/02/26/us/26identity.html

Liptak, Adam, and Julia Preston. 2009b. "Justices Limit Use of Identity Theft Law in Immigration Cases." *New York Times*, May 4. Available at http://www.nytimes.com/2009/05/05/us/05immig.html

Maslin, Janet. 1992. "Whose Life Is It, Anyway?" *New York Times*, August 16, p. 12.

Massachusetts Executive Office of Public Safety. 2007. *Identity Theft*. Available at http://www.mass.gov/?pageID=eopssubtopic&L=3&L0=Home&L1=Crime+ Prevention+%26+Personal+Safety&L2=Identity+Theft&sid=Eeops

Mayer, Caroline E. 2001. "Time Limit on ID-Theft Suits Upheld." *Washington Post*, November 14, p. E01.

Mayer, Caroline E. 2003. "FTC Says Identity Theft Is Rampant; 10 Million Cases in the Past Year, Survey Concludes." *Washington Post*, September 4, p. E05.

Mayer, Caroline E., and John Schwartz. 2000. "ID Theft Becoming Public Fear No. 1; Federal Hot Lines Clogged With Calls." *Washington Post*, July 13, p. E01.

Maze, Rick. 2007. "No More GWOT, House Committee Decrees." *Military Times*, April 4. Available at http://www.militarytimes.com/news/2007/04/military_ gwot_democrats_070403w

McCarthy, Ellen. 2005. "Cash, Charge or Fingerprint?; Retailers Experiment with Biometric Payment to Speed Up Service and Prevent Fraud, a Move that Worries Some Privacy Advocates." *Washington Post*, June 9, p. D01.

McCorkle, Richard C., and Terance D. Miethe. 2002. *Panic: The Social Construction of the Street Gang Problem*. Upper Saddle River, NJ: Prentice Hall.

McIntyre, David J., Jr. 2003. "Identity Thieves Are Usually Way Ahead of the Law." *Arizona Republic*, January 19, p. V3.

McLeod, Ramon G. 1996. "Beyond Credit Card Theft/Victims Struggle to Erase Blots on Identity, Reputation." *San Francisco Chronicle*, August 30, p. A26.

McLeod, Ramon G. 1997. "New Thieves Prey on Your Very Name, Identity Bandit Can Wreak Credit Havoc." *San Francisco Chronicle*, April 7, p. A1.

McNally, Megan M. 2008a. *Trial by Circumstance: Is Identity Theft a Modern-Day Moral Panic?* PhD Dissertation. Newark, NJ: Rutgers University.

McNally, Megan M. 2008b. "Charting the Conceptual Landscape of Identity Theft." In *Perspectives on Identity Theft*, ed. Megan M. McNally and Graeme R. Newman, 33–55. Crime Prevention Studies, Vol. 23. Monsey, NY: Criminal Justice Press.

McNally, Megan M., and Graeme R. Newman, eds. 2008. *Perspectives on Identity Theft*. Crime Prevention Studies, Vol. 23. Monsey, NY: Criminal Justice Press.

McRobbie, Angela. 1995. "Folk Devils Fight Back." In *The Sociology of Crime and Deviance: Selected Issues*, ed. S. Caffrey and G. Mundy, 249–257. Kent, UK: Greenwich University Press.

McRobbie, Angela, and Sarah L. Thornton. 1995. "Rethinking 'Moral Panic' for Multi-Mediated Social Worlds." *British Journal of Sociology* 46(4): 559–574.

Medine, David. 1998. *Prepared Statement of the Federal Trade Commission on "Identity Theft" Before the Subcommittee on Technology, Terrorism and Government Information of the Committee on the Judiciary, United States Senate*. May 20. Available at http://www.ftc.gov/os/1998/05/identhef.htm

Meece, Mickey. 1998. "Productivity; Many Buying Home Shredders to Thwart Garbage Snoops." *New York Times*, June 4, p. 6.

Menefee, Sami. 1998. "Identity Theft Reaches Epidemic Proportions—SFPD." *Newsbytes News Network*, March 23.

Merton, Robert K. 1957. *Social Theory and Social Structure*. New York: Free Press.

Michigan State Police. 2007. *Identity Theft, the Fastest Growing Crime in the Nation*. Available at http://www.michigan.gov/msp/0,1607,7-123-1584_3471_4715- 99574—,00.html

Mierzwinski, Edmund. 2004. "Preemption of State Consumer Laws: Federal Interference is a Market Failure." *Government, Law and Policy Journal* 6(1): 6–12.

Miller, Maeve Z. 2007. "Why Europe Is Safe from Choicepoint: Preventing Commercialized Identity Theft Through Strong Data Protection and Privacy Laws." *George Washington University Law Review*, 395.

Monahan, Mary. 2007. *More Good News from the FTC.* February 8. Available at http://www.javelinstrategy.com/2007/02/08/more-good-news-from-the-ftc/

Moore, David W. 2001. *Only One in Five Americans Without a Credit Card. Gallup Poll News Service.* May 10. Available at http://poll.gallup.com/content/default.aspx?ci=1744&pg=1&VERSION=p

National Cyber Security Alliance. n.d. *Top 8 Cyber Security Practices.* Available at http://www.staysafeonline.info/practices/one.html

National Institute of Justice. 2007. *Identity Theft—A Research Review.* Washington, D.C. Available at http://www.ncjrs.gov/pdffiles1/nij/218778.pdf

Nelson, Scott Bernard. 2000. "Money Matters/Identity Crisis; The Imposters—More People Seeing Their Good Names Sullied by Thieves." *Boston Globe*, August 27, p. G4.

Nesbitt, Frank. 2005. *Identity Theft Exists:—But Is It the Real Threat that Those Scaremongering for Profit Would Have It?* Unpublished thesis for postgraduate MA in fraud management. United Kingdom: University of Teesside.

Neuffer, Elizabeth. 1991. "Victims Urge Crackdown on Identity Theft; Say Officials Often Fail to Act on Complaints." *Boston Globe*, July 9, p. 13.

Newman, Graeme R., and Megan M. McNally. 2005. *Identity Theft Literature Review.* Unpublished report prepared for the National Institute of Justice. Available at http://www.ncjrs.gov/pdffiles1/nij/grants/210459.pdf

Newport Beach Police Department. 2007. *Identity Theft.* Available at http://www.nbpd.org/news/displaynews.asp?NewsID=18

New York Senate Majority Task Force on the Invasion of Privacy. 2000. Available at http://www.senate.state.ny.us/Docs/nyspriv00.pdf

New York State Consumer Protection Board. 2007. *A Consumer Guide to Preventing and Responding to Identity Theft.* Albany, NY. Available at http://www.consumer.state.ny.us/pdf/id_theft_online_version.pdf

Nirode, Jodi. 1998. "Identity Crisis: Theft of Names on the Rise." *Columbus Dispatch*, September 24, p. 1A.

O'Brien, Timothy L. 2004. "Gone in 60 Seconds." *New York Times*, October 24, p. 1.

O'Connor, Rory J. 1996a. " 'Identity Theft' Becomes a Growing Problem—Ambitious Thieves Saddle Victims with Unpaid Debts." *Seattle Times*, August 22, p. A 10.

O'Connor, Rory J. 1996b. "Identity Crisis: Thieves Get Credit, You Get Bills." *Miami Herald*, August 21, p. 1A.

O'Harrow, Robert, Jr. 2003. "Identity Crisis; Meet Michael Berry: Political Activist, Cancer Survivor, Creditor's Dream. Meet Michael Berry: Scam Artist, Killer, the Real Michael Berry's Worst Nightmare." *Washington Post*, August 10, p. W14.

O'Harrow, Robert, Jr., and John Schwartz. 1998. "A Case of Taken Identity; Thieves with a Penchant for Spending Are Stealing Consumers' Good Names." *Washington Post*, May 26, p. A01.

Oldenburg, Don. 1997. "Identity Theft and Other Scams." *Washington Post*, November 3, p. D05.

Oldenburg, Don. 2001. "Avoid an Identity Crisis." *Washington Post*, August 29, p. C12.

Oldenburg, Don. 2003. "Identity Theft: It Pays to be Diligent." *Washington Post*, January 7, p. C09.

Oldenburg, Don. 2004. "'Phishing' on the Rise, But Don't Take the Bait." *Washington Post*, November 9, p. C10.

Pankratz, Howard. 1999. "Police Seek Three Indicted in Identity Theft." *Denver Post*, August 6, p. B-01.

Pastrikos, Catherine. 2004. "Identity Theft Statutes: Which Will Protect Americans the Most?" *Albany Law Review* 67: 1137–1157.

Perl, Michael W. 2003. "It's Not Always About the Money: Why the State Identity Theft Laws Fail to Adequately Address Criminal Record Identity Theft." *Journal of Criminal Law & Criminology* 94(1): 169–208.

Perry, Nancy J. 1995. "How to Protect Yourself from the Credit Fraud Epidemic." *Money*, 24: 38–39, August.

Pierce, Scott D. 1991. "GMA Looks Into Loss of Privacy." *Deseret News*, November 11, p. C6.

Popkin, Helen A. S. 2008. "Sing It, FreeCreditReport.Com Guy! Talk About 'Identity Theft!' That Singer in Those Commercials Isn't Even Real!" August 7. Available at http://www.msnbc.msn.com/id/26061279/ns/technology_and_science-tech_and_gadgets/#

Poynting, Scott, Greg Noble, Paul Tabar, and Jock Collins. 2004. *Bin Laden in the Suburbs: Criminalising the Arab Other*. Sydney Institute of Criminology Series No. 18. Sydney, Australia: Sydney Institute of Criminology.

President's Identity Theft Task Force. 2007. *Combating Identity Theft: A Strategic Plan*. Available at http://www.idtheft.gov/reports/StrategicPlan.pdf

Preston, Julia. 2004. "Man Admits Role in Ring that Stole Credit Identities." *New York Times*, September 15, p. 7.

PrivacyGuard. 1993. *Membership Information*. CUC International Inc.

"Protect Yourself from Identity Theft." 2003. *Washington Post*, May 22, p. T19.

Rawe, Julie. 1999. "In Brief; Losing Your Name." *Time Magazine* 154(17): 135.

"Recovering from ID Theft Can Be Difficult, Costly, Victims Report." 2005. *Insurance Journal National News*, July 26. Available at http://www.insurancejournal.com/news/national/2005/07/26/57597.htm

Richards, Bob. 1998. "You Can Take Steps to Prevent Identity Theft." *The Capital Times*, February 28, p. 1C.

Rivlin, Gary. 2005. "Purloined Lives." *New York Times*, March 17, p. 1.

Rothe, Dawn, and Stephen L. Muzzatti. 2004. "Enemies Everywhere: Terrorism, Moral Panic, and U.S. Civil Society." *Critical Criminology* 12(3): 327–350.

Rother, Caitlin. 1995. "Are You a Victim of Identity Theft?" *San Diego Union-Tribune*, February 6, p. B2, B4.

Rubin, Sabrina. 1999. "'She Stole my Identity!'" *Cosmopolitan* 227(2): 196.

Rusch, J. J. 2001. *Making a Federal Case of Identity Theft: The Department of Justice's Role in Identity Theft Enforcement and Prevention*. Available at http://www.usdoj.gov/criminal/fruad/fedcase_idtheft.html

Ryst, Sonja. 2006. "The Booming Biz of ID Protection." *Business Week Online*, January 10. Available at http://www.businessweek.com/technology/content/jan2006/tc20060110_146542.htm

Safire, William. 2000. "Essay; Defend Your Identity." *New York Times*, May 11, p. 31.

Safire, William. 2004. "Cut and Run." *New York Times*, May 2, p. 22.

Sanko, John J. 2002. "ID Thieves Hit Castle Rock Man; So Far, $1,183 Worth of Bad Checks Found Written in His Name." *Rocky Mountain News*, November 28, p. 32A.

Saunders, Kurt M., and Bruce Zucker. 1999. "Counteracting Identity Fraud in the Information Age: The Identity Theft and Assumption Deterrence Act." *Cornell Journal of Law and Public Policy* 8(3): 661, 663.

Schrager, Adam. 2006. *Governor Aims to Crack Down on Internet Luring and Identity Theft. KUSA-TV report.* May 10. Available at http://www.9news.com/news/article.aspx?storyid=22696

Schumer, Charles E. 2002. *The Growing Menace of Identity Theft to New York Consumers.* Available at http://www.senate.gov/~schumer/SchumerWebsite/pressroom/special_reports/identity%20theft%20fact%20sheet%20SI%2012-13-02.pdf

Schwanhausser, Mark. 1995. "Armed With Your Social Security Number, a Crook Can Hijack Your Financial Identity." *San Jose Mercury News*: 1F.

Schwanhausser, Mark. 1999. "Identity Crisis—ID Theft Can Rob You of Your Money—and Your Sanity." *Chicago Tribune*, May 11, p. 1.

Sears. 1993. *Credit Alert.* Cendant Membership Services, Inc.

Second meeting of the Core Group of Experts on Identity-Related Crime, Vienna, Austria, 2–3 June 2008. *Final Report.* 2008. Available at http://www.unodc.org/documents/organized-crime/Final_Report_ID_C.pdf

Shafer, Jack. 2006. *The (Ongoing) Vitality of Mythical Numbers: Does ID Theft Really Cost $48 Billion a Year?* June 26. Available at http://www.slate.com/id/2144508/

Sheehan, Kathy, and Jennifer Preston. 1983. "Identity Crisis/Mystery Professor's Repertoire Grows: Investigators Find 14 Sets of ID." *Philadelphia Daily News*, March 23, p. 5.

"Shredders Manage a Variety of Tasks." 1998. *Office World News*, September.

Silva, Jerry, and Chris Pratt. 2004. "Five Certainties in the Uncertain World of Identity Theft." *TowerGroup ViewPoint* 113: 1–6.

Singer, Heidi. 2007. "Identity Crisis—246,000 Hit in Theft Epidemic." *New York Post*, February 8, p. O14.

Singletary, Michelle. 2001. "Identity Theft: Your Money and Your Life." *Washington Post*, February 4, p. H01.

Singletary, Michelle. 2003. "Identity Thieves Preying on Seniors." *Washington Post*, August 10, p. F01.

Singletary, Michelle. 2005. "When ID Theft Starts at Home." *Washington Post*, February 13, p. F01.

Smith, Marcia S. 2005. *Identity Theft: The Internet Connection.* CRS Report for Congress. Available at http://italy.usembassy.gov/pdf/other/RS22082.pdf

Sowers, Carol, and Patricia Biggs. 2002. "Drug-Linked 'Epidemic' Ruins Lives." *Arizona Republic*, October 13, p. A1.

Spinner, Jackie. 1999. "County Takes on Identity-Theft Issue; Pr. George's Would Aid Fraud Victims." *Washington Post*, September 22, p. B04.

Sproule, Susan, and Norm Archer n.d. *Measuring Identity Theft in Canada: 2008.* Consumer Survey, McMaster University, Working Paper #23. Available at http://www.merc.mcmaster.ca/working-papers/23.html

Stabile, Carol A. 2001. "Conspiracy or Consensus? Reconsidering the Moral Panic." *Journal of Communication Inquiry* 25(3): 258–278.

Stanley, Rick. 2001. "Identity Crisis; Cyberthieves Are Taking Credit for Your Good Name—and All They Need Is Nine Numbers." *Buffalo News*, July 1, p. E1.

Steinhardt, Barry. 2000. *Testimony of Barry Steinhardt, Associate Director, American Civil Liberties Union Before the Subcommittee on Government Management, Information and Technology of the House Committee on Government Reform.* May 18, 2000. Available at http://www.aclu.org/privacy/gen/15150leg20000518.html

State of California. 2005. *Locking Up the Evil Twin: A Summit on Identity Theft Solutions. Perspectives and Recommendations from Governor Arnold Schwarzenegger's March 1, 2005, Summit.* Sacramento, CA.

Sullivan, Bob. 2004. *Your Evil Twin: Behind the Identity Theft Epidemic.* Hoboken, NJ: John Wiley & Sons.

Sullivan, Bob. 2005. *Instant Credit Means Instant Identity Theft.* May 25. Available at http://www.msnbc.msn.com/id/6762127/

Summers, Lawrence H. 1999. *Generating Economic Opportunity for All Americans; Treasury Secretary Lawrence H. Summers Remarks to the Enterprise Foundation's Annual Enterprise Network Conference, Arlington, VA.* October 13. Available at http://www.ustreas.gov/press/releases/ls153.htm

Suzukamo, Leslie Brooks. 2004. "Identity Crisis: Credit Scams Are Exploding Across the Nation, with Sophisticated ID Thieves Finding Victims Among Careful and Savvy Consumers." *St. Paul Pioneer Press*, September 26, p. A1.

Swartz, Jon. 2003. "Hackers Evolve from Pranksters into Profiteers." *USA Today*, March 17, p. 3B.

Swartz, Jon. 2005a. "Identity Thieves Can Lurk at Wi-Fi Spots." *USA Today*, February 7, p. 1B.

Swartz, Jon. 2005b. "Meth Addicts Hack into Identity Theft." *USA Today*, September 30, p. 1B.

Swartz, Jon. 2005c. "2005 Worst Year for Breaches of Computer Security." *USA Today*, December 29, p. 1B.

Swecker, Chris. 2005. *Statement of Chris Swecker, Assistant Director, Criminal Investigative Division, Federal Bureau of Investigation Before the Senate Judiciary Committee.* April 13. Available at http://www.fbi.gov/congress/congress05/swecker041305.htm

Synovate. 2003. *Federal Trade Commission—Identity Theft Survey Report.* McLean, VA. Available at http://www.ftc.gov/os/2003/09/synovatereport.pdf

Synovate. 2007. *Federal Trade Commission—2006 Identity Theft Survey Report.* McLean, VA. Available at http://www.ftc.gov/os/2007/11/SynovateFinalReportIDTheft2006.pdf

"The Great Imposter Returns!" 1961. *New York Times*, October 22, p. BR49.

Thompson, Kenneth. 1998. *Moral Panics.* London: Routledge.

Travelers Insurance of Florida. 2007. *Identity Theft Insurance 101.* Available at http://www.travelersfl.com/TrvFlportalmain.asp?startpage=/iwcm/TravFlorida/buyins/idtheft101.html

"'True Name' Credit Card Fraud Is Stealing Good Credit Ratings from a Lot of People." 1988. *Deseret News*, October 16, p. B12.

United Nations Office on Drugs and Crime. 2007. *The United Nations Study on Fraud and the Criminal Misuse and Falsification of Identity.* PowerPoint presentation accessed online March 1, 2010.

U.S. Bureau of Justice Statistics. 2005. *Criminal Victimization in the United States, 2003 Statistical Tables.* Washington, D.C.: U.S. Department of Justice, Office of Justice Programs, Bureau of Justice Statistics.

U.S. Bureau of Justice Statistics. 2006. *Criminal Victimization in the United States, 2004 Statistical Tables.* Washington, D.C.: U.S. Department of Justice, Office of Justice Programs, Bureau of Justice Statistics.

U.S. Defense Advanced Research Projects Agency. 2003. *Report to Congress Regarding the Terrorism Information Awareness Program: Executive Summary.* Available at http://www.globalsecurity.org/security/library/report/2003/tia-exec-summ_20may2003.pdf

U.S. Department of Homeland Security. 2006. *MATRIX Report: DHS Privacy Office Report to the Public Concerning the Multistate Anti-Terrorism Information Exchange (MATRIX) Pilot Project.* Washington, D.C.: Privacy Office, U.S. Department of Homeland Security.

U.S. General Accounting Office. 1998. *Identity Fraud: Information on Prevalence, Cost, and Internet Impact Is Limited.* Briefing Report to Congressional Requesters. Available at http://www.gao.gov/archive/1998/gg98100b.pdf

U.S. General Accounting Office. 2002a. *Identity Theft: Greater Awareness and Use of Existing Data Are Needed.* Report to the Honorable Sam Johnson, House of Representatives. June. Washington, D.C. Available at http://www.consumer.gov/idtheft/reports/gao-d02766.pdf

U.S. General Accounting Office. 2002b. *Identity Fraud: Prevalence and Links to Alien Illegal Activities.* Before the Subcommittee on Crime, Terrorism, and Homeland Security and the Subcommittee on Immigration, Border Security, and Claims, Committee on the Judiciary, House of Representatives. June. Available at http://www.consumer.gov/idtheft/reports/gao-d02830t.pdf

U.S. General Accounting Office. 2002c. *Identity Theft: Prevalence and Cost Appear to Be Growing.* Report to Congressional Requesters. March. Washington, D.C. Available at http://www.gao.gov/new.items/d02363.pdf

U.S. General Accounting Office. 2002d. *Identity Theft: Available Data Indicate Growth in Prevalence and Cost.* Before the Subcommittee on Technology, Terrorism, and Government Information, Committee on the Judiciary, U.S. Senate. February. Available at http://www.gao.gov/new.items/d02424t.pdf

U.S. House of Representatives. 2003. *House Report 108–283: Making Appropriations for the Department of Defense for the Fiscal Year Ending September 30, 2004, and for Other Purposes.* Washington, D.C.

U.S. House of Representatives. Committee on Government Reform. 2006. *Congressional Preemption of State Laws and Regulations.* Washington, D.C.

U.S. Office of Community Oriented Policing Services. 2006. *A National Strategy to Combat Identity Theft.* Washington, D.C.

U.S. Postal Inspection Service. 2004. *2003 Annual Report of Investigations.* Available at http://www.usps.com/postalinspectors/ar03/ar03main.htm

U.S. Postal Service. 2003. *Operation Identity Crisis: Making the Mail Even Safer.* Press release available at http://56.0.134.24/mailerscompanion/oct2003/mc1003art2.htm

U.S. Senate. 2007. *Designating March 2007 as "Go Direct Month."* Senate Resolution 67. February 1.

Utah Bureau of Criminal Identification. 2006. "Identity Theft." *Utah Bureau of Criminal Identification Newsletter* 106(4): 4.

Van der Meulen, Nicole. 2007. "The Spread of Identity Theft: Developments and Initiatives Within the European Union." *Police Chief* 74(5).

Van Dyke, James. 2007. *The Hype on Synthetic Fraud Is Based on Synthetic Reasoning*. March 21. Available at http://www.javelinstrategy.com/2007/03/21/the-hype-on-synthetic-fraud-is-based-on-synthetic-reasoning/#more-663

Vancheri, Barbara. 2000. "Stamping Out Evil; Showtime Delivers Postal Inspectors Movie to Pittsburgh for Advance Screening." *Pittsburgh Post-Gazette*, March 7, p. D-1.

Vasquez, Chris. 2005. "Meth Is Taking a Toll on Pinal County." *Arizona Republic*, September 15, p. A22.

Victor, Jeffrey S. 1998. "Moral Panics and the Social Construction of Deviant Behavior: A Theory and Application to the Case of Ritual Child Abuse." *Sociological Perspectives* 41(3): 541–565.

Waddington, P. A. J. 1986. "Mugging as a Moral Panic: A Question of Proportion." *British Journal of Sociology* 37(2): 245–259.

Wagner, Dennis. 2005. "Passing the Buck—Drug Addicts, Armed with Printers, Making Valley a Hotbed for Bogus Bills." *Arizona Republic*, March 21, p. A1.

Wakin, Daniel J. 2001. "The Nation: Identity Crisis; National I.D. Cards: One Size Fits All." *New York Times*, October 7, p. 3.

Washington, April M. 2006. "Owens Signs Anti-Crime Bills into Law: Identity Theft, Foreclosure, Mortgage Fraud Targeted." *Rocky Mountain News*, May 31, p. 3B.

Weicher, Neil. 2007. "Educating Students About ID Theft." *BusinessWeek*, May 8. Available at http://www.businessweek.com/technology/content/may2007/tc20070508_560383.htm?chan=top+news_top+news+index_technology

Weisburd, D., E. Waring, and E. F. Chayet. 2001. *White-Collar Crime and Criminal Careers*. Cambridge, U.K.: Cambridge University Press.

Welch, Michael, Eric A. Price, and Nana Yankey. 2002. "Moral Panic Over Youth Violence: Wilding and the Manufacture of Menace in the Media." *Youth & Society* 34(1): 3–30.

Weston, Liz Pulliam. n.d.a. *Beef Up Your Credit Score in 5 Steps*. Available at http://articles.moneycentral.msn.com/Banking/YourCreditRating/BeefUpYourCreditScoreIn5steps.aspx

Weston, Liz Pulliam. n.d.a. *The Basics: What Europe Can Teach Us About Identity Theft*. Available at http://moneycentral.msn.com/content/Banking/FinancialPrivacy/P116528.asp

"What Can We Do About the Frauds?" 1864. *New York Times*, November 6, p. 4.

White Canyon Software. n.d. *Personal Identity Theft Protection Software*. Accessed March 20, 2007 at http://www.whitecanyon.com/mysecurityvault-pro-password-manager.php

White, Ed. 2003. "Identity Crisis—Thievery Creates Mystery Bills, Tax Mess for Single Mother." *Grand Rapids Press*, November 8, p. A1.

Wiles, Russ. 2000. "Precautions, Vigilance, Insurance Help Fight Identity Theft." *Arizona Republic*, June 11, p. D1.

Wiles, Russ. 2001. "New Books Address Analysts, Fraud, Taxes, Arizona Estate Planning." *Arizona Republic*, December 15, p. D1.

Wiles, Russ. 2003. "ID Theft Begins When You Share Sensitive Info." *Arizona Republic*, January 18, p. D1.

Wiles, Russ. 2005. "ID-Theft Services Added to Workplace Benefits." *Arizona Republic*, July 24, p. D6.

Williams, Jack. 1999. "Identity Theft: The Fuse Has Been Lit." *Boston Herald*, April 23, p. O37.

Wilmouth, Rex, Dan Grossman, and Gail Hillebrand. 2005. "Bill Would Allow Credit Report 'Freeze.'" *Rocky Mountain News*, February 28, p. 34A.

WFSB. 2006. *Packaging Material Contains Crime Report Info: Company to Stop Using Vendor's Shredded Paper in Packages*. Eyewitness News, Channel 3. Hartford, CT. December 18. Available at http://www.wfsb.com/iteam/10562661/detail.html

Wolf, Mark. 2004. "Protecting Your Identity; How to Safeguard Personal Information as Fraud Escalates." *Rocky Mountain News*, June 7, p. 3D.

Yavorsky, Sarah. 1997. "Forget Cops and Robbers: Its Age of the Inside Job." *American Banker* 162(99): 15.

Yip, Pamela. 1999. "Identity Crisis: Act Quickly to Recover Financial Good Name If It's Stolen—But Expect a Long Road." *Dallas Morning News*, October 25, p. 1D.

Yip, Pamela. 2001. "Banks, Customers Warned About Worthless Checks." *Dallas Morning News*, May 28, p. 1D.

Young, Jock. 1971. "The Role of the Police as Amplifiers of Deviancy, Negotiators of Reality and Translators of Fantasy: Some Consequences of Our Present System of Drug Control as Seen in Notting Hill." In *Images of Deviancy*, ed. S. Cohen, 27–61. Middlesex, England: Penguin Books Inc.

Zug.com. n.d. *The Credit Card Prank*. Available at http://www.zug.com/pranks/credit/

Index

About the Author

MEGAN McNALLY received her PhD in criminal justice from Rutgers University. She is the coeditor of *Perspectives on Identity Theft*, and coauthor of the National Institute of Justice *Identity Theft Literature Review*.